D0849735

STUDIES IN THE HISTORY
OF CHRISTIAN MISSIONS

R. E. Frykenberg
Brian Stanley
General Editors

STUDIES IN THE HISTORY OF CHRISTIAN MISSIONS

Susan Billington Harper

In the Shadow of the Mahatma: Bishop V. S. Azariah and the Travails of Christianity in British India

D. Dennis Hudson

Protestant Origins in India: Tamil Evangelical Christians, 1706-1835

Kevin Ward and Brian Stanley, Editors

The Church Mission Society and World Christianity, 1799-1999

PROTESTANT ORIGINS IN INDIA

Tamil Evangelical Christians, 1706–1835

D. Dennis Hudson

William B. Eerdmans Publishing Company
Grand Rapids, Michigan / Cambridge, U.K.

Curzon Press Ltd
Richmond, Surrey, U.K.

Published jointly 2000 by
Wm. B. Eerdmans Publishing Co.
255 Jefferson Ave. S.E., Grand Rapids, Michigan 49503 /
P.O. Box 163, Cambridge CB3 9PU U.K.
and by
Curzon Press Ltd.
15 The Quadrant, Richmond, Surrey, TW9 1BP, UK

Printed in the United States of America

05 04 03 02 01 00 7 6 5 4 3 2 1

Library of Congress Cataloging-in-Publication Data

Hudson, D. Dennis.
Protestant origins in India: Tamil Evangelical Christians, 1706-1835 /
D. Dennis Hudson.
p. cm. (Studies in the history of Christian mission)
Includes bibliographical references and index.
Eerdmans ISBN 0-8028-4721-8 (cloth: alk. paper)
1. Tamil (Indic people) — Missions — History.
2. Protestant Churches — Missions — India, South — History.
3. Protestants — India, South — History.
4. India, South — Church history. I. Series.

BV3255.T3 H83 2000
266'.00954'8— dc21

00-26467

British Library Cataloguing-in-Publication Data

A catalogue record for this book is available from the British Library.
Curzon Press ISBN 0-7007-1244-5

Dedicated to the memory of

The Rev. J. D. Manasseh and 'Achi' Dayamani Manasseh,

and of Anjala Richard,

descendants of Vedanayaga Sastri,

and to the honor of

their family and mine

in Chennai, in Tamilnadu, in India

and now the World.

Contents

Preface

This book has evolved slowly. Growing out of a long interest in the encounter of Protestant Christianity with Tamil religions and culture, it began as 'Luther's Voice in India', my brief contribution to a symposium in October of 1984 commemorating the 400th anniversary of Luther's birth. The symposium was held at Smith College, Northampton, Massachusetts, where I teach. Nine years later I returned to that unpublished paper and made it the basis of a more extended contribution to the May 1993 seminar 'Social Dimensions of Religious Movements', part of the multidisciplinary team project on 'Socio-Religious Movements and Cultural Networks in Indian Civilization', coordinated by J. S. Grewal and held at the Indian Institute of Advanced Study, Rashtrapati Nivas, Shimla. That study was then published as 'The First Protestant Mission to India: Its Social and Religious Developments', in the *Sociological Bulletin* (Journal of the Indian Sociological Society) 42, nos. 1 and 2 (March-September 1993): 37-62.

Responses to that study by Tamil Protestants in Madras, eager to learn more about the history of their religious community, encouraged me to pursue it further. Robert E. Frykenberg of the University of Wisconsin at Madison provided that opportunity when, in 1994, he invited me to join his international 'Christianity in South India Project', sponsored by the Pew Memorial Trust. I presented portions of the expanded study in January 1997 during that project's 'Research Colloquium' at the Asha Nivas Conference Center in Madras. The critical responses I received there enabled me to bring it to its present and final form.

The question in the subtitle of the original version, 'Is the Kingdom of God Food and Drink?' comes from Romans 14:17. There the apostle Paul discusses an issue the first Protestants of India found important in the eighteenth century: To what had they converted when German Pietist Lutherans baptized them in the Danish colony at Tranquebar? Was it a style of living that prescribed certain foods and certain modes of social behaviour, as was true for the Muslims of India, or was it something else? What did it mean to follow the command, 'Love your neighbour as yourself', and who was to decide?

The question of what constitutes the Kingdom of God, posed in Lutheran terms, continued in Tranquebar and Tanjore throughout the eighteenth and into the early nineteenth century, when these Christians encountered differing Calvinist or Reformed terms newly brought from Europe. Controversy about the social implications of the Christian faith broke out among Tamil-speaking Protestants, and with that controversy this book ends. A later volume in this series will bring the discussion down to 1900 in Tamilnadu.

One feature of my approach needs explanation. I have retained the eighteenth- and ninteenth-century terms found in the historical records to designate the people discussed; I have not translated them into contemporary terms. For example, 'Malabarian', 'heathen', 'pagan', 'pariah,' and 'Moor' or 'Mahometan' will generally appear instead of 'Tamilian', 'Hindu', 'Dalit', and 'Muslim.' I have intentionally kept the original terms because they convey the way Europeans and Malabarians of the period thought of each other and of themselves and because they retain the tone of those views. At the same time I have tried to use the Tamil terms used by Christians, Muslims, Saivas, and Vaishnavas of the same period for the same reasons. One interesting aspect of the study is the way changing nomenclature reflects changing perceptions of oneself and of others.

Throughout this volume, my intent is neither to applaud nor to denigrate the views of any of the participants I discuss, but to present each group on its own terms as best I can. My purpose is to gain some understanding of their respective points of view as they interacted with one another. Nevertheless, I do write in a specific context, and I am primarily interested in the Tamil-speaking peoples, not in the Europeans. This work is not meant to be a history of Christian missions. I have therefore used the European sources, and the Europeans themselves, as means to understand the Tamilians, resulting inevitably in some distortions or at least one-sidedness. For example, this narrative surprisingly has turned out largely to be about Velalans. They are a ritual class *(varṇa)* of castes *(jāti, kula)* who, along with the Brahmin ritual class of castes, formed the elite of the period. In classical vedic terms, the Velalans were classified ritually as Sudras, the lowest in status of four *varṇas,* of which the Brahmins were the highest; yet Sudra Velalans and Brahmins had long composed the Tamil-speaking aristocracy. The Velalans will receive extended treatment in Chapter 4.

On the other hand, the important low-status castes known as 'pariahs' or 'untouchables', or, in modern terms, 'Dalits', will barely be touched because the sources I have used provide little information about them. Someone else, I hope, will tackle that interesting and important subject — perhaps through archival work in India and Sri Lanka, at the University of Halle in Germany, at the British Library in England, and at archives in Copenhagen, Basle, and wherever else missions have kept their records.

This study interprets people in eighteenth- and nineteenth-century, Tamil-speaking, South Asia as they appear to me at the beginning of the twenty-first century in New England. It is largely suggestive and certainly not exhaustive. I hope it will stimulate others to think about these matters and research them more thoroughly. In most cases, Tamil and Sanskrit words have been rendered into forms that are easily recognized by those familiar with those languages, even when the transliteration system is not exact. Inconsistencies are inevitable, especially because I have rendered personal names in contemporary forms (in quotations I have retained their forms as found in the sources). I ask the reader to please indulge me in this matter, for, to put it mildly, the study of South Asia is linguistically complex.

I acknowledge, finally, the debt I owe many for their help in bringing this study to completion: to Smith College for their generous support of faculty research, to the Fulbright Program, to The Indian Institute for Advanced Study at Shimla, to the Pew-supported research project directed by Robert E. Frykenberg, and to his own enthusiastic interest and encouragement; to John B. Carman and Ineke Carman at Harvard Divinity School for their continuing interest; to Indira Viswanathan Peterson and Daniel Jeyeraj for their scholarship; and to Leslie Tagore, Anjala Richard, N. R. D. Ezekiel, Christodoss Kannappa, Priscilla Christodoss, Divakar Masilamani, Jamie Myerhoff, Zoe Sherinian, and Narelle Bouthillier for their critical readings and responses at different stages. I am, finally, most of all indebted to Lori, Jake, and Alexa for their patient and loving tolerance whenever, over the years, I have withdrawn into my office and into my own world to think and write about these matters. Without them I would never have finished.

D. Dennis Hudson
Smith College

CHAPTER 1

Beginnings

On July 9, 1706, two Germans landed on the southeastern coast of India in the Danish colony called Tranquebar. Nearly two hundred years after Martin Luther had begun the Reformation of European Christianity in Germany they had come to be his Evangelical voice to Indians of all sorts. When they landed, Bartholomaeus Ziegenbalg was 24 and Heinrich Pluetschau was 29. King Frederick IV of Denmark, as head of the Lutheran Church of Denmark and Norway, had commissioned and financed them, but as Daniel Jeyeraj discovered, the king had done so without consulting the Directors of the Danish East India Company in Copenhagen. The offended Directors therefore sent a secret instruction ahead of the missionaries to the Danish factory in Tranquebar to 'hinder the beginning, growth and establishment' of the missionary work (Jeyaraj 1997a: 67-77). Accordingly, when they landed, the two young men were surprised by a hostile reception and soon were outside the Danish fort in a marketplace with nowhere to go.

Where were they? They were on the coast of the ancient Tamil-speaking Chola empire centered at Tanjore called 'Cholamandalam', which the Europeans knew as Coromandel (Yule and Burnell: 256-58). They were in a town on a strip of coastal land three miles by five, which the Danish East India Company had been renting from the kings of Tanjore for 86 years. When Roelant Krappe, a Dutch merchant-sailor in charge of a Danish East India Company ship, had been attacked by the Portuguese in 1618 while trying to help the king of Ceylon, the Tanjore king Raghunatha Nayakan (1600-1630) gave him refuge (Jeyaraj 1997b). Two years later, Krappe negotiated a treaty with the king allowing the Company to use the strip of Tanjore land named for its main town 'City of Waves' or Tarangampadi. The Company paid fees to the

Tanjore ruler gleaned from its own taxes on the 15 towns and villages in the Tranquebar region, and from trade (Fenger: 1-6). By 1706 the town of Tranquebar had a population of about 18,000 (Ziegenbalg 1957: 35), and Tranquebar colony a total population of about 30,000 dispersed in 15 settlements (Lehmann 1956b: 1-4).

On the east the Bay of Bengal bounded the colony, and the Tanjore kingdom, about 100 miles long and 70 wide, bounded it on the west. The kingdom contained three notable palaces, four fortified towns, many large temple ('pagoda') towns, and resthouses for travellers supported by local 'pagans' of means, each about four miles apart and open to all for any length of time, 'let him be Heathen or Mahometan, black or white Christian' as Ziegenbalg would later report (Ziegenbalg 1717: 6-7).

Tanjore, the walled capital, lay 60 English miles to the northwest of Tranquebar. It contained a spacious palace and the monumental Brihadesvara temple built for the god Siva by a Chola ruler around 1000 C.E. Whoever ruled Tanjore controlled the rich resources of the Kaveri River delta and enviable wealth. As Ziegenbalg would report in 1709, Tanjore's Maratha king drew 'above thirty Tuns of Gold in Money' each year out of his dominions and was said to possess 'above Thirty Hundred Thousand Tuns of Gold' in his treasury. He kept 140 elephants for battle and over 300 imported horses; with his funds he could raise 'a most numerous Army' in a short time.

Warriors had fought over the region for centuries, and a complex linguistic, dynastic, and religious culture had emerged among the predominantly Tamil-speaking peoples of the region. The Marathi-speaking family that now ruled Tanjore and worshiped Siva had descended from warriors of the Bhonsle dynasty of Maharashtra; they had conquered the fortified capital in 1674. But Telugu-speaking Nayakas from the Andhra region, who worshiped Krishna or Vishnu, had preceded them as part of the earlier Vijayanagara realm centered in Karnataka; their Telugu-speaking presence was now permanent. The Vijayanagara realm had replaced the even earlier Cholas, and they carried on their predecessor's patronage of Sanskrit as an elite literary and religious language. When the Mughal rulers and the French and British of the East India Companies joined the ancient struggle over Tanjore, Persian, French, and English were added to the Portuguese, German, Danish, and Dutch already there. Yet for the vast majority of peoples on the subcontinent, and across the straits in the kingdom of Jaffna *(Yāḻpaṭṭiṇam)* on the northern peninsula of Ceylon, many dialectical versions of Tamil remained the spoken language, and its poetic versions the literary language. It is not surprising that language would become an important issue in the early development of Protestant culture in India.

When Tanjore's Maratha king sought to form an army, he drew upon the earlier Vijayanagara system of a 'lord' *(nāyakaṉ)* governing subordinate war chiefs *(pāḷaiyakkaraṉ)*. Those war chiefs used armed men as a tax-gathering military force housed in 'war camps' *(pāḷaiyam)* placed throughout the kingdom (Caldwell 1881a: 102-5). 'Vijayanagar was perhaps the nearest approach to a war-state ever made by a Hindu kingdom,' K. A. Nilakanta Sastri observed, 'and its political organization was dominated by its military needs' (Nilakanta Sastri: 297). A town called 'the fortified war camp' *(Pāḷaiyankōṭṭai)*, later important to this narrative, signifies the importance of warriors to the diffusion of the Evangelical message and its institutions.

Although the Maratha king of Tanjore was a Saiva who had inherited the Vaishnava court of the Telugu Nayakan, he was by this time subordinate to Muslim authority and impelled by its demands. In about 1699, the Tanjore king Shahji besieged the town of Tranquebar with 'forty Thousand Men' for nine months; he left only when his terms were agreed to and he was paid a 'Sum of Money.' The reason, Ziegenbalg would later explain, was his subordination to the Mughal emperor in Delhi:

> He is obliged to pay Annually a very great Sum of Money to the Mogol, to whom he is Tributary. Thus is he no Sovereign King, but a Vassal of the great Mogol. And such are all the other Kings and Princes upon the other Coasts, since they all pay Tribute to the Mogol. . . . At present there is no Sovereign King in all East-India, except in the Island of Ceylon, who is called Kandiarasha [*Kaṇḍya-rājā*], and is altogether independent. (Ziegenbalg 1717: 7-8)

A year after the missionaries arrived, the Mughal emperor Aurangzeb died; he had ruled and plundered the central Deccan area of the subcontinent for 25 years. The Mughal empire was now bankrupt, and as its administration and discipline disintegrated, an independent, Muslim-ruled principality emerged at Hyderabad in the Deccan. Through its local subordinate, the Nawab of Arcot, who formerly represented the 'Great Mughal' at Delhi as viceroy *(nawāb)*, Hyderabad influenced Tranquebar and Tanjore throughout the century, producing a renaissance of classical culture in the region. The British called the Nawab of Arcot's region the 'Carnatic' (from *Karṇāṭaka*), and the court music produced in the region from the seventeenth century became known as 'Carnatic music.' Music would join language as an important issue in a developing Protestant culture.

Rather arbitrarily, Protestant origins in India were thus planted in a complex cultural soil fertilized by generations of warfare and trade between

Arabs, Persians, Europeans, and the multilingual and multireligious kingdoms of south India and Ceylon. Although Tranquebar was on the eastern coast of Cholamandalam, in the 16th century the Portuguese had extended to it a name non-Indians had long used for the western coast; they called it 'Malabar' and its population 'Malabaris.' A Portuguese-based patois soon developed to bridge the linguistic gap between the Danish and German spoken by Europeans and the various forms of Tamil and Telugu spoken by those whom Europeans referred to as 'pagans' and 'Moors.' And that patois was the language of the growing number of Eurasians, or 'Luso-Indians', who were known as 'Portuguese.'

Three years after his arrival, Ziegenbalg described the population of the colony to correspondents in Germany in terms of skin color. The Europeans are white, he said, the 'Portuguese' are half-white, the 'Moors' are yellow, and the majority population, the 'Malabarians', are dark brown' (Lehmann 1956b: 17; Ziegenbalg 1717: 2). Yet, as Simon Casie Chitty observed in 1834 about the 'Malabarian' majority, skin color depended on contact with the sun, which was itself was a function of economic class and social custom.

> Their complexion varies from a dark brown to black, but when not exposed to the heat of the sun, as is the case with the majority of the Brahmans and the women of the superior classes, it often approaches to a yellow tint. (Chitty 1988: 62-63)

On the day they landed, the two young Germans Ziegenbalg and Pluetschau, somewhat at a loss about what to do after their expulsion from the Danish fort, stood for some time in the Tranquebar marketplace. A German-speaking Dane then came and took them home. He later rented them a house in a low-status neighbourhood of Eurasians and slaves of the Europeans. The slaves were members of crews that had been captured, baptized, and then sold; or were individuals sold by parents under financial duress; or were people who had been stolen or kidnapped; or were people bonded to land caught in political turmoil (Fenger: 12-13; Thurston: 6:114; Manickam: 47-51). Many appear to have been Roman Catholics. Battles between Nayakan and Mughal forces had created famines and dislocations in the Tanjore kingdom, and people had fled to the coastal towns. Philippus Baldaeus wrote in 1660 about 'the poor Country Wretches' who fled to coastal Nagapattinam for lack of food that,

> you saw the streets cover'd with emaciated and half starv'd Persons, who offer'd themselves to Slavery for a small quantity of Bread, and you might have bought as many as You pleased at the rate of 10 Shillings a Head;

> about 5000 of them were there bought and carried to Jafnapatnam, as many to Columbo, besides several thousands that were transported to Batavia. (Sathianathaier: 76)

It was from that socially marginal, dependent, Portuguese-speaking, Catholic and 'pagan' setting of slaves and Eurasians that the two Pietist Germans commissioned by Denmark's Lutheran king began to address the 'Evangelisch' message to India.

Protestant Predecessors

Ziegenbalg and Pluetschau were not, of course, the first Protestant spokesmen in India, nor were their converts the first Tamil-speaking Protestants. The Dutch Reformed Church had already made an impact on Catholics in the previous century. In 1613 the Dutch East India Company had established a trading post at Pulicat, about 30 miles north of Madras. Abraham Rogerius had served there between 1630 and 1640 as the first Reformed minister to the Dutch and to the 'Luso-Indian' community. Study rather than conversion, however, was Rogerius's primary approach to the 'pagans'; he produced the most authentic description of India's religions published in Europe until William Jones founded the Asiatic Society in Bengal in 1784 (Mitter: 51-55, 146-47).[1] Similarly, from 1656 to 1662 the Reformed minister Phillipus Baldaeus served as the Dutch chaplain in Jaffna and on the Pandya coast, and he, too, wrote reports, though they were largely plagiarized from a treatise of 1609 by the Jesuit Jacopo Fenicio that had been translated into Dutch from Portuguese (Mitter: 57-59, 297-98 n. 277; Arasaratnam: 11-14).[2] But in contrast to

1. Guided for a decade by the Brahmin Padmanabhan (probably a Sri Vaishnava), Rogerius published *De Open-Deure tot Verborgen Heidendom (Open-Door to Secret Heathendom)* in Leiden in 1651 (Arasaratnam: 12). It was translated into English as *A Door open'd to the Knowledge of occult Paganism: Or, a true Representation of the Life, Manners, Religion, and divine Service, of the Brahmins, who inhabit the Coast of Coromandel, and the neighbouring Countries* (Amsterdam, 1670), and reprinted as *A Dissertation on the Religion and Manners of the Bramins. Extracted from the Memoirs of the Rev. Abraham Roger, a Hollander.*

2. Baldaeus's publication appeared in Amsterdam in 1672: *Naauwkeurige Beschyvinge van Malabaren Choromandelen het machtige Eyland Ceylon. Nevens een omstandige en grondigh doorzochte ontdekking en wederlegginge van de Afgoderye der Oost-Indische Heydenen* (Amsterdam, 1672) (Extract description of Malabar and Coromandel — and the powerful island Ceylon. Together with a detailed and thoroughly investigated discovery and refutation of the idolatry of East Indian heathens).

Rogerius, Baldaeus had worked vigorously to turn the Tamil-speaking Catholics of the Jaffna kingdom into Protestants.

The kingdom of Jaffna, south of Tranquebar, on the northern end of the island of Ceylon, had long been an extension of Tamil culture across the Palk Strait, and had old cultural and trade ties to the Tanjore kingdom. By 1621 the Portuguese had taken control of Jaffna and were consolidating the Catholicism that had taken root, in part, through vigorous and ruthless conversion (De Silva: 114-19, 122-29). When the Dutch East India Company took Jaffna away from the Portuguese in 1658, it outlawed Catholicism and used the Company clergy to turn Catholics into Protestants.

Yet, though the Company controlled and used the Dutch Reformed Church, it gave it little financial support. When he became the Company chaplain, Phillipus Baldaeus took over the kingdom's 34 'Malabar' churches, and in place of the Roman Catholic sacrifice of the mass put the Dutch Reformed liturgy. Its centerpiece was the sermon expounding the 'Law of God' according to Calvinist principles. Baldaeus reported that they replaced the Catholic altar with the tablets of the Law, and severely simplified and intellectualized the liturgy:

> In the Churches of Jafnapatnam the ten commandments, written in large Malabar characters, are hung up on a table, on both sides whereof are the Our Father and the Creed. Every Sunday the people come to Church about ten a clock, and after they have sung a psalm, the school-master reads a sermon in the Malabar language, for which purpose a certain number of sermons are allotted to each Church, to be read in the absence of the minister. This done, they conclude with singing another psalm. (Baldaeus: 30)

Baldaeus noted in 1672 that, with not more than two or three ministers serving churches once served by at least 40 under the Portuguese, it was impossible to give individual instruction to the church members. Their greatest difficulty, he lamented, was instructing the young and old individually, 'which is best done by way of question and answer, which makes the deepest impression upon the minds of these tender christians' (Baldaeus: 31). Tamil was difficult for the Dutch ministers to learn, and each one had to visit the country churches constantly and preach three times on Sunday and once midweek. They had little energy or time left to proselytize the 'pagans' or 'Moors.'

An officially established Reformed Church with a puritanical liturgy, a doctrinal and intellectual emphasis, and few ordained ministers would not gain deep and independent roots in Ceylon. The Dutch government judged the bulk of Protestants there to be 'Calvinists and Christians only in name' (De Silva: 196-97). By 1796, when the British replaced the Dutch, Protestant culture in the whole of Ceylon was in decay, with 'heathenism' and Catholicism the beneficiaries (Baldaeus: vi-x, 43-48).

Nevertheless, the eighteenth century saw significant developments among Ceylon's Tamil-speaking Protestants. As official patron, the Dutch East India Company in 1737 established a printing press at its Colombo headquarters to publish Christian literature in the island's major languages, Sinhalese and Tamil (De Silva: 197). Records of 1743 reveal that 53,219 Reformed Church members lived in Colombo's predominantly Sinhala-speaking area, and that some belonged to a Tamil-speaking elite that would not develop on the subcontinent.

Two intermarried families, which were apparently Velalan, are noteworthy. A member of one family, Simon De Melho, held the position of 'Chief Tamil Mudeliar of the Gate' and was on the personal staff of ten Dutch Governors. His second son (Philip De Melho, whom we will discuss later) became the first Ceylonese native ordained according to the rules of the Church of Holland. A member of the other family, Philip Jurgen Ondaatje, was Translator to the highest judicial body, and his son became the Clergyman of Colombo and Rector of the Seminary. His daughter married Philip De Melho. One of their sons studied in Holland, as did several Protestant 'Malabarians' of eighteenth-century Ceylon (Chitty 1859: 70-71). In contrast, no Malabarian of the Danish mission studied in Europe, although a Tamil boy named Timotheus traveled in Europe with Pluetschau in 1711, and a Tamil boy named Peter Malaiappan went there with Ziegenbalg in 1715 (Lehmann 1956b: 95-96).

In the old Jaffna kingdom, which was predominantly Tamil-speaking, there were 200,233 Reformed Church members dispersed in 37 churches throughout five provinces, four times the number in Colombo. Yet by 1815, J. A. Dubois estimated that in the whole of Ceylon there were only 160,000 Christians, two-thirds (106,000) of whom were Catholics and the remainder (53,000) Calvinists (Dubois: 55). Yet, significantly, there were Tamil-speaking Protestant Brahmins in Jaffna, but not across the Palk Straits in Coromandel. Those Jaffna Brahmins articulated an early Protestant self-understanding that we will see repeated throughout this study, but voiced later on the subcontinent by Velalans in Tranquebar and Tanjore. Since Brahmins and Velalans comprised the learned elite and social aristocracy among non-Muslim Tamil speakers in both Jaffna and 'Malabar', it is not surprising that their values and views were much the same, even when translated into Christian terms.

Baldaeus reported in 1672 that he had baptized a learned Brahmin, 46 years old, who then wrote a Sanskrit poem entitled 'History of the Life and Passion of our Saviour' (Baldaeus: 6). He described a small island 'inhabited by Brahmins turned christians, who lead very sober lives' (Baldaeus: 25). He also described Protestant Brahmin culture:

> The Brahmins living in Jaffnapatnam, or any other part of the Indies, are for the most part men of great morality, sober, clean, industrious, civil, obliging, and very moderate both in eating and drinking: they use no strong liquors, wash or bathe twice a day, eat nothing that has had or may have life, yet are much addicted (like all the rest of the Indians) to pleasure.

Such vegetarian Protestants also kept other traditional customs:

> Notwithstanding they are christians, they carry still certain beads, and (as Rogerius observed, fol. 71.), like those of Coromandel, never marry out of their families, but frequently their brothers' and sisters' children; though else they are great enemies to incest, but excuse this near alliance by the great value they put upon their generation, which they deduce from Bramma, and some learned men from Abraham and Ketura, whose children, according to Gen 25. v. 6, went into the eastern country.

Cross-cousin marriages, a typical and ancient custom on both sides of the Palk Strait, allowed them to keep their lineages 'pure.'[3] Like most Brahmins, they traced their ancestry to the god Brahma, but some who knew the Bible traced it to the patriarch Abraham through Keturah; he had married Keturah after his first wife Sarah had died. To separate Keturah's six sons and their descendents from Isaac, his son by Sarah, Abraham sent them 'eastward to the east country' (Genesis 24:1-6). A variation of that Christian tradition was reported in 1834; it placed Brahmin origins even earlier in the biblical narrative. Some Brahmins said that the Seven Sages, the progenitors of their ancestral lineage according to traditional belief, were in fact the seven sons of Japheth, the eldest of Noah's three sons at the time of the great Flood (Genesis 9:18–10:32; 1 Chronicles 1:1-27) (Chitty 1988: 15).

According to Baldaeus, Protestant Brahmins understood the biblical Law of the Reformed Church, yet they interpreted it their own way through a reasoned analysis of the 'essence of Christianity' as it appeared to them in Scripture. For them, that essence did not consist in 'meat and drink', but

3. Margaret Trawick lucidly discusses Tamil kinship patterns in Trawick: chap. 4.

rather in a way of life that emerged from their 'nature' and level of 'education':

> Though they bear the name of christians, and know how to discourse rationally of the ten commandments, and the other points of the christian doctrine, they still retain many of their pagan superstitions. If you tell them of the christian liberty in victuals and drinks, they reply, that they are not ignorant of it, but as the essence of christianity does not consist in eating and drinking, so they did not think themselves obliged to feed upon such things as are contrary to their nature and education, being from their infancy used to much tenderer food, which agrees best with their constitution, and makes them generally live to great age. (Baldaeus: 35-36)

To those Protestant Brahmins, the 'freedom' from culinary obligations and restrictions that the European Protestants found appealing was not at all attractive. They understood perfectly well the Protestant insistence that all foods are ritually 'clean' and that purification through fasting and dietary restrictions is irrelevant in matters of salvation and may lead the faithful to rely on 'works' rather than on 'grace', as they said the Catholics did. But the Protestant Brahmins also believed that such Evangelical 'freedom' did not *require* them to eat and drink in the manner of other Christians, whether Tamil-speaking or European. Instead, they ate according to their 'nature' and level of 'education.' Both 'nature' and 'education' imply specific marriage patterns and diet, a common South Asian concept of 'habituation' (*paḷakkam* in Tamil) that will later appear among Protestant and Catholic Velalans on the subcontinent. We will discuss *paḷakkam* in greater detail in Chapter 10. With that background, let us now return to Tranquebar in 1706.

CHAPTER 2

Spreading the Word

Ziegenbalg and Pluetschau had not come to Tranquebar to serve the Europeans or to study India even though, in 1713, Ziegenbalg would produce the best scholarship on India's religions for many decades, unpublished until 1867 (Mitter: 59). They had come to address 'pagans' and 'Moors' with the Protestant message, and were the first Europeans sent to India or Ceylon expressly for that purpose. The various trading companies of Protestant Europe had long employed chaplains for their personnel in the colonies, and in Tranquebar the Danes possessed their own Lutheran church with two pastors. Yet no Malabarians belonged to their congregation, nor, apparently, did any Eurasians. There was also a Catholic church, and the Eurasians and Malabarian slaves who were Catholics were served by a Jesuit under the jurisdiction of the Portuguese Bishop of San Thome in Mailapore (Mayilapuram, now in Madras) (Fenger: 29-30; Dubois: 52-54). No 'pagans' or 'Moors' had yet voluntarily sought baptism from Protestants.

Two years after Ziegenbalg and Pluetschau arrived, three other Germans, J. E. Gruendler, P. Jordan, and J. G. Boevingh, came to Tranquebar. Over the next 131 years of the Danish-Halle mission, 51 other Europeans would continue what they had begun. In this chapter, however, our attention will not be on those missionaries but on the responses to them and their message by Tamil-speaking people of the early eighteenth century. How did Malabarians establish themselves as Evangelical Christians in Tranquebar and Tanjore? How did they view themselves socially and religiously? How did others, who were divided among a variety of religious and caste cultures, view them? Available evidence will not allow us to answer these questions completely, but even incomplete answers will lead us toward understanding what

Tamil-speaking people heard and what they responded to, positively or negatively, in the earliest effort to communicate the Evangelical message specifically to them.

Ziegenbalg's view of the people he sought to convert was a Pietist theology of culture not incompatible with Enlightenment ideas in Europe about universal reason:

> God is all wisdom and does not need man's help. Yet he walks around in the whole world so to speak offering his grace and his wisdom to men. And if He did not precede men in this work, nobody would feel even the desire for wisdom, let alone seek it and achieve it as they ought. (Gensichen: 40)

In his view, God's wisdom had long been at work among the Malabarians. The very fact that they — or any people — desired to be wise and to know truth and reality was evidence of God's ever-present grace. His task was to give them the 'good news' that would lift their veils of ignorance and enable them to understand fully what they already knew in part. Once the veils were off, people would be able to apply that 'good news' to their lives and their society in ways that flowed from their own informed judgment. For the most part, then, people of good faith equally committed to the 'good news' might disagree honestly about how it applied to their specific contexts. His pastoral task was not to make everyone conform to the same application of the Christian faith, but to enable differing applications of it to coexist harmoniously in a single community of faith.

Ziegenbalg's views account in part for the criticism the German Halle mission received in the next century from British Christians. Many of the British said that the German Lutherans had allowed too much caste observance into the church. In 1835 T. B. Macaulay in Calcutta published his famous 'Minute on Education', which stated his intent to create 'a class of persons, Indian in blood and colour, but English in taste, in opinions, in morals and in intellect.' They would, he thought, mediate between the British rulers and the millions they governed (Kuriakose: 125). Therefore, it is not surprising that the year before, Macaulay had said that the Evangelicals in Tanjore 'are a perfect scandal to the religion they profess' (Manickam 1988: 46). Their observance of caste distinctions within the sacred arena of worship was obviously not British.

Language and Velalans

Ziegenbalg and Pluetschau had been commissioned to spread the 'good news', and to do it effectively they first had to study the relevant languages. Both studied Portuguese, and Ziegenbalg also took up Tamil, drawing upon the linguistic and literary learning of Velalans belonging to the high-status Malabarian 'aristocracy.' After ten weeks Ziegenbalg described himself as surrounded by cultured men of high social standing. They considered themselves aristocratic 'sons of Goddess Earth' (as we will see later), yet Brahminical tradition ranked them ritually as Sudra, the lowest of four ritual classes *(varṇa)* according to the 'revealed' knowledge called Veda. Learned aristocrats they may have been, but since Veda classified them as Sudras, Velalans could gain direct access to the vedic rites and knowledge taught by Brahmin priest-teachers *(ācārya)* only after special rites of purification and consecration *(dīkṣā)*. It was the Velalans — high in Malabarian social status but low in vedic ritual status — who introduced Ziegenbalg to the complex weave of cultures in which he and Pluetschau were now entangled.

Yet Ziegenbalg and Pluetschau had become involved with the Velalans unwittingly. Right at the boat, before the two Germans had even touched the soil of Coromandel, a Portuguese-speaking Malabarian of about 20 years named Mudaliyappan offered himself as their servant. That 'heathen' Velalan introduced them to the rich feast of Velalan culture and to their first surprising taste of what they had come to save people from. Two months after they met, Ziegenbalg wrote to Halle the following about him (as translated three years later):

> As soon as we came to Anchor here, a pretty young Man of the Malabarian Race coming to our Ship, made some Inquiry about us, and asked me: Whether I would not take him to be my Servant? Whereupon I consulted with my Colleague, and we both thought it to be a Providence; and so took him into our Service. His Name is Modaliapa, of about Twenty Years of Age. His Mother being still alive, is of good Extraction; her Grand-Father having been a Prince of this Country. (Ziegenbalg 1718: 1:41-50)

How did Mudaliyappa communicate with Ziegenbalg on board the ship anchored off Tranquebar? The missionaries knew German, of course, and had studied Danish on the ship, but they knew no Portuguese or Tamil. The young man, who knew Tamil and Portuguese, must also have known some Danish, for, as it turned out, his deceased father had once worked for the Danish East India Company:

> His Father served the East-India Company here, and got a great deal of Wealth: But before he died, he gave all away to the Company, with this Request, that they would employ his Son in their Service, and see him well educated. And he deposited a certain Sum of Money for this Purpose. But all being come to nothing, both his own and his Mother's Estate being lost or consumed, this young Man hath been reduced to such a low Condition, that he is fain to go to Service for his Livelihood.

Ziegenbalg and Pluetschau immediately set to learning Portuguese from Mudaliyappa. He taught them from a Portuguese New Testament that a former Catholic priest, who had become a Protestant in Batavia, had translated from the Dutch (Fenger: 82-83), and from a Portuguese grammar written by a French Catholic missionary (Ziegenbalg 1957: 42-43). Nine weeks later Ziegenbalg began translating Christian ideas and prayers into Portuguese, which he then had put into Tamil.

About eight days after Mudaliyappa began teaching the missionaries, he asked them in Portuguese whether he might always stay with them and go to Europe one day. They said that he would first have to become a Christian and learn German. Mudaliyappa replied that:

> As for the Christian Religion, he would first be instructed in the fundamental Principles thereof, and get a competent Knowledge of our way of Worship. But as for the High-Dutch, he fell to it immediately, beginning now [two months later] to read and speak many things pretty well.

At that early stage, however, the missionaries' Portuguese was scant, and to explain Christian doctrine to Mudaliyappa they had to 'make use of Images, and to convey the Signification of things to his Mind by outward objects and Representations.' In the most important matters, such as the doctrine of 'the only true God, and his Son Jesus Christ, with the Holy Spirit: Likewise in the Doctrine of our Misery and fallen Condition, etc.' they brought in others to explain.

Sixteen days after their arrival, on July 25, a man visited who spoke both German and Portuguese. Through him, more serious theological discussions took place with Mudaliyappa. The latter now said that he believed in only one God, who had created him and everything else, 'and to this God he belonged, as well as the Blanks [Whites] or Christians, notwithstanding the Blackness of his bodily Shape, whereby he was distinguish'd from them.' He did not believe 'the Malabar Idols to be true Gods, and consequently as such to be worshipped', for 'a Man could be no God, much less coin Gods to himself.' But regarding Jesus Christ and the doctrine of the Christian religion, Mudaliyappa was not yet sure:

> I am, quoth he, not fully instructed in this matter, and therefore can't at present give any satisfactory Account thereof; but I heartily desire to have it explained to me, and to be taught such Things as I am yet unacquainted with.'

When pressed to convert, Mudalyiappa said that first he needed to be thoroughly convinced by Christian doctrine because, 'It wou'd but make a great Noise among the Malabarians, if he should suffer himself to be baptized so soon, and yet at the same time not to be able to give any sufficient reason for his doing so.' Then, in a further discussion of his own background, it became clear that the reason his conversion would create turmoil was that he had been an aristocrat:

> He told us: 'That his Neck, Hands and Feet, had formerly been all adorned with Gold Chains; but that he was brought now to such a low Ebb, as to be willing to serve others, tho' he himself had heretofore a long Train of Slaves attending him.' He said: As a Man had brought nothing into the World, so he could take nothing with him at his going out on't, besides his own Soul, and the good he had done during his Stay in it.

So far, however, Mudaliyappa had not said anything about religion that was not also believed by many 'pagan' Malabarians, as Ziegenbalg would soon learn.

On the next day Ziegenbalg went on a walk with Mudaliyappa, presumably still with the visitor as translator. During the conversation Mudaliyappa pointed out that 'almost all the Christians led a more vicious Life than the Malabarians did themselves.' Ziegenbalg could only respond that he should not pay attention to the scandalous life of those Christians, but rather to '*our* Life and Doctrine.' Ziegenbalg and Pluetschau were so impressed by Mudaliyappa's sincerity and commitment to them that from that day on, they 'spared to Labour, carefully to instruct him in the Word of God.'

They were astonished in the days that followed at the sophistication of the questions Mudaliyappa posed. They learned that he had already studied for five years in 'Malabarick-Schools' and was 'pretty well versed in their Theology, Philosophy, Arithmetick and fair Writing.' By September Mudaliyappa had learned enough German, and they enough Portuguese, that they could 'make shift to understand one another'; and Mudaliyappa also interpreted for them to the Malabarians. Ziegenbalg had by now hired a full-time schoolmaster for him, with the idea of sending him to Europe. There, Ziegenbalg thought, Mudaliyappa could correspond in Tamil with his own people in India and publish books in Tamil about Christianity.

That never happened, but Mudaliyappa did prove to be useful. On August 6, the King of Tanjore sent an officer to visit the new missionaries. They talked through an interpreter and kept up a correspondence after he left. On October 16 they sent Mudaliyappa to the officer 'about the Dispatch of a certain Affair' (Ziegenbalg 1718: 1:53). Whatever that affair was, Mudaliyappa's status as an educated Velalan no doubt facilitated its resolution with the officer and the king's court.

By September Ziegenbalg and Pluetschau had hired a Tamil tutor to teach them and other students in their house. The tutor was a 70-year-old 'heathen' poet and writer who knew no Portuguese. Not able to talk to Ziegenbalg directly, he introduced him to Tamil writing and reading, but not to vocabulary and linguistic structure (Lehmann 1956b: 21). That was remedied, however, when the missionaries employed a Velalan named Aleppa, who spoke Portuguese, Danish, Dutch, and German well (Lehmann 1956b: 23-24). Aleppa's son would later become Pluetschau's servant; perhaps he was Seperumal, the first free Malabarian who would be baptized by the missionaries (Lehmann 1956b: 9). As Aleppa developed Ziegenbalg's knowledge of Tamil, the elder teacher was able to explain Tamil texts to him, write down new words and expressions for him, and put complex poetry into colloquial speech (Lehmann 1956b: 24).

Insight into 'Heathen Darkness'

Ziegenbalg gleaned further insights into 'heathen darkness' from that elderly Velalan. The two of them reveal an intriguing Velalan-European interaction. In a letter to Germany dated 25 September 1706, Ziegenbalg wrote that Tamil should be taught in Europe, not only because 'the Malabarees are a great and innumerable people', but also because

> we should thus be able to understand from their writings the mystery of their theology and philosophy out of which one might extract much that is good and sensible. Indeed, I must confess that my 70 year old tutor often asks such questions to make me realize that in their philosophy everything is by no means so unreasonable as we in our country usually imagine about such heathen. . . . My old tutor often spends the whole day with me in discussion,

> through which I have already obtained quite an insight into their gods and idol worship. I intend to make a Christian of him, and he hopes that I may eventually become a Malabaree. Therefore he tries to show me everything very plainly, so that I could not wish it better. (Lehmann 1956b: 10)

Ziegenbalg's view that his tutor was trying to make him a 'Malabari' probably meant that the old man wanted to make the European 'civilized in the manner of a Velalan', for as we will see later, 'Malabari' was used commonly to denote Velalans and others of comparable status.

Unwittingly, the missionaries had surrounded themselves intellectually and domestically with men of high social status in Malabarian society rather than with the low-status people the Europeans called 'pariahs.' And it would be important to Tanjore Evangelical Velalans a century later that, even though they had been 'heathens', it was Velalans who had cooked the food, maintained the house, and taught language and culture to the first Evangelical missionaries.

Through Mudaliyappa, the elderly tutor Aleppa, and others, the two missionaries were gaining entrance to a sophisticated religious environment. In his letter of October 16, Ziegenbalg reported that they had composed a small tract that contained the 'Substance of the Christian Principles', the 'Lord's Prayer', and a 'petition for true conversion.' They wrote it in Portuguese, had it translated into Tamil, and then copied it by hand onto palm leaf books, which were now being disseminated among the Saivas and Vaishnavas. The 'pagans' who read the tract, however, were more advanced in their thinking, and more like the Christians, than the missionaries had thought:

> As for these Malabar-Heathens, we must needs say, they are a People of a great deal of Wit and Understanding, and will not be convinced but with Wisdom and Discretion. They have an exact Analogy and Coherence in all the fabulous Principles of their Faith. As for a Future Life, they have stronger Impressions than our Atheistical Christians. They have many Books, which they pretend to have been deliver'd to them by their Gods, as we believed the Scriptures to be delivered to us by our God. Their Books are stuffed with abundance of pleasant Fables and witting Inventions concerning the Lives of their Gods. They afford Variety of pretty Stories, about the World to come. And at this rate, the Word of God, which we proposed, seems to them to contain nothing but dry and insipid Notions.

He was impressed, moreover, by the discipline of their daily life and by the humility of their devotion:

> However, in the midst of these exorbitant Fancies and Delusions, they lead a very quiet, honest and virtuous Life, by the meer Influence of their natural Abilities; infinitely outdoing our false Christians, and superficial Pretenders to a better sort of Religion. They are wont to pay a great Deference to their Gods. When lately in the abovesaid Translation of the Christian Principles, a passage happened to be, shewing how we might become Children and Friends of God, our Schoolmaster startled at so bold a Saying, and offer'd to put in, instead of that Expression, that God might allow us to kiss his Feet.

Nevertheless, he and Pluetschau were certain that it was right to destroy 'idol worship', intellectually and literally, and that certainty led them further into the 'heathen darkness' they had come to dispel. During a walk in the colony, Ziegenbalg reported, they came to a temple of the Goddess *(Devī)*, consort of Siva the Ruler *(Īśvara)*, whose guardians were depicted by painted clay images:

> Yesterday taking a Walk in the Country, we came to an Idol-Temple, wherein Ispara's [Isvara's] Lady (he being one of their first-rate Gods) is worshipped. Her Ladyship was surrounded with abundance of other Gods made of Porcellain. We, being deeply affected with the Sight of so foppish a Set of Gods, threw some down to the Ground, and striking off the Heads of others, endeavour'd to convince this deluded People that their Images were nothing but impotent and still Idols, utterly unable to protect themselves, and much less their Worshippers.

Remarkably, that violent outburst did not evoke an equivalent response in the 'heathens' present. Instead, one 'pagan' scholar-teacher *(upadhyāyaṉ)*, no doubt restraining his agitation, told Ziegenbalg and Pluetschau that the pottery figures they had destroyed were of the guardians of the gods, not of the gods themselves. Nevertheless, the missionaries persisted in arguing the 'foolishness' of such images:

> But one of their Wathyjan [*Upadhyāyaṉ*], or Doctors of Divinity, happening to be present, replied: They did not hold 'em to be Gods, but only God's Soldiers, or Life-Guard-Men. At last, we convinced him so far, that he was forced to own these things to be meer Fooleries; but said withal, that the Design of 'em was to lead the meaner and duller sort of People, by looking on these Images, up to the Contemplation of the Life to Come. (Ziegenbalg 1718: 1:55-57)

The missionaries may have thought that they had argued the scholar into an admission he might not otherwise have made, but more likely their persistence led him to fall back upon an esoteric teaching found in the liturgical texts and practices called Āgama. In its respective versions, Agama underlies the religious systems *(samayam)* of the Saivas *(Śaivasamayam)* and the Vaishnavas *(Vaiṣṇavasamayam);* five years later Ziegenbalg would write about the ideas and practices of Agama with greater insight.

In his 1711 monograph 'Detailed Description of Malabarian Hethenism' *(Ausführliche Bescreibung des Malabarischen Heidenthums),*[1] Ziegenbalg explained the four types of religious practice Agama teaches, each of which requires a rite of initiation and a specific ritualized style of life (Ziegenbalg 1926: 26-29). The first two types are 'disciplined behaviour' *(caryā)* and 'liturgical ceremony' *(kriyā);* they focus on the rites of temples and images. The third type is 'unified consciousness' *(yoga);* it seeks to unify body and mind in the art of 'visualization' *(dhyāna),* often in the context of temples, images, and liturgies. The fourth type is 'esoteric knowledge' *(jñāna);* devotees achieve it by renouncing all rites, temples, and images as 'falsehood' *(mithyā)* or 'delusion' *(māyā)* when compared with 'the Absolute' *(parāparam).*

The word *parāparam* denotes a realm *(vastu)* beyond discursive thought, and may be glossed in two ways. First of all, it designates 'that which is beyond *(parā)* the beyond *(parāt)*', suggesting the realm of being from which heaven, atmosphere, and earth themselves emerge. Secondly, it designates 'that which is simultaneously beyond *(parā)* and not-beyond *(aparā)*', meaning that most essential mode of being which is both transcendent and immanent. As Ziegenbalg noted (1926: 39-41), the realm of absolute being *(parāparamvastu)* cannot be worshiped directly; it is unmanifest, but can only be worshiped by means of the manifest, for which reason it may be called 'Siva' or 'Vishnu' or 'Devi.' But from the esoteric point of view, in the end any manifest form is 'stupidity' *(Thorheit)* (Ziegenbalg 1926: 48).

The 'pagan' scholar-teacher *(upadhyāyaṉ),* it now appears, brought an end to their argument at the Goddess temple by appealing to esoteric thought *(jñāna).* From absolute being's point of view, all forms of matter *(mūrti)* are constructions of delusion *(māyā);* sacred forms in particular are meant to point beyond themselves to *parāparamvastu.* The pottery images of the guardians smashed by the missionaries were merely symbols point-

1. In 1926 W. Caland edited and published it in Amsterdam as *Ziegenbalg's Malabarisches Heidenthum.* For a detailed discussion of the Saiva Agama as prescribed for priests, see Davis 1991.

ing the 'meaner and duller sort of People' beyond themselves to Siva, the *parāparam.*[2]

The 'pagan' scholar's restrained response to that violent iconoclasm, I think, is noteworthy. Ziegenbalg did not say what kind of Devi temple they had encountered in their walk through the Tranquebar colony, but we can identify it as a temple of Ankalamman from his 1713 monograph, 'Genealogy of the Gods of Malabar' *(Genealogie der Malabarischen Götter).*[3] Ankalamman, he reported, manifests Siva's transcendent power *(parāśakti)* and, as a protector, receives offerings at least every Friday and an annual feast of cooked rice and sacrificed animals (Ziegenbalg 1867: 167-68). Commonly, her icon is carved of wood. Inside her shrine with her are wooden images of other deities (he listed eight), all of whom are worshiped. But in the open air outside, both within and beyond the temple's enclosing wall, are various large and small images made of clay *(Thon).* They, he said, do not receive veneration (Ziegenbalg 1867: 164-65). Those clay images are what Ziegenbalg and Pluetschau smashed.

The low status of those clay images accounts in part for the scholar's restrained response to their destruction; the guardian beings they embodied were not especially powerful or dangerous and could be appeased with relatively inexpensive rites. The fact that this particular Ankalamman temple stood in the Danish colony was another factor. From the Malabarian point of view, the recently arrived Germans belonged to the same 'caste' as the Danish rulers; and in traditional thought the ruler was responsible for the temples, in this case, the Danes. If a member of the ruling 'caste' behaved in such a manner, it was prudent to respond with restraint. Yet, if they had been in the Tanjore kingdom at the time, the response of the *upadhyāyaṉ* and those with him might have been quite different. Indeed, the missionaries may have felt free to act that way because of their presumed safety as members of Tranquebar's ruling 'caste.'

Yet even that *upadhyayaṉ* may not have been so restrained in Tranque-

2. In this Saiva case, the scholar might have appealed to the esoteric *Śvetāśvatara Upaniṣad,* which explains that *parāparamvastu* (or *brahman*) is tripartite: Ruler *(pati),* Goddess *(pāśa),* and Soul *(paśu).* As Siva's power *(śakti),* the Goddess is the material bond *(pāśa)* that causes death and birth through delusion *(māyā).* Siva the Ruler is her master *(pati),* and he uses her for his own ends, which includes liberating individual souls from her bondage. When a liberated soul sees the Goddess, the Ruler, and all souls in their true relationship to each other, undefiled by deluded perception and free of death and birth, it sees *parāparamvastu* as it truly is.

3. Edited by W. Germann and published in 1867 in Madras as *Genealogie der Malabarischen Goetter.*

bar had the missionaries dared to walk inside the temple and attack Ankalamman herself. An attack on the 'Mother of the Universe' was unlikely to elicit merely a theological response.

Mutual Perceptions

By October the two Pietists had been in Tranquebar for four months, and 'Heathens' like the *upadhyāyan̠* must have found them intriguing. They were a new type of European. From any 'well-born' Malabarian point of view, they were viewed as living and working in dismal circumstances among refugees, slaves, and poor Eurasians. In mid-October, for example, they set up a 'Charity-School' for Malabarian boys. They planned to meet all their students' expenses because they would either come from families who had lost all means of support after they had converted to the Evangelical Church, or they would themselves be purchased, an investment for the mission's future. Purchasing children, however, could be expensive, even though (or perhaps because) the Danish East India Company was regulating the market. As Ziegenbalg noted in his letter of October 16, 1706,

> For the right settling and increasing whereof [the Charity-School], we must buy such Children, (and this now and then at a high Rate too,) as their Parents are willing to part with; which one time Necessity obliges them to; another time perhaps some other Reasons, which God knows. For the East-India Company has made an Order, not to buy any Children from those Kidnappers, that secretly use to convey away young Children, to the great Grief of their Parents, and to sell 'em again, for a little Money, to accomplish some sinister End or other they have in view. (Ziegenbalg 1718: 1:60-61)

In addition to their resident students, they also urged Europeans working for the Danish Company in Tranquebar to send their slaves to the school as non-resident day students. In that same letter Ziegenbalg reported:

> A few Days ago we delivered a Memorial to the [Danish] Governour here, intreating him, to order all the Protestant Inhabitants of this Place, to send their Slaves two Hours a Day, on purpose to be instructed in sound Principles of Religion, and afterwards initiated by Baptism into the Communion with Jesus Christ. Hereupon the Governour visited us himself, and promised to send 'em shortly. (Ziegenbalg 1718: 1:53-54)

While high-status Malabarians and Europeans agreed that the Charity-School was a sign of the dismal economic and social circumstances of the mission, they agreed on little else.

Each viewed the other as belonging to a degraded civilization. Throughout his career Ziegenbalg reported that from the viewpoint of 'heathen' Velalans and Brahmins, European Christians were barbaric. A lengthy quote from one of his letters makes the point vividly:

> Their minds are aroused by the European Christians into such bitterness and resentment, because they often treat the heathen most unmercifully, and treat them as just black dogs; on top of that they offend them by their behaviour. Wherefore, as I was once speaking with several heathen and addressed them sharply to penetrate their conscience, they replied thus: As certainly and surely as you Christians with your drinking and gluttony, with your adultery, with your dancing and gambling, with your swearing and cursing, and with your evil and sinful life, hope to be saved, so certainly and surely we consider that we shall be saved by our quiet and retired life, even if our religion should be false and all lies. Here I was shocked and asked them what in their hearts they thought about us Christians? They did not want to answer, but I promised them, they should not suffer anything bad on account of it. On this assurance, they said that they had thought the Christians were rather stupid and without learning, because they gave no thought to God or to the future life. I asked how they could think that, when they saw that we had a church in which three times a week we sang and preached, all the Europeans attending the divine services. Yes, they saw and heard this, but they had thought that the preachers in the church taught how one could anyway indulge in drinking, gluttony, gambling, adultery, and do all sorts of evil things to the black people. . . . Because when they saw our actions, they found that the Christians did such things right after Church. . . .' (Lehmann 1956b: 40)

In another letter, quoted in a letter from Copenhagen dated June 14, 1709, Ziegenbalg said that the Malabarians were particularly

> offended with that Proud and insulting Temper, which is so obvious in the Conduct of our [European] Christians here. 'Tis true, they too much value themselves on one Hand on account of their Parts, Wit, and Abilities; and on the other, make too little of the poor Heathens, whom they treat with a haughty Look, call 'em Dogs, and other Names, and show 'em all the Spight and Malice they are able to contrive. Yea, some of our [European] Chris-

> tians are arrived to such a Pitch of Haughtiness, as to continue utterly ashamed of the Heathens even then, when they are brought over to Christianity by Baptism, and initiated into our holy Faith: Much less will they be induced to live with them as with Brethren in Christ; a Name so much used and beloved among the Christians in the primitive Days.
>
> Many of the Heathens, it is true, are convinced of the Soundness of the Doctrine we have all along proposed to them; but casting their Eyes upon the profligate Manners of those that profess it, they are at a stand, and do not know what to betake themselves to. They suppose that a good Religion and a disorderly Conversation, are Things utterly inconsistent one with another. And because they see the Christians pursue their wonted Pleasure presently after divine Service, some of the Heathens have from thence taken up a Notion, as if we Preachers, in our ordinary Sermons, did teach People all those Debaucheries, and encourage 'em in so dissolute a Course of Life. (Ziegenbalg 1718: 2:27-28)

Consequently, Ziegenbalg elsewhere reported,

> The name of Christ has become so hated and despised among them because of the offensive and shameful life of the Christians that they think a worse people could not be found in the whole world than the Christians. Therefore they will neither eat nor drink with any Christian nor permit such in their house. (Lehmann 1956b: 10)

Nevertheless, Ziegenbalg said, he and Pluetschau were not viewed with hostility by the Malabarians, but rather by the Europeans. Fourteen months after their arrival he wrote in a letter dated September 12, 1707:

> Heathens and Mahometans are kind enough to us, and love to be in our Company; notwithstanding we have all along laid open to them the Vanity of their idolatrous and superstitious Worship. But those [Europeans] that pretend to be Christians, and are worse than Heathens at the Bottom, have shewn us all the Spite and Malice they ever cou'd. However, there is a Remnant left among them too, that love to be sincerely dealt with. (Ziegenbalg 1718: 1:73)

Ziegenbalg also said that the Velalans who worked for him at home had 'great regard' for him and appreciated his 'genuine love for them'; therefore they were willing to introduce him to their knowledge. The elderly poet in particular appears to have thought that, if Ziegenbalg would apply that knowledge to his life, he would become truly 'civilized', a path that some European Catholics had already followed.

In the seventeenth century the Jesuit Robert de Nobili (1577-1656) had lived the life of a radical renouncer *(sannyāsin)* in Madurai and was famous (and notorious) among Catholics for doing so (Neill 1984: 279-309; Cronin). Similarly, in 1710 the Jesuit Joseph Constantius Beschi joined the mission Nobili had founded in Madurai and likewise adopted the vegetarian lifestyle of a 'pagan' religious leader. His model, however, was not the *sannyāsin,* but the householder teacher-priest *(ācārya),* even though he was celibate. He continued the practice when he moved to the Tanjore region in 1720. One hundred and twenty years later, a Catholic Velalan named A. Muttusami Pillei (i.e., Pillai), described Beschi's home life this way:[4]

> From the time of his arrival in this country, he abstained from the use of flesh, fish, etc., and employed two Tamil youths to dress his food according to the Hindu custom, partaking of it only once in the day. When at home, he wore on his head a velvet cap; the remainder of his dress consisted of a cloth, with a narrow red border, tied round the waist by another cloth of a light purple colour, and of sandals for his feet — his costume was the same as that worn by the Hindu devotees.

When he went out in public, Beschi dressed and behaved like a royal acharya (or *rājā-guru*) of the Saivas and Vaishnavas:

> When abroad, he wore a long gown of light purple colour, with a waistband of the same colour; on his head was a white turban, covered with a purple cloth, in his hand he carried a handkerchief of the same colour — his ears were adorned with a pair of pearl and ruby ear-rings — his forefinger with a gold ring. A long cane in his hand, and a pair of slippers on his feet, completed his out-of-door dress. His conveyance was a palankeen, having a tiger's skin for him to sit upon, two persons attended on either side

4. The account by A. Muttusami Pillei was published as 'A Brief Sketch of the Life and Writings of Father C. J. Beschi or Viramamuni, Translated from the Original Tamil,' *Madras Journal of Literature and Science* (April 1840): 250-300. A. Muttusami Pillei was the 'Manager of the College of Fort St. George and Moonshee to the Tamil Translator to Government.' He began the Tamil original in 1822, based on 1798 manuscripts by the poet Saminada Pillei. A Tamil version of his account, including Beschi's instruction to catechists, *Vētiyar-oḻukkam,* appeared serially as '*Vīrmāmunivar carittirvaralāṟu:* Life of Beschi' and '*Vētiyar-oḻukkam,*' in *Utayatārakai — Morning Star,* published in Jaffna, January 12, 1843–December 28, 1843.

> of the palankeen to fan him — a third person carried a purple silk umbrella, surmounted with a golden ball, whilst two others carrying a bunch of peacock's feathers proceeded in front, and whenever he alighted from the palankeen he sat down upon the tiger's skin. In order to preach the gospel with full effect, and to make converts to Christianity amongst the heathens, he made himself perfect master of the Hindu sciences, opinions and prejudices, and conformed to their customs in matters of indifference. (Muttusami Pillei: 254)

In contrast to those two famous European Catholics of the Madurai mission, Ziegenbalg and other German Evangelical missionaries in Tranquebar dressed as they had in Europe. Ziegenbalg reported that, 'Europeans go about here dressed as in Europe, each one according to the custom of his country, only that in the warm season one has to wear [indoors] very light silk clothes like the Indians.' In public, it meant for him a wig, his collar buttoned to the top, and a long black overcoat over a coat of European cloth (Lehmann 1956b: 19).

After the missionary C. T. Walther arrived from Germany in 1725, he discovered that Europeans were so strange to villagers that they startled not only them but also their animals. In the words of Daniel Jeyaraj:

> When Europeans tried to enter the villages they met with [a] very unusual welcome. The villagers feared them and ran away from them. Even hens, dogs and cows made loud noise when they saw the Europeans. In their appearance, skin and dress, and in their food and habits, they remained, as far as the Tamilians were concerned, foreigners. (Jeyaraj 'Ordination': 8)

One of the reasons Ziegenbalg's elderly tutor may have tried to 'civilize' him in the manner of a Velalan was to enhance the missionary's enjoyment of life. As Ziegenbalg regretfully observed about the 'heathens', 'Their books are all filled with cheerful and attractive things, so that in contrast the living Word of God seems to present only dreary matters' (Lehmann 1956b: 10).

First Baptisms

The first committed responses to Ziegenbalg and Pluetschau's preaching and teaching came from the Eurasian 'Portuguese.' The missionaries gave them the individual catechetical attention that Baldaeus had found wanting in Jaffna. They used Portuguese to teach three slaves of the Danish Commandant, and, shortly thereafter, two more. They did not baptize them quickly, but only after six months of instruction for two hours a day, an intensive indoctrination of individual catechumens in belief and practice that expressed the religious 'individualism' characteristic of Pietist thought. They wanted 'genuine' piety firmly grounded in each person.

The five slaves were baptized in May 1707 (Lehmann 1956b: 37-38; Paul 1961: 3). The rites took place not in the missionaries' house, where their congregation met, but in the Danish church. On Wednesdays Ziegenbalg preached there in German to the many German soldiers of the factory. That was the first time that Protestant slaves and masters in 'Malabar' had worshiped together within the same liturgical boundary; thus, the Evangelical pattern of 'sitting together separately' had been inaugurated. Yet, as we will shortly see, that practice quickly changed. In contrast to the practice of Evangelical Malabarian 'aristocrats' and their Evangelical Malabarian 'servants' over the following years, the Protestant European masters and their Protestant Malabarian servants would not long 'sit together separately' for worship.

Ziegenbalg's Wednesday preaching in the Company church reflected the official status of the Pietist mission within the Church of Denmark, even though in its place of worship, its authority, and its finances, it functioned independently of the Company. Missionary identification with the Company, however, posed a problem in recruiting converts. The congregation had grown too large for Ziegenbalg and Pluetschau's house, but where would they go? According to one author, the baptism of the five slaves had prompted the missionaries to build their own place for worship because the Europeans did not want to worship with their own servants.[5] That may have been true, but Ziegenbalg also believed that worshiping with Europeans hindered conversion. On September 12, 1707, speaking of Malabarian men rather than of women, he wrote that

> the Heathens [are] too shy, to venture into the Churches of the Blanks, (so they call the Christians) since these were generally adorned with fine Cloaths, and all manner of proud Apparel; but they themselves black, and wearing nothing but a thin Cloth to cover their Body. (Ziegenbalg 1718: 1:70)

5. 'The Europeans of the place, both Germans and Danes, did not . . . relish the idea of their own domestic servants becoming Christians and coming to worship with them in the same church. They refused to let the missionaries bring these new converts to Zion Church for worship and reserved the church exclusively for the use of Europeans' (Paul 1961: 8).

He wrote to the King of Denmark a week later that he had often been told that Malabarians would not convert because they did not want to be with the 'civil servant Christians' who 'naturally' made them fearful and timid.[6]

Consequently, in June of 1707 the two Pietist Germans and their congregation laid the foundation of the 'New Jerusalem Church', built of stone on the main street of the Malabarian village. They began to worship in it two months later. In September of 1707 they baptized the first free Malabarian who was not 'Portuguese.' He appears to have been Ziegenbalg's 30-year-old Velala servant named Seperumal (Ziegenbalg 1957: 55).[7]

After 14 months in Tranquebar, Ziegenbalg and Pluetschau now possessed a new church building of stone, a congregation of 75 (37 of whom were baptized), and held worship services in Tamil and Portuguese.[8] The congregation, however, only partially represented the colony's population. It consisted of former Catholics and 'pagans', of Eurasians and Indians, of slaves and 'pariahs', but few Velalans. There were no former Muslims, no Brahmins, and no Europeans other than the missionaries. It was economically and socially dependent on the Danish fort, on mercantile trade, and on the mission's institutions, which depended on contributions from Europe and were expensive. One year later, for example, the school divided into two, one a 'Portuguese school' taught by Pluetschau, who also taught Danish and German, and the other a 'Malabarick school' where Ziegenbalg taught. Eight children were 'freely boarded and provided with all Necessaries' (Ziegenbalg 1718: 2:6-7).

New Jerusalem's pastors, though German, followed the Danish Lutheran rite, which linked their congregation to the Company's official Zion Church, whose Europeans followed the same rite. Their New Jerusalem congregation, however, consisted largely of the servants and slaves of the European civil and military servants of the Company. Since it belonged to the Tranquebar colony rather than to the kingdom of Tanjore, the New Jerusalem congregation was subject to the civil authority of the Danish Commandant. When a larger New Jerusalem Church was built in 1718, it made that political fact clear to all: the crown of its patron, the King of Denmark and Norway, hung above its entrance.[9]

6. '. . . vor welchen sie eine naturliche Fürcht und Scheu haben' (Ziegenbalg 1957: 54).

7. In this letter he is identified as 'about 25 years old', and no name is given. Arno Lehman identified him as Seperumal, age 30, who took the name Andreas (Lehmann 1956a: 70).

8. Ziegenbalg 1957: 59-60. A list for 1707 gives a total of 35 (presumably baptized): 16 'Portuguese' and 19 'Tamil' (Lehmann 1956b: 122).

9. See the plate in Lehmann 1956a: 79.

The congregation grew during the remaining 12 years of Ziegenbalg's life. By 1712 there were 202 members, 117 of them Malabarians and 85 'Portuguese.' In 1720, the year after his death, 250 people remained out of the 450 who had been recruited: 147 of them were 'sudra' (Velalans), and the remainder belonged to low-status 'pariah' castes.[10] There were schools, and in 1716 a seminary began that lasted until 1780. It started with eight young men. According to a letter of 1717 in the Halle archives studied by Daniel Jeyaraj, the seminary was meant to train schoolteachers and catechists, and eventually 'pastors for the black.' As a Pietist seminary that viewed the natural world as a source of the knowledge of God as well as the Bible, its curriculum included 'Bible knowledge, exegesis, catechism, systematic theology, geography using globes, Church history, medicine, and mathematics.' But its emphasis was on the Bible and its exegesis (Jeyeraj 1998: 7; Lehmann 1956b: 146).

A printed report of 1725 gives an idea of the occupations of Malabarian Evangelicals in Tranquebar town. Of 87 adults, five served the Danish company, six were soldiers or sailors, others served the mission as catechists, clerks, or teachers, and the remainder sought work with the Europeans and gained food however they could, some earning a little by knitting stockings, a skill taught to children of the mission's schools. Of the 'Portuguese' adults, 13 were soldiers and sailors, and the rest served the company and earned money by knitting stockings and weaving reeds (Lehmann 1956b: 43).

The Protestants of the Danish fort thought the Evangelicals were a disreputable lot, and the conflict of interest between the Danish Commandant and the missionaries was obvious. The Commandant's job was to use Malabarians to make profits for Company investors in Denmark, while the missionaries' job was to profit in souls for God in heaven. That conflict led the Commandant eventually to jail Ziegenbalg for four months, from November 11, 1708, to March 26, 1709. The occasion, according to Daniel Jeyeraj, was Ziegenbalg's intercession for justice on behalf of a widow humiliated by a Roman Catholic and the local Danish government (Jeyeraj 1997a: 71). The Commandant's antagonism to Ziegenbalg led him to report that

> the whole congregation of this missionary consists (despite their boasting) only of . . . slaves among the people and a group of evil, ill-bred creatures, who are drowned in sin and wickedness and must be maintained by them with food and clothing, together with some small children of whom one

10. Lehmann (1956b: 111) noted that many had died, some had moved away, and others had relapsed into their former faith or had joined the Catholic congregation.

can have, in this present famine, as many as one wants to feed. (Lehmann 1956b: 75)

The Commandant's further views were summarized by Arno Lehmann:

> [The missionaries] gave out too much relief, collected money without permission, and were constantly pressing for donations; they showed an excess of missionary zeal even against the laws of nature and of the country. They had the idea that a master was not entitled to sell his slave if he had become a Christian and he no longer suited his master. He, the Commandant, never doubted the good intentions of the most gracious King and the proper calling of the missionaries for the conversion of the heathen. But he did doubt the correctness of their methods and procedure, and discovered in the missionaries a pedantic pride, concealed selfishness, injustice and tyranny. (Lehmann 1956b: 75)

Spread of the Mission by Europeans

Still, the Danish-Halle mission spread beyond Tranquebar. In 1726 the missionary Benjamin Schultze left Tranquebar for Madras and established an Evangelical congregation in a house in 'Black Town' where 'pagans', Muslims, and Armenian Christians lived. In the 'white town' near Fort St. George, where the English and some Portuguese lived, stood an English church and a French Catholic church with a congregation of about 1,000 Indians. To the south lay the Vaishnava temple town of Triplicane (Tiruvallikkeni) and the Saiva temple town of Mailapore (Mayilapuram). In 1752 the Tamilian and 'Portuguese' Evangelical congregation moved westward from 'Black Town' into a confiscated French Catholic church and residence near the village of Vepery, which today is a major center of Protestants in Madras (the metropolis now known as Cennai) (Lehmann 1956b: 130-34). About 62 years later, in 1814, two 'new missionaries' named C. T. Rhenius and L. P. Haubroe would antagonize Velalans in the Vepery congregation and set off a controversy about 'sitting together separately' that would reverberate southward in Tranquebar and Tanjore (Manickam 1988: 47).

The British in Madras, who were Anglicans, found the German Evangelical missionaries appealing, and in 1728 the Society for Promoting Christian Knowledge began sponsoring Schultze's school and congregation. A decade later it sponsored German missionaries southward along the coast at Cuddalore (Kutalur), where Fort St. David stood, beyond the French colony of Pondicherry. About 50 miles south of Cuddalore in Tranquebar, the German missionaries stationed there spread their work southward along the coast, and from 1732 they were involved with Protestants of the Dutch colony at Nagapattinam, an ancient port to Ceylon, Batavia, and points further east (Lehmann 1956b: 139). Gradually, Anglicans, Dutch Reformed, and German Evangelicals had formed a collective 'Protestant' presence in colonial factories on the Coromandel Coast, and from there they would slowly move inland.

By 1732 the Tranquebar Evangelical mission consisted of 1,478 members: 287 were 'Portuguese', 546 were Malabarians, and 645 resided in the kingdom of Tanjore. There were three Malabarian schools and two 'Portuguese' schools, with a total of 196 children of both sexes, according to a report of 1733, 'fed, clothed and taught gratis' (Paul 1961: 14). Twenty-five native catechists, assistant catechists, and schoolmasters assisted nine European missionaries; 16 worked in Tranquebar and its environs, and nine worked in the outlying country (Lehmann 1956b: 145; Paul 1961: 9).

One year later (1733), the first Malabarian Evangelical pastor was ordained at the New Jerusalem Church in the presence of seven German missionaries, two Danish ship chaplains, two Danish pastors of the Zion Church, four Malabarian catechists, six Malabarian assistant catechists, the Dutch catechist delegated by the Nagapattinam governor, and many Malabarian lay people. He would be the first of 14 in the original Tranquebar mission (1706-1825), all of them Velalans. The first non-Velalan pastor, B. Samuel of Manigraman, was not ordained until 1890.[11] The story of that first pastor, Arumugam Pillai, who took the baptismal name of Aaron, brings us to the next chapter and the subject of Pietism in Malabarian lives.

11. The second was Diogo or Diago (1709-1781), born to a Catholic family and ordained in 1741. The third was Ambrose (d. 1777), also born a Catholic, who was ordained in 1749. The fourth was Pulleimuttu (c. 1731-88), the son of a 'pagan' headman from near Nagapatanam, who had been abducted to Tranquebar as a slave. He was baptized as Philipp, served as a catechist, and was ordained in 1772. The fifth was Rajappen, ordained in 1778, and the sixth was Sattyanathan, ordained in 1790. In the time of the old Tranquebar Mission, 14 Malabarians were ordained, all of whom were 'caste people', i.e., 'Sudras.' In the 216 years between 1733 and 1949, 140 Tamil pastors are listed in the Tamil Evangelical Church (Lehmann 1956b: 147-52).

CHAPTER 3

Pietism in Malabarian Lives

The Pietist version of Evangelical, or Protestant, Christianity began with two Germans, but spread by means of Malabarians, whose lives it transformed. In this chapter we will explore Pietism and the means by which Ziegenbalg disseminated it in Tamil. We will also consider how two Tamil-speaking men adapted it to their lives. One man was a high-status Velalan; he became the first ordained Protestant pastor on the Indian subcontinent. The other man was a low-status Servaikaran;[1] he was a soldier who took the Evangelical message to people and places the Germans could not reach, and he experienced the consequences of the status that allowed him to do so. Right from its introduction into India, people of both high-status and low-status castes led Protestant Christianity, which, given Malabarian society and mission interests, produced social and ecclesiastical complications that will be discussed in the following chapters.

Aaron, the First Ordained Malabarian Pastor[2]

Aaron was the first Protestant pastor or 'priest' of India. He was born in 1698/99 in Cuddalore, the location of Fort St. David, as a Saiva Velalan named

1. Servaikaran is a title for Akampatiyar, an agricultural caste in the Tanjore and Madurai districts, known as having been palace servants of ancient chieftains (*Tamil Lexicon,* loc. cit.). In another form, Servaikkaran, it may designate the captain of a division of an army.

2. The following account is based on Jeyeraj 1998: 1-79; and Paul 1961: 4-24.

Arumugam Pillai. His father, Sorcanada Pillai (Cokkanatha Pillai), was said to have been a wealthy merchant, and Arumugam was educated enough to read and write. In 1717, when he was 17 or 18 years old, a Velalan catechist from Tranquebar named Savarimuthu arrived in Cuddalore to look after a charity school that the British governor had newly established across from Sorcanada Pillai's house. Not long after that his son began reading the Tamil books recently printed at Tranquebar.

In 1718 Arumugam's father lost his business and the family was impoverished. Sorcanada Pillai wanted his son to take up manual labor in the fields, but Arumugam resisted that idea and, with the help of relatives, went south to Tranquebar. There he met Savarimuthu, who took him to meet Ziegenbalg. Arumugam Pillai then began to study with Ziegenbalg, and not long afterward received baptism. He received the name of Aaron, presumably an allusion to Aaron of the Bible, the first priest of Israel, the people God was believed to have created as his own. Apparently, Ziegenbalg had hoped that the young man would likewise become the first 'priest' of the people God would create among the Malabarians.

In that same year Aaron began teaching writing and arithmetic in the Tranquebar school, and he married a colleague's daughter named Rachel. In the following year he was appointed assistant catechist at the New Jerusalem Church, newly built to replace the smaller original building. The latter building of 1707 was now used to tutor new converts, catechumens, and adult Malabarians, as Ziegenbalg and the more recently arrived J. E. Gruendler wrote in 1718, 'that they may each in their turns be daily instructed in the principles and practice of a true Christianity' (Jeyeraj 1998: 75 n. 18). By 1719 Aaron was about 21 years old, married, and well launched on an ecclesiastical career.

The mission could not survive without Malabarian catechists. As Daniel Jeyaraj noted, besides teaching Christian doctrine, they superintended the spiritual lives of Christians in the villages, visited the sick and needy, administered aid to the poor, conducted marriages and funerals, and preached sermons (Jeyeraj 1998: 10). Importantly, they could go where Europeans could not. In 1727, for example, when Europeans were not allowed to cross the border to Tanjore on pain of death, Aaron freely went to Tanjore to investigate the Evangelicals who had appeared there (as will be discussed below). He delivered books and tracts and carried a letter from the missionaries to a member of the Maratha court.

Moreover, they could solve traditional issues with traditional means. By 1729 Aaron had been appointed a full catechist, and specific villages were under his jurisdiction. The next year he took charge of the Mayavaram area, within the

Tanjore kingdom, where there were 177 Christians, mostly Velalans, but — in a reversal of caste norms — a low-caste catechist named Sattianadan (Satyanathan) had been appointed their leader. Consequently there was strife. But two years after Aaron took charge, the strife seems to have subsided and there were 381 Christians, with more to follow in 1733 (Jeyaraj 1998: 11).

In the meantime Rachel had died in childbirth, leaving Aaron in 1731 with three children. At missionary suggestion, a year later he married Anandaj, the daughter of a widow. Together they had two additional children.

It was becoming clear that a Malabarian would have to be ordained a priest, because there were few missionaries coming from Germany, and those in Tranquebar had tied themselves up in disputes with each other. They did agree, however, to choose three Velalan catechists as candidates: Savarimuthu, Aaron, and a former Catholic named Diago. Savarimuthu claimed old age and bowed out at the end, leaving the choice between Aaron and Diago. The method of selection followed Lutheran polity of the time: All constituent families of the Tranquebar congregation cast votes through each family's head. The result was a tie that was finally broken in Aaron's favor (Lehmann 1956b: 147-48).

Aaron's pastorate was intended for Malabarians; whether he ever administered the sacraments to Europeans is not known. Geographically, it covered a wide area, and two catechists assisted him, both former Catholics. From 1737 he had a horse. The Tamil name used for a European pastor was *aiyar* ('noble' or 'respected', from *arya* and *ayya*), an honorific commonly used as a caste title for Smartha Brahmins (as Aiyar) and for Sri Vaishnava Brahmins (as Aiyangar). Malabarians in Tranquebar sometimes applied the title to Aaron as 'Aaron Aiya', but in the villages he was known more commonly as *nāṭṭuguru* (country teacher) or as *nāṭṭaiyar* (country *aiyar*) (Jeyaraj 1998: 25; Paul 1961: 12 n. 1).

While he was serving as priest, Aaron's family was infused with the mixed sorrow and joy that was not unusual in a Malabarian householder's life of the time. Four years after ordination, his second wife, Anandaj, died, leaving him now with five children. In the next year, 1738, he married again, and two more children were born. On June 23, 1745, while his third wife was pregnant, he gave one of his daughters in marriage to a son of Diago, also a Velalan. Diago had by now been ordained as the second Evangelical priest. But two days after the wedding, Aaron died. He left a richly textured household, consisting of a widow with eight children fathered by a single man with three different wives. As inferior 'bride-givers', they all were linked patrilineally to Diago as the head of a superior 'bride-receiving' patrilineage within the same Velalan caste. Yet Diago was of junior status professionally to

S. Aaron of Cuddalore, the first Evangelical clergyman in India, is depicted here for a German audience after his 1733 ordination. The copperplate engraving, in color, was made in Halle from a written description sent from Tranquebar. His dress is the Persian style used in Coromandel courts influenced by Moghul rule. The Tamil text of the Bible he holds is from Acts 11:18: 'And they glorified God, saying, "Then to the Gentiles also God has granted repentance unto life."' Complementing that text, the German inscription above identifies Aaron as the means of repentance for Malabarian 'heathens': 'Herr Aaron. National Land-Prediger unter den heidenische Malabaren in Ost-Indien.' [The photo is taken from Lehmann 1956b: facing p. 96.] For a Tranquebar critique of the depiction, see J. Müller-Bahlke: 95.

the deceased father.[3] For a life to be lived satisfyingly in such a complex network of kinship and professional status, caste custom was an indispensable guide.

The trauma of repeated spousal deaths, especially in childbirth, was not unique to Aaron in those days, and Malabarian values encouraged a widower to remarry rather than remain alone, to take pleasure in family, and to produce children. As the ancient *Tirukkuṛāl* said, 'the man who lives the householder life well on earth attains a place among the gods in heaven' (50), but while he is here, his wife's splendour is his blessing, and their happy children his jewels (60). Great esteem for the householder life and its propagation was no doubt an important reason, besides conversion, that 32 years after Ziegenbalg and Pluetschau had landed, the Tranquebar mission could count 3,186 living members from a total of 4,609 (Lehmann 1956b: 161).

Lutheran Pietism

What was the message to which those members of the Evangelical mission had responded so positively? Aaron stated it succinctly in his Tamil ordination examination of 1733, which Daniel Jeyaraj recently found in the archives of the Leipzig Mission. It was the doctrine and way of life of the Evangelical Lutheran Church of Germany with a Pietist slant. Let us examine it by beginning with Aaron's statement of the doctrine.[4]

The doctrine centered on 'Christ the Word' in the context of the belief that God is 'three-and-one.' Preexistent with God, who is the creating Father, Christ, who is the Son or 'Word', had centuries ago incarnated as the man Jesus. Christ Jesus taught and performed miracles, but when he died, he rose from the dead and visibly ascended into heaven to sit at the Father's right hand. His human nature as Christ Jesus is omnipresent on earth, but is invisible, for it is Spirit. Christ Jesus will become visible at an unknown time, and then he will return to judge the living and the resurrected dead. On that future Judgment Day, the only hope anyone will have of a favorable judgment

3. For a discussion of 'bride-giving and receiving' in Tamil culture, see Trawick: chap. 4. The genealogy of Aaron and his descendents down to the present is charted by J. E. David and Sundar Clarke in Jeyaraj 1998: 147-79.

4. Daniel Jeyaraj (1998: 41-54) reprinted the Tamil examination report he found in the Archives of the Leipzig Mission, Leipzig, Germany, with his English translation as Appendix III. The following is summarized from Aaron's answers to questions put to him by the examining pastors in Tranquebar, supplemented by reference to 'The Augsburg Confession' of 1530.

will be if he or she possesses faith in Christ Jesus as the Father's incarnate Son, a faith that the omnipresent Spirit gives.

By what means does God as Spirit give faith? Through accurate knowledge of God the Father and of his preexistent 'Word.' First, God graciously spoke that Word through the people of Israel and their prophets, and then God lovingly embodied it as the man Jesus. Knowledge of God the Father's spoken and incarnate Word therefore comes through the record of that revelation, which is the written Bible. It consists of two covenants or 'testaments', the first with the people of Israel, the second with those who cling to the crucified and resurrected Christ Jesus in faith. Nowadays, insisted the Evangelicals, the Bible, whether read or preached, is the only means by which the Spirit will graciously instill faith; and only faith will dispel the dark sin innate to human birth that leads to condemnation on Judgment Day. It is therefore imperative that the Bible be translated into all the languages of the world, for the eternal salvation of souls depends on it.

The Roman Catholics, the Evangelicals said, had corrupted true Christian faith. They had kept the Bible away from the people, and 'the struggle of godly *bhakti*' *(tēva paktiyiṉ pirayācam),* as Aaron described that faith, had disappeared from the Church (Jeyaraj 1998: 46). Nevertheless, in sixteenth-century Germany, the omnipresent human Christ Jesus had used Martin Luther and his co-workers to reform the Church. Now, in the eighteenth century, Christ was using European 'gurus' to bring 'the struggle of godly *bhakti*' to the ignorant people of India, Catholics included.

That much was an orthodox version of Luther's Evangelical message. The Pietist slant, which Ziegenbalg, Pluetschau, and others brought, modified the forensic metaphor of judgment by adding the biological metaphor of rebirth (Tappert: 1-28). The metaphoric labor of birth explains, perhaps, what Aaron meant by 'the struggle of godly *bhakti*,' for Pietism required energy, effort, and sacrifice — all three the possible meaning of *pirayācam*, translated here as 'struggle.'[5]

Pietists in seventeenth- and eighteenth-century Europe drew upon medieval mystics and vernacular devotional practices in small groups of believers, both inside and outside local congregations, to create a relatively informal, but vigorous and controversial, movement within the established and government-supported churches of the Protestant Germans, Swiss, and Dutch. Without abandoning a concern for forensic righteousness, they more

5. *Pirayācam* is the Tamil form both of Sanskrit *prayāsa*, 'endeavour, effort,' and of Sanskrit *prayāja*, 'a sacrifice' (*Tamil Lexicon* V: loc. cit.). Jeyaraj left the word out of his translation (1998: 51).

often spoke of 'rebirth, 'new man', 'inner man', 'illumination', 'edification', and 'union of Christ with the soul' (Tappert: 27) to describe the direct, inner, personal, and individual experience of the living, yet invisible, human Christ that was their goal.

Philip Jacob Spener (1635-1705), who provided Pietists with intellectual and organizational leadership, was pivotal to the movement's widespread dispersion along the trail of international trade and colonial expansion laid by Protestant countries. Through his baptism of Count Nicholas von Zinzendorf (1700-1760), Spener linked the Pietists to the Moravians. Through von Zinzendorf and the Moravians, he linked them to the Anglican brothers John Wesley (1703-91) and Charles Wesley (1707-88), and to the English Methodists. Through August Herman Francke (1663-1727), Spener's informal successor at the University of Leipzig and later at the new Saxon university at Halle, he linked them to the Danish royal court, to Ziegenbalg and Pluetschau, and through them to the Malabarians. And finally, through the deputation by Francke's son of Henry Melchior Muhlenberg (1711-87), Spener linked the Pietists to Lutherans in North America (Tappert: 21-24).

In Tranquebar, Ziegenbalg and Pluetschau followed the six proposals Spener had stated in part 3 of his highly influential German book of 1675, *Pia Desideria.*[6] It has been translated as *Heartfelt Desire for a God-pleasing Reform of the True Evangelical Church, together with Several Simple Christian Proposals Looking toward This End.* Spener's goal was to instill in Christians the warm feeling of self-disciplined piety through small groups focussed on prayer, Bible study, and mutual moral support. He believed that such warmth would infuse life into churches now chilled by their establishment as the 'official religion' of the state. In Tranquebar the Danish Lutheran Church of the Fort was the 'official' religion, and the New Jerusalem Church of the Malabarians was the Pietist alternative. Its German pastors attempted to implement Spener's six proposals among their Malabarian congregations.

Of Spener's six proposals, the first was that more extensive use should be made of the written Word of God outside of the sermon. It should be done through household, private, and small-group readings of the Bible. The second was that believers should exercise their spiritual priesthood with each other (apparently a form of 'mutual counseling'). The third was that they should practice their faith daily. The fourth, of a more controversial nature in the Danish colony, was that they should argue religion with those who are in error, but do so carefully. The fifth was that they should train 'truly Christian' men for the ministry in schools and universities. And the sixth was that, in

6. Described by Tappert: 14-20, 29. Part III consists of pp. 87-122.

those places, they should teach preachers how to make their sermons cultivate faith, and the fruits of faith, in their audience.

At the New Jerusalem Church, Ziegenbalg and Pluetschau put those proposals into practice through Bible translation, intensive catechism and Bible study, the discipline of believers, the establishment of schools for both boys and girls, the founding of an advanced seminary, and Ziegenbalg's scholarly efforts to dispute 'Pagan' and 'Moorish' beliefs. Following Luther, they taught their Tranquebar congregation that if faith were genuine, the Word of God working in their hearts would transform their everyday life; once they recognized sin, they would renounce it voluntarily. Life by customary law enforced by external authority (whether by caste, family, or crown) was to give place to Christ's love expressing itself through them, an experience given by the faith that itself is a gift.

Outside the basic discipline required by baptism into the Danish Lutheran Church, the Pietist German Lutheran missionaries made no effort, as did later German and British 'Calvinists', to legislate an ideal social relationship between believers in the New Jerusalem Church. In particular, they did not employ external authority or force to erase caste distinctions in the matter of 'sitting together separately' during worship. Whatever changes in caste observance that might emerge among the congregation, they believed, should come from an inward 'rebirth' of the heart, not from an external application of law.[7]

In the Indian context, loving faith that clings to the feet of a personal saviour is called *bhakti*. Aaron had used the term 'the struggle of godly *bhakti*' to describe true Christian faith. Like Pietism, capitalism, and Company colonialism in the seventeenth, eighteenth, and nineteenth centuries, *bhakti,* too, was transcultural. In Germany, Johann Sebastian Bach (1685-1750) expressed his Evangelical *bhakti* through weekly cantatas addressed to God as Father, Son, and Holy Spirit. A few decades later, in Tiruvayaru outside Tanjore, Tyagaraja (c. 1759-1847) used 'Carnatic' classical music to express his *bhakti* in Telugu and Sanskrit to God as Rama. At the same time Muttuswami Dikshitar (1775-1835) in nearby Tiruvarur used it to express his *bhakti* in Sanskrit to the Goddess as 'Auspicious Knowledge' *(Śrī Vidyā),* as did Syama Sastri (1763-1827). As a temple priest in Tanjore, he used 'Carnatic' music to express his *bhakti* for the Supreme Mother he served as Kamakshi (Rangaramanuja Ayyangar: 193-206).

During this period the 'Evangelical poet' named Vedanayaga Sastri

7. See K. Graul's statement in *Explanation concerning the Principles of the Leipzig Missionary Society, with regard to the Caste Question* in Kuriakose: 149-50.

(1774-1864) brought Pietist *bhakti* into 'Carnatic' music through his own literary and musical creativity focussed on Jesus. We will discuss Sastri at length later, but it is noteworthy that his adaptation of European Pietism to Malabarian music had its instrumental parallel: the European violin entered into early nineteenth-century 'Carnatic' music as an 'Indian' instrument. Tuned in the 'Carnatic' manner, and held between the right heel and the chest, it allowed for the graces and embellishments of melody *(gamaka)* played like other stringed instruments — for example, the ancient South Indian *bahuvīṇā,* or the *dharnurvīṇā,* or the North Indian *saraṅgī* (Sjoman and Dattatreya: 58-59).

Interestingly, all those musicians — Bach, Tyagaraja, Muttuswami Dikshitar, Syama Sastri, Vedanayaga Sastri — who expressed a similar *bhakti* focussed on differing images of God did so within similarly 'holistic' social ideologies that had developed in very different civilizations.[8] *Bhakti* and Pietism may be seen as similar in their effort *(pirayācam)* to nurture the 'inner person' within a 'holistic' society and to modify that society without destroying its 'holism.' In the case of Europe, however, one of Pietism's unintended consequences was to assist in the larger cultural disruption of the 'whole' in favor of the 'individual.'

Within its European context, Pietist devotion cultivated an individualistic experience and conscience, and an interest in nature and practical knowledge. In a university milieu, those elements of Pietist devotion would later open themselves to Enlightenment rationalism and deistic theism.[9] By stressing the individual's inner experience of 'true belief' and the belief that God actively seeks each individual soul — as Ziegenbalg had put it, God 'walks around in the whole world so to speak offering his grace and his wisdom to men' — Pietism unwittingly fit a notion of individual value and autonomy that was developing socially through a laissez-faire capitalism represented by the East India Companies.

In 1710, for example, Francke in Halle, Germany, began publishing the *Königlich-Danischen Missionarien aus Ost-Indien eingesamdte Ausführliche*

8. For example, Saxony, where Bach lived, was a cluster of independent duchies and free cities, united only by the fact that the Elector resided in Dresden. Except for two trips to Berlin, Bach spent his entire life within 100 miles of his home and depended on court and church patronage. Similarly, the Tamil-speaking realms consisted of various kingdoms, landholdings *(zamīndāri),* and colonies; likewise, musicians were patronized by courts and religious institutions. In both places, the value of the individual was located within the encompassing value of the social order (as argued by Louis Dumont 1977: 4).

9. Lehmann 1956b: 172-73; Pelikan: chaps. 1–3; Dillenberger and Welch: 122-27, 151-59; and Peterson 1996.

Berichte ('The Collected Detailed Reports from the Royal Danish Missionaries in East India') to advertise and raise money for the Tranquebar mission. Those reports, known informally as the 'Halle Berichte', circulated in an international subculture of commercial Protestant piety, linking the Evangelical Ziegenbalg in Tranquebar to the Puritan Cotton Mather in Boston, to the Anglican Archbishop of Canterbury, to the Society for Promoting Christian Knowledge in London, to Count Zinzendorf in Saxony, and to John and Charles Wesley's mother (Lehmann 1956b: 97-105).

Using Louis Dumont's terms, we may think of Pietism as a religious dimension in Protestant Europe's development from medieval 'holism' to modern 'individualism.' Holism, according to Dumont, assumes the reality of social relations and bases its power over people on immovable wealth. Individualism, in contrast, assumes the reality and value of the autonomous individual and bases its power over people on movable wealth (Dumont 1977: chap. 1). Pietism provided a religious basis for the idea of the individual involved in the world in a manner commensurate with the commercialism of the East India Companies. On the one hand, it provided a contrast to the sacramental concerns of Roman Catholic missions, which it viewed as heretical in any case. On the other hand, it contrasted to the established 'worldliness' of the Calvinist Dutch Reformed Church in Ceylon and of the Lutheran scholastic orthodoxy of the Danish East India Company. Pietism encouraged 'romantic enthusiasts' who sought moral perfection, which was the way Ziegenbalg and Pluetschau had been viewed in Copenhagen before they left for India (Lehmann 1956b: 6).

In an account published in 1717, Ziegenbalg described an event that succinctly summarized his Pietist message to the Malabarian people (Ziegenbalg 1717: 38-40). One day he walked with colleagues to the town of Anandamangalam, ending up in the house of a Brahmin priest attached to its large temple. Brahmins had gathered there, and one of them was writing accounts ('Accompts'). Ziegenbalg therefore drew upon accounting as a way to explain his message to the gathering townspeople.

He first spoke about the 'spiritual Accompts' due to God on the last Day when all the dead will be raised to life and summoned to Christ the judge to give an account of all their thoughts, words, and actions. In preparation for that Day, he explained, they must know who that God is. Moreover, they must have someone to mediate with him on their behalf because they are too sinful to stand before his justice themselves. No one is qualified to mediate (and by no means the gods Vishnu, or Isvara, or Brahma, he stressed) except Jesus Christ. He is qualified because he is God's own son who has become a man, has taken everyone's sins upon himself, and has suffered and satisfied God's justice on their behalf in order to redeem them from sin, death, the devil, and hell.

Through faith in that saviour, he continued, people must turn themselves to God, give up communion with wicked people and devils, and enter into close union with God. Then, not only will their sins be pardoned but they will also be given the power to flee from sin and do good. And then they will be able to keep a strict and daily account of all their actions; morning and evening they will consider the manifold mercies God has given them and the sin and ungratefulness of which they are guilty. That consideration will inspire them to pray fervently for mercy to resolve firmly to sin no more. Such an account, he noted, will be pleasing to God.

Moreover, he concluded, all that is required is 'Singleness of Heart, joined to a hearty Love to that Truth', a truth that is so 'plain' that people of the 'meanest Capacity, and even Children', may understand it. Once faith is received, all that is required is the continuous cultivation of the inner experience of it together with repentance that is expressed through ethical living:

> If you suffer Faith and unfeigned Repentance to be wrought in your Souls; a Faith, I mean, attended with a constant Exercise of good Works, and with a continued Perseverance to the End; there is no doubt but your Souls shall be saved by Virtue of our Religion. But if you barely change the Name, and not the Heart, then the coming over to our Religion, and the taking upon you the Name of a Christian, will do you no good at all.

Ziegenbalg wanted to get his religion to the 'pagans' and 'Moors,' for by doing so, he believed, he would be responding to their desire for wisdom that was itself a sign of God's earlier work among them (Gensichen: 40). Believing they lacked the full story that would complete their wisdom, he did everything in his power to tell it to them.

Besides itinerant preaching, Ziegenbalg communicated his message in written forms. Assisted by Catholic Tamil books, he rendered Lutheran and Pietist doctrinal and liturgical works into Tamil, for example, Martin Luther's 'Small Catechism' (Gensichen: 33). He used the everyday spoken Tamil of Tranquebar, not the poetry of the elite, even though custom did not consider colloquial spoken Tamil proper for books. He had up to 12 copyists transcribe his translations, tracts, and letters onto palm leafs, which he had distributed to interested Muslims and Hindus who could read. Hundreds, and perhaps thousands, of palm leaf texts circulated, including, in one example, a translation of Matthew's Gospel with an exposition of Christian doctrine and a letter explaining conversion (Gensichen: 30).

In 1713 Ziegenbalg began to use a Tamil printing press sent from the Pietist center at Halle. Its first product, he reported, was 'a booklet dedicated to the heathen, and consisting of eight chapters, in which is shown how great a horror heathenism is and how those who live in it may be saved and go to heaven.'[10] According to Han-Werner Gensichen, although Catholic Tamil writings of the sixteenth century were the first printed books to appear outside of Western Europe, and even though there had been four Catholic printing presses in India since 1548, Ziegenbalg's pamphlet of 1713 'inaugurated the modern era of Tamil book-printing and printing in Indian languages as a whole' (Gensichen: 34). Notably, a century and a half later, the Saiva reformer Arumuga Navalar would use the modern Tamil press Ziegenbalg inaugurated to argue that the 'heathens' were not Saivas or Vaishnavas, but the Protestants themselves (Hudson 1992: 27-51; 1991: 23-51).

Ziegenbalg's widely distributed Tamil literature was of interest to many and effective. Several letters that addressed questions to the 'heathen' about their beliefs may be the first written questionnaires ever distributed in India. They produced two batches of letters written in Tamil on palm leaves, which Ziegenbalg translated and sent to Halle. The batch sent in 1713 consisted of 58 replies; the batch sent in 1714 was made up of 46 replies. A. H. Francke removed five of the replies and published edited versions of the remainder, in 1714 and 1717 respectively, as 'Malabarische Korrespondenz' ('Tamil Correspondence') (Grafe: 45-47). They contain an abundance of information, some of which we will discuss shortly.

One result of Ziegenbalg's literary dispersion was the appearance of Evangelicals in the Tanjore capital, a major step taken by Malabarians in spreading the religion among themselves. But it was one not taken by the aristocratic Velalans, but by 'pariah' soldiers. The Maratha king of Tanjore, Shahji (reigned 1684-1711), did not allow missionaries to work inside his kingdom; some Malabarian Catholics therefore lived in Tanjore without a church or a priest.[11] Ziegenbalg had attempted to walk to Tanjore in 1709, but he turned back after learning on the way that 'no white European could travel in the country unless he had a passport issued by the King or one of his highest officials', and that the King had killed a few Portuguese priests and imprisoned others who then died (Lehmann 1956b: 124-25). The danger was vividly real. Sixteen years earlier the Marava ruler of Uraiyur west of Tanjore had executed

10. The booklet was reprinted in 1729 and 1745 and then forgotten until a copy turned up in 1965 in Czechoslovakia on a rubbish heap (Gensichen: 31.)

11. In 1708 Ziegenbalg had been asked by the Tanjore Catholics for help during a persecution, and many wanted to settle in the Danish territory, but he had his own difficulties with the Danish Commandant and was unable to help (Fenger: 38).

the Jesuit John De Brito in public and had left his decapitated body, severed of hands and feet, hanging on a post as food for animals and a warning to others (Neill 1984: 307; Farnum: 153-57).

Ziegenbalg's Tamil publications, however, did reach Tanjore. During the reign of Sherboji (1712-27), the king's maternal uncle had read some of the literature and was interested enough to correspond with the missionary Benjamin Shultze; and in 1721 he sent him a Brahmin emissary, a contact that would later bear fruit (Paul 1967: 29).

Rajanayakan: The Catechist

Four years later a Catholic named Rajanayakan (or Rajanaikan) (1700-1771), who was of a 'pariah' caste from Sinneyanpalaiyam and a subordinate officer *(sērvaikāraṉ)* in Sherboji's army, read Ziegenbalg's 1714 printed translation of the four Gospels and the book of Acts (Paul 1967: 17-47).[12] As he later reported about himself, Rajanayakan was a third-generation Catholic in a family that 'loved the holy [Francis] Xavier very much, and built a chapel to his honour, in which service was performed morning and evening' (Paul 1967: 25). By the age of 22, he and his younger brother Chinappan (or Sinappen) had learned to read and began reading palm leaf books about the lives of the saints, the miracles of the Virgin Mary, and Christ. The story of Christ's passion, he recalled, 'caused such an emotion in my heart that I began to meditate on what sin really is and began to fear His judgment.' He wanted to know the history from Christ back to Moses, but the Catholic catechists he approached knew of no books to give him. Then he obtained Ziegenbalg's printed translation of the Gospels and of Acts from a 'Catholic mendicant monk' named Sittanandan; he thought it was a Catholic publication because the title page with the information that it had been printed in Tranquebar had been torn out.[13] Parts of it moved him greatly:

> When I had thus obtained the book my longing was satisfied by it. I used to read it all day and then from the evening till midnight by a light. When I had read it through, the Lord had given me great light in understanding it. . . . The texts which struck me most while I was reading poured like oil upon my faith and caused it to burn brightly. (Paul 1967: 26)

12. A second edition by Ziegenbalg and J. E. Gruendler was published in 1722: *Novem Jesu Christi Testamentum/Ēcukkiṛisttu nātarāṇava . . . vētaposttakam* (Barnett and Pope: 61a).

13. The title page is reprinted in Lehmann 1956a: 38.

The next year, in 1726, when floods had created a severe famine, the king sent Rajanayakan as head of a detachment of soldiers to guard crops near Tranquebar. While encamped in tents he obtained other writings disseminated from Tranquebar, this time through a Catholic villager. One writing was Ziegenbalg's 1713 tract against 'heathenism' *(akkiyāṇam, ajñāna)* entitled 'This Book Reveals How Detestable Ajnana Is and How Those in Ajnana Can Be Saved.' Ziegenbalg described the booklet as 'consisting of eight chapters, in which is shown how great a horror heathenism is and how those who live in it may be saved and go to heaven' (Gensichen: 31; Grafe: 59). Another writing was Ziegenbalg and Gruendler's 1716 translation of J. A. Freylinghausen's 'Theologica Thetica' *(Vedasāstiram)* (Barnett and Pope: 96). A third was Ziegenbalg's 1717 printed letter to Malabarians. Rajanayakan also had access to the 1720 and 1726 editions of Ziegenbalg and Gruendler's translations of the Old Testament (Barnett and Pope: 58).

That was the first time Rajanayakan had learned about Evangelicals. The Catholic villager explained to him that there were two kinds of Christian priests and that the 'German priests' were 'those who do not pray to our Holy Mother.' Rajanayakan eventually contacted the Tranquebar missionaries directly through letters, and they sent him Luther's larger catechism, the New Testament, and part of the Old, along with directions on how Scripture was to be read. Eventually the missionaries appeared in Rajanayakan's camp. After repeated discussions with him in his tent, he was convinced that they preached the truth.

After Rajanayakan returned to Tanjore, he taught Protestant doctrine to three 'pagan' soldiers. In 1727, the four of them went to Tranquebar and, after the three 'pagans' received intensive instruction, all four were baptized. Apparently, the Pietist Lutherans did not regard the Catholic baptism that Rajanayakan had received to be valid, another sign of the heretical camp to which they assigned the 'Popists.' When he again returned to Tanjore, Rajanayakan converted a Catholic catechist named Surappan and his son named Sattianadan (Satyanathan). They likewise went to Tranquebar for baptism. Those six converts — three baptized 'pagans' and three rebaptized Catholics — then began to spread the Evangelical message in Tanjore. Rajanayakan urged the Tranquebar missionaries to extend their work there. Accordingly, the Germans sent Aaron, who at this point was a catechist, and he carried books and tracts for distribution and a letter from the missionaries to the Maratha king, Tukkoji (r. 1727-35). In response, Tukkoji invited the missionaries to join him the following year during a festival in Tanjore.

Thus it was that in July of 1728, the missionary Friedrich Pressier traveled in Tukkoji's own carriage to the wedding of the king's son in Tanjore. There he met the Evangelicals, who apparently lived outside the city walls. Some of them were 'sudras' (Velalans), whom the missionary was allowed to meet upstairs in the royal house where he stayed; but, according to Lehmann, the 'pariah' Evangelicals had to remain outside, and he could speak to them only from an upstairs window (Lehmann 1956b: 140).

In the meantime the ex-Catholic Sattianadan received further instruction in Tranquebar, was made a catechist, and was sent back to Tanjore to take charge of the developing congregation. Most of the Tanjore converts at that time, it appears, were Velalans, but Sattianadan was a 'pariah.' His low-caste status created a controversy among the Evangelicals in the area that Aaron would be sent to resolve in 1730.

Rajanayakan, who had begun the Tanjore congregation, now left the service of its Maratha king to serve the Marava ruler of Ramanathapuram to the south. There he disseminated Protestant literature among soldiers and villagers, persuading some and alienating others, especially Catholic priests and catechists. He seems particularly to have irritated the Jesuit missionary Beschi with his successful propagation of 'heresy.' Beschi responded in 1728 with the Tamil work 'Exposition of Revelation' *(Veda Viḻakkam),* in which he first attacked Lutheran teaching before defending the veneration of saints and the Virgin Mary, the use of images, and other Roman Catholic matters.[14] He also ridiculed the Tamil language the Tranquebar Pietists had used for the Bible. In 1859 Simon Casie Chitty translated Beschi's comments in chapter 16 of 'Exposition of Revelation' this way:

> Can those books be fairly called the Word of God, which the Tranquebarians, who do not at all write correctly in Tamil the name of their country, have handed down to us pretending that they have translated the Holy Scriptures in Tamil, whilst ignorant of that language, they have to the bitter paining of our ears, written them in barbarous words. By this means, the truth of God's word has been darkened, and by depriving it of its excellence, been tarnished, even as if a costly bright gem were buried in mire, or poison mixed with ambrosial sweet or a beautiful picture stained with ink.' (Chitty 1859: 75 n.)

14. Muttusami Pillei (259 and n.) noted that 'This work was composed by Beschi in consequence of an attempt made by the Danish missionaries to circulate, in the vicinity of Tirookavaloor, where Beschi resided, a translation of the New Testament. The missionaries had deputed a zealous catechist for that purpose, and provided him with a large supply of their own version.' Most likely, the zealous catechist was Rajanayakan.

Finally, Rajanayakan left military service to pursue work as an Evangelical propagandist full-time. By this time Chinappan, his younger brother, and two other Catholic soldiers, named Savarimuttu and Sandiyar, had also converted. The missionaries in Tranquebar eventually dedicated Rajanayakan and his brother as catechists, and sent them both to serve in Tanjore.

Meanwhile vigorous Catholic opposition to their work emerged. According to a letter Rajanayakan wrote from Tanjore to the missionaries after he had returned from his dedication as catechist while he had been in Tranquebar, Beschi at Ellakurichi had mustered the Catholics at Tanjore to oppose him (Paul 1967: 33-35; Neill 1985: 87-88). Then the Catholic catechist at Tanjore led men from 18 villages to Rajanayakan's native village. As he wrote, they

> troubled my parents very much and wished to pull my house down; but the inhabitants of all castes interfered to prevent this outrage. This happened on the very day that I started from Tranquebar. As they could not succeed in pulling my house down, they declared that I had lost my caste, and forbade my relations to hold any intercourse with me. Now that I have arrived in Tanjore many despise me and behave towards me as enemies. They threaten the heathen telling them not to speak to me, which distresses my parents very much. I wished to let you know this and beg you to send me some good advice. (Paul 1967: 33)

The missionaries wrote Beschi to ask him to put a stop to the physical violence, with little effect. Repeated attempts were made on Rajanayakan's life, and one altercation in 1731 killed his father.

Nevertheless, Rajanayakan and his brother continued to gain converts from among the 'pagans' and Catholics, and congregations developed both in Tanjore and in the strong Catholic center of Madewipatnam. For example, a 'native physician' named Joseph, who had been a schoolmaster, went as a catechist to Rajanayakan's village of Sinneiyanpalaiyam (Paul 1967: 38).

At the end of 1717, only 15 Evangelicals resided in the Tanjore territory, but eleven years later there were over 100. Two years after that, 367 Protestants lived in the vicinity of the capital. Yet it would be 12 years before they were meeting for worship inside Tanjore's walls, in a school Rajanayakan had opened in 1742. In 1744 a prayer hall was built for 'sudras in a sudra' street, which meant that the Velalans were now worshiping in their own neighbourhood.[15]

15. In 1755 a prayer hall was built outside the city, and in 1761 a little church was erected, wiped out, it appears, in the siege of 1771 (Lehmann 1956b: 140-41).

During that time, Rajanayakan proselytized the Muslims of the lower classes, Muslim officers in the Mughal army, and Muslim servants in the Tanjore court. He distributed Arabic language New Testaments and tracts to them, but whether any ever converted is not known (Paul 1967: 42-43).

In 1749 the French besieged Tanjore to aid a claimant to the Arcot Nawabship against the British. Rajanayakan's house was demolished during the siege, but he remained with the Evangelicals and took refuge in the fort, an act of pastoral faithfulness that made him a leader among 'pariahs' of all religions. According to J. F. Fenger, after the siege,

> nine pariah suburbs of Tanjore chose him as their umpire in all their disagreements, and gave him full permission to publish the Gospel among them. Shortly after being chosen as umpire, he allowed himself to be appointed by the King of Tanjore as headman of the people who bury their dead. (Paul 1967: 44)

Appointment by the Maratha king as headman of those who buried, rather than burned, the dead suggests that Rajanayakan had been given the authority to mediate periodic disputes between the 'right hand' and 'left hand' divisions of 'pariah' castes. In that region the agricultural Velalans customarily supported the Valangamattar, the Paraiyans of the 'right hand' *(valaṅkai);* the mercantile Chettis and Beri Chettis, however, together with the artisan Kammalans (goldsmiths, brass-smiths, carpenters, stonemasons, and blacksmiths) supported the Pallans of the 'left hand' *(iṭaṅkai).*[16] As we will see, the Evangelical Velalans and their traditional 'right hand' Valangamattar allies eventually formed a single congregation in a single church building in Tanjore. On the one hand that union articulated their traditional 'right-hand' caste alliance, but on the other hand it continued a potential for inter-caste divisiveness, a topic to which we will return later.

In 1758 the French again besieged Tanjore, and again Rajanayakan stayed on. This time his work received the support of the German officer in command of the Maratha king's troops. The officer gave him a house near the garrison, and Rajanayakan held morning and evening prayers there for whatever 'pagan' and Christian soldiers wanted to attend (Paul 1967: 45).

By now, however, Rajanayakan's relations with the Tranquebar missionaries were seriously strained. The question of ordaining him a pastor or 'priest' had naturally arisen, and the declining health of Tanjore's Velalan pastor Aaron was the occasion for an answer. As we recall, Aaron had replaced

16. Thurston and Rangachari: 1:213-17; 3:107, 117-18; 5:472-75; 7:366.

the 'pariah' catechist Sattianadan in order to satisfy the Velalans, who had increased in number under his pastorate. Yet, as the missionaries had explained in a letter of about 1739 to the Principal at Halle, who had posed the question about ordaining Rajanayakan, his 'pariah' status prevented them from ordaining him, even though he appeared qualified:

> Not you only, but several of us, desired to ordain Rajanaiken to the office of priest. This might be done if he were to confine his labour to the Pariahs. It is true, there are several very honest and respectable persons among them, like Rajanaiken himself; still, from the general low character of those people, the Christians of higher caste avoid coming into contact with any of them. We take great pains to lessen these prejudices among our Christians; still to a certain degree they must be taken into consideration. Rajanaiken is very useful and successful, in his labour as a catechist, in his four districts. But we should greatly hesitate to have the Lord's Supper administered by him lest it should diminish the regard of Christians of higher caste for that Sacrament itself. (Paul 1967: 40)

A Velalan like Aaron could serve the Lord's Supper to Velalans and to 'pariahs', but a 'pariah' could serve it only to 'pariahs.' A 1732 report had said that 'sudras' (Velalans) and 'pariahs' possessed catechists of their own castes, especially in the country, though if necessary Velalans could be appointed for 'pariahs' (Lehmann 1956b: 146). The Jesuit Beschi followed the same practice, and his own catechist was a Velalan.[17]

Therefore, to assist the ailing Aaron, in 1741 the missionaries in Tranquebar ordained Diago, a former Catholic Velalan, as the second Malabarian pastor or 'priest.' They then sent him to the Tanjore kingdom. Evangelicals in the kingdom by then numbered 2,469, divided into administrative 'circles' centered in Tanjore, Tirupalatur, and Kumbhakonam (Lehmann 1956b: 149-150).

The 1739 missionary judgment of Rajanayakan as 'very honest and respectable' had changed by the 1758 siege of Tanjore 19 years later. According to Arno Lehmann, Rajayanakan had incurred debts 'mostly due to drinking, through which the missionaries were put to indescribable grief' (Lehmann 1956b: 152). Two years later, he and his brother Chinappan were suspended from the mission 'because of much unfaithfulness and offences which they created recently . . .' (Lehmann 1956b: 166). Their 'unfaithfulness' may refer

17. He was Savarimuttu ('Chowrimootoo') Pillai, who had two sons, Dayiriyam Pillai and Amirda Pillai (Muttusami Pillei: 265, note).

to contacts they made with the Moravians — the more radical Pietists of Count Zinzendorf's realm — who had stopped in Tranquebar on their way to the Nicobar Islands. But they remained for 50 years, in a settlement near Poreyar about a mile from Tranquebar town (Walker: 331-32, 450-54; Dubois: 20-21; Hough: 107-8). In 1760 Rajanayakan, Chinappan, and other presumably 'pariah' catechists met with the Moravian theologian Voelker to consider joining them. The Moravians had treated Rajanayakan warmly, had sat with him to drink tea and coffee, had served breakfast to him, and so, a Lutheran report to Halle said,

> [he] was completely bewitched. . . . Rajanayakan and his brother Sinappan, whom we had to suspend . . . were actually willing to bring the Christians under their care to the Moravian community. They were not accepted, mainly because Voelker could speak very little Tamil. (Lehmann 1956b: 166)

The fact that Voelker's two interpreters had been raised in the Tranquebar school, where they had learned German, seemed to have made no difference.

It is difficult to separate Rajanayakan's estrangement from the Tranquebar mission from his confined position within the mission administration as a 'pariah.' A pious and courageous man deemed 'very honest and respectable' and worthy of consideration for ordination might well be troublesome two decades later to foreign employers who now thought of him as someone who would be 'bewitched' by Europeans treating him warmly in a way that suggested social equality. It was true that a 'pariah' administering the Lord's Supper would not be acceptable to the Velalans — just as an Indian-American or an African-American serving the Lord's Supper would not have been tolerable to most European-Americans of the time. Rajanayakan and Chinnapan, it appears, had explored the possibility that the Moravians could be Protestant patrons who would allow them their leadership of Evangelical 'pariahs', but without the traditional subordination of 'pariahs of the right hand' to Velalans, as was practiced in the Tanjore congregation.

Religious Discussions

In addition to itinerant preaching and making tracts and books, Ziegenbalg communicated his message by studying Tamil writings assiduously and by discussing religious matters with Malabarians whenever he could. The intent of his study was to understand 'pagan' ideas in order to refute them in favor of the 'true Gospel.' Wherever he traveled, which was usually by foot or ox-cart, he and his later colleague, J. E. Grundler, discussed religious matters in Tamil and afterwards wrote detailed accounts of their conversations in German. From 1715 Francke edited and published 54 of those conversations in the 'Halle Berichte', 34 of which — along with 19 abridged letters written by 'pagans' — were then translated into English and published in London in 1719 (Grafe: 43-50).

In 1708 and again in 1709, Ziegenbalg visited the Dutch to the south in Nagapattinam. After his abortive effort to walk to Tanjore, in 1710 he went northwards in a caravan to the English in Madras. He took nine and a half days to pass through Sirkali, Cidambaram, Porta Nova, Cuddalore, Pondichery, Sadraspatnam, and St. Thomas Mount. Wherever he traveled, he distributed literature to the Brahmin and Velalan literati, and gathered names for future correspondence. While he was in Tranquebar, whenever he could he talked with the men who frequently came to his house and with those he met on his walks through the colony: in marketplaces, in front of temples, on the streets during festivals, in public resting places, and in private homes.

He would begin those discussions with the notion of wisdom he believed they shared, and then he would move on to his particular message. 'To start with the crucified Jesus is not possible', he explained to Danish supporters. 'One has to begin with the book of Nature, from there move on to the Holy Scripture, and on that basis proclaim the crucified Jesus, as the circumstances and the occasion present themselves' (Lehmann 1956b: 37). He used reason to bludgeon through what he thought to be the blind ignorance of 'heathenism' *(ajñāna)*. Yet, as a result of his studious efforts to understand whatever wisdom he believed the Malabarians to have, Ziegenbalg ended up producing for Europe the most accurate studies of the 'pagans' in India since Rogerius. Not until he began sending his voluminous reports and studies of Malabarian culture and religion to Halle did the Pietists in Germany have an opportunity to gain a clear idea of the Malabarian religions from which they were trying to save people. But Pietist authorities at Halle suppressed his reports: 'The missionaries were sent out to exterminate heathenism in India', A. H. Francke said, 'not to spread heathen nonsense all over Europe' (Lehmann 1956b: 32). Consequently, the full extent of his serious scholarly studies of 'Malabarian' religion and culture in the early eighteenth century did not appear in public until late in the nineteenth and early in the twentieth century. *Genealogie der Malabarischen Goetter* ('The Genealogy of the Gods of Malabar'), which he wrote in 1713, was recovered from the Halle archives, edited by W. Germann with notes and additions, and published for missionary use in Madras in 1867; an expanded English translation by G. J. Metzger also appeared in Madras in 1869.[18] *Malabarisches Heidenthum* ('The Heathenism of Malabar'), which he wrote in 1711, remained in manuscript form until W. Caland published it in Amsterdam in 1926 as *Ziegenbalg's Malabarisches Heidenthum.*

Exposition through Liturgy

In still another approach to disseminating the Evangelical message, Ziegenbalg welcomed Hindus and Muslims to the liturgies of the church in Tranquebar, the context in which it was heard in its fullest resonance. He and Pluetschau conducted their rites and ceremonies in the New Jerusalem Church, a stone building 20 feet by 50, white washed, containing a stone altar and a stone pulpit, but purposely bare of pictures, images, and crucifixes (Ziegenbalg 1717: 53-54). When the congregation gathered, Ziegenbalg reported,

> Those women and men who wear European clothes sit on benches and stools, but those men and women who wear Indian clothes sit on mats and down on the paved floor. No one but Heathens and Moors, who do not belong to the congregation, stand at the four windows and doors.[19]

The men and women of the congregation sat apart, and, as we will later discuss, the high-caste members sat on mats while the low-caste members sat directly on the paved floor. Caste distinctions, it appears, were recognized in the sacred arena of the Evangelicals right from the beginning. Attendance was high, partly because mission employees did not want to risk losing their jobs (Lehmann 1956b: 45).

In that context Ziegenbalg articulated the Evangelical message vigorously. On Sunday he led worship and the rite of the Holy Supper, preached doctrinal sermons, and catechized the members present. On Wednesday he reviewed for them the Sunday sermon and catechized them again. On Friday he drilled them in Luther's Catechism according to Philip Spener's interpreta-

18. The 1869 English translation has been reprinted as Bartholomaeus Ziegenbalg, *Genealogy of the South-Indian Gods* (New Delhi: Unity Book Service, 1984).

19. The quotation is from Ziegenbalg 1957: 90. Lutz's translation (of Lehmann 1956: 73) omitted the distinction between those who sat on mats and those who sat on the paved floor (*'. . . aber auf den Matten und unten auf dem Pflaster sitzen diegenigen Manns- under Weibspersonen . . .'*). He said that they all sat on mats (Lehmann 1956b: 45).

tion as he had translated it into Tamil.[20] 'Pagans' and Muslims attended all of those occasions, he reported, sometimes by the hundreds.

The 'pagans' and 'Moors' gazing through the windows and doors of the tiny New Jerusalem Church metaphorically create the context within which the small congregation developed and spread over the decades. The Malabarian Evangelicals were well aware of their gaze. What did the gazers see? How might they have thought about what they saw and heard? How would their gaze have affected the congregants' view of themselves as they applied their faith to their lives? To answer those questions, we now need to turn to the 'pagans' and the 'Moors.'

20. Barnett and Pope (15b) lists a Tamil translation by Ziegenbalg entitled *Martin Luther . . . Jñānopatēcem . . .* and describes it as 'A catechism of Protestant doctrine, based upon P. J. Spener's "Einfache Erklaerung der Christlichen Lehre," embodying and amplifying Luther's Kleiner Catechismus. Translated into Tamil by B. Ziegenbalg. Revised by A. Blomstrand. Third edition' (Tranquebar, 1872), 160.

CHAPTER 4

'Mahometans' or 'Moors'

In this chapter and the next, we will discuss those who watched through the doors and windows of the newly built church. Let us begin, however, by briefly considering the returned gaze of the missionaries inside. Over the decades, the intellectual stance towards non-Christians taken by Ziegenbalg, Pluetschau, Grundler, and other early Pietist missionaries, being that of Europeans in a European colony, must have influenced Malabarian views of themselves. We will not be able to trace in full the complex influences and developments that contributed to 'modern consciousness' among the Tamil-speaking people, but we will offer some ideas to add to the studies done so far.[1]

Bartholomeus Ziegenbalg provides a useful beginning. He was a Protestant European educated at a German university at the end of the seventeenth century, and he was interested in the religions of the world. The religions he encountered in Tranquebar fascinated him, and he worked hard to understand them. Nevertheless, he had come there to abolish them in favor of Evangelical Christianity, and he studied them for that purpose. In that respect, interestingly, he was no different from India's intellectuals of the time, for Saivas, Vaishnavas, Buddhists, Jainas, and Muslims customarily studied each other only for the sake of apologetics, not for disinterested 'scientific' knowledge.

Ziegenbalg had very clear views about the world's religions, which he outlined for a German audience in the 1711 introduction to his monograph,

1. The premodern setting has been explored by Rao, Shulman, and Subrahmanyam. For eighteenth- and nineteenth-century studies, see Grafe; Hudson 1972, 1982, 1985, 1992, 1994a, 1995b, 1998); and Young and Jebanesan. Bayly expanded the arena by bringing in Muslims and Catholics. Ramaswamy focussed on language and nationalist ideas to bring the study closer to the present.

'Detailed Description of the Heathenism of Malabar' *(Ausführliche Bescreibung des Malabarischen Heidentums).* The study was not published in Europe until 1926, but no doubt he 'published' his views verbally in Tranquebar as soon he could speak Portuguese and Tamil.

Ziegenbalg began by explaining to the Europeans at home that all the people of the world are divided into four main religions. There are Jews, Christians, 'Mahometans', and heathens (Ziegenbalg 1926: 9-11). The Jews, he said, form the numerically smallest people *(Volck),* but they are spread throughout the world. The Christians are more numerous; they occupy all of Europe and are also found in the other three parts of the world. The 'Mahometans' are a still larger people *(Volck);* occupying almost three-quarters of the world, they are found everywhere. Nevertheless, the heathens, who occupy most of the world, are numerically the largest people *(Volck)* of all.

Among those four great world religions, he continued, the devil *(Teufel)* has been very active, confusing the souls of people in order to bring them to eternal damnation. For example, the devil caused the Jews to throw out the kernel of the Scriptures God had revealed through Moses, but to keep the chaff. They divided into sects, killed their own prophets, and then their expected messiah. Moreover, due to the blindness of the devil, they are without faith to this day and await another messiah.

He then turned to the Christian religion. It was founded on the Word of God as spoken through the prophets of the Jews in the Old Testament, he said, but it originated with God in the fulfillment of the Old Testament through his son Jesus Christ, as described in the New Testament. The apostle Paul spread the 'good news' *(evangelium)* about Jesus Christ in order to bring all peoples of the world together in a church. That church exists to this day, and, according to God's promise, it will exist until the end of the world. The gates of hell will never overwhelm it.

Nevertheless, he continued, the devil has also worked among the Christians. He created sects and corrupted teachings. Some Christians held onto the pure teaching of the Word of God, but most went over to 'an ungodly and heathen' life and became lost through the doctrine of *'opus operatum.'* Ziegenbalg meant the Roman Catholic doctrine of the sacraments.

As defined by thirteenth-century European Scholastics, when the priest's intent is right and the recipient's desire is true, five material sacraments convey the grace of God by the fact of their reception *(ex opere operato)* (Walker: 247). Martin Luther in the sixteenth century, however, said that, according to the apostle Paul, faith is a personal transforming relationship of the soul with Christ; it leads to the forgiveness of sins, and comes from God by means of the Word. The sacraments, of which Luther said there are only two, attest or seal God's promise of union with Christ and forgiveness of sins, and they strengthen faith. But the manipulation of material substances does not control God's grace (Walker: 308). God's grace is a gift given freely, beyond human or 'priestly' control. *Opus operatum,* in Ziegenbalg's mind, was the doctrine the Saiva and Vaishanava priests also followed, for just as the devil had deceived them, so he had deceived the Roman Catholics.

Regarding the 'Mahometans', Ziegenbalg's disdain was unmitigated. Following European custom, he did not refer to them as they did to themselves, as 'those submitting to God' (Muslims, Mussulmans, Moslems), but as 'those who follow the doctrine of Muhammad' (Mahometans, Muhammadans, Mohammadans). That offended Muslims, of course, because they believed themselves to be following God by means of the Qur'an he revealed by means of Muhammad as prophet. Ziegenbalg also referred to them as 'Moors', which originally designated Muslims of ancient Mauritania in Northwest Africa, who had conquered Christian Spain. Among Europeans, the word 'Moor' had negative connotations, including dark skin (explicitly so in 'blackamoor'), although by Ziegenbalg's time, Europeans knew there also were 'white Moors' (*Oxford English Dictionary:* 'moor').

Furthermore, Ziegenbalg had no respect for Muslim belief or behaviour. He said that 'Mahometan' histories drew on the Old and the New Testaments but that they were mixed up. The origin of their religion, its propositions, and their own sinful lives, he said, reveal that the 'Mahometans' are a people existing under the power of darkness and in slavery to the devil. Led astray by him into error and sin, he concluded, body and soul, 'Mahometans' are lost forever.

For the last category of religions, Ziegenbalg used the word 'heathen' as equivalent to 'pagan' or 'gentile.' It denoted nonmonotheistic people, and connoted 'ignorant' and 'uncivilized.' All heathens, Ziegenbalg said, are under the rule of the devil, whom they worship as a god. He leads them into idolatry and superstitious rites. The devil is the father of them all, but they have divided into many sects, and in Africa, in America, and in East India they differ in their gods and teachings. Among the East Indian heathens, moreover, there are also many sects. One of the largest of them, he said, the Europeans call 'Malabaren.' But they, too, are divided into many smaller sects, as well as into many languages.

Ziegenbalg concluded by stating his mission. Now that God had brought him to Tranquebar, his task was to reveal 'heathen Blindness' and make known the 'Light of the Evangelii', so that heathens may convert from Satan to God, and from darkness to light. It was to that end, he explained, that he studied their books and discussed religion with them.

The 'Mahometans' or 'Moors'

To explore the metaphorical 'gaze' of those standing at the door and windows of the New Jerusalem Church, let us turn to the Muslims, who were well established in Tranquebar. As Susan Bayly noted, a chain of Muslim trading towns had grown up along the east coast, from Pulicat north of Madras down to the southernmost Tamil ports; some of the richest were in the Tanjore delta area where Tranquebar is located (Bayly: 77-82). Tranquebar town contained a large mosque, and nearby Poreyar contained several, including a fine new one. A Sufi lived not far away. At Nagore, southwards along the coast near Nagapattinam, stood the dargah or tomb of the Sufi master Shahul Hamid Naguri, an international pilgrimage center that the Tanjore rulers had patronized. It was believed that the Telugu Nayaka Vaishnavas had patronized it, and it was also believed that the Dutch East India Company Christians had patronized it; but everyone knew that the Maratha Saivas had patronized it munificently after they took Tanjore from the Nayakas in 1674 (Bayly: 91-94, 216-21).

Among Muslims, the endogamous Tamil-speaking Maraikkayar dominated. They were a Sunni elite of merchants and shipowners who sustained close ties to Arab centers of trade and pilgrimage and to Muslim communities in southeast Asia and along the west coast of India northward to Gujarat. They followed the Shafi'i school of Quranic law, which linked them in religious law to Arabia. They distinguished themselves from the Labbais, also Tamil-speaking Sunnis, who included fishermen and pearl divers, cultivators, weavers, artisans, and petty traders, some dealing in fish and leather. The Labbais followed the Hanafi school, which similarly linked them to the Deccan, to Central Asia, and to Iran (Bayly: 79-81).

When, in 1709, Ziegenbalg described the Muslims in the colony as 'yellow' in pigmentation (Ziegenbalg 1717: 2), he probably meant the Maraikkayar elite who claimed descent from Arab settlers and regarded the Labbais as 'mere converts' (Bayly: 80). The Labbais, who lived on the fringes of Tranquebar town's Muslim society, may have appeared to him as indistinguishable from the 'dark brown' Malabarians. The Labbais in the region had a close relationship to the low-status Kammalan castes of the 'left hand' division (Thurston and Rangachari: 3:116-17). We will discuss the 'right hand' and 'left hand' divisions of castes in Chapter 5.

Yet Ziegenbalg's perception of Muslims as different from the majority population may have been the way the Maraikkayar elite represented themselves to him, as not really 'of Malabar.' Nevertheless, in contrast to Bengal's Muslims, who favored Arabic, Persian, or Urdu as their language and identified the Bengali vernacular with non-Muslims (Roy: 65-72), Tamil was the language of both Maraikkayar and Labbai. By this time a Maraikkayar of coastal Kilakkarai, who claimed kinship with the ancient Pandya kings, had commissioned a courtly poem *(kāppiyam, kāvya)* of 5,000 stanzas on the life of the Prophet Muhammad called the *Sīṛāppurāṇam;* it alluded explicitly to another Tamil courtly work, the *Rāmāyaṇam* by Kambar (Bayly: 83, 86). Its author, Umaru Pulavar (c. 1665-?), was developing at the time the literature of what might be called a 'Muslim *maṇipravāḷa*', an Arabic-Tamil literary language written in Arabic script.[2]

Despite the fact that the language of most Muslims was Tamil, Ziegenbalg nevertheless assumed that the Muslims in Tranquebar had their own language, even though, he said, they did not speak it often, and they sent their children to Tamil schools. Perhaps because they used Arabic script to write their Tamil, he thought Persian or Urdu was their language. In answer to the question from Europe, 'Are the Malabarians for the most part Heathens or Mahometans?' he wrote:

> I have never seen as yet a Malabarian that was a Mahometan. The Mahometans here, are generally Blackamoors: Though they are settled every where among the Malabarians, yet do they make a particular Body of Men, or a quite different sort of People from the Heathens. And since the Malabarick Language has the Ascendant here above all others, they very seldom speak their native Tongue, and suffer their Children to frequent the Malabarick Schools, without obliging their Masters to teach them the Tenets of the Mahometan Faith. So that the Moors or Mahometans understand the Malabarick Language, both as to read, write, or to speak it; yet are they no Malabarians, but vastly different from them, as well with respect to their Religion, as likewise to their Complexion, their Shape, and Apparel. Many Hundred Thousands of those Moors inhabit the Coast of Coromandel, enjoying everywhere great Power and Liberty: For as they depend on the great Mogol, so he doth always protect them against the Insults of the Heathenish Kings, if they should offer to molest them.

2. Among Tamil-speaking Muslims it is known as *Fatha at-Dayyan* (Arabic-Tamil). According to Abdul Majeed Mackeen, it is a 'a type of Tamil written in Arabic script drawing on such Arabic terms as constituted the religious and cultural vocabulary of a non-Arabic speaking community' (Lebbai: v). *Maṇipravāḷa* commonly refers to the language of the Sri Vaishnavas, in which the 'jewels' *(maṇi)* of Sanskrit are placed in the 'coral' *(pravāḷa)* bed of Tamil linguistic structure; it was written in *grantha,* or Telugu, or Tamil script (see Venkatachari).

By the time Ziegenbalg and Pluetschau had landed, Mughal rule, with its use of Persian and Urdu, was close at hand. The Mughal emperor in Delhi had used the Nizam of Hyderabad to claim the whole of the Tamil country as a Mughal province; the Maratha-built fortress in Vellore was now under Mughal control; and the Nawab of Arcot's authority was about to be established as paramount in the 'Carnatic' (Bayly: 151-52).

Returning to Ziegenbalg's church, the Muslim men standing on its edges to watch the liturgies, who believed themselves to belong to 'the definitive religion' *(al Dīn)*, must have seen things both familiar and strange (Al Fārūqī: 107). They were accustomed to weekly communal gatherings for the rituals of prayer *(ṣalāt)* and to daily individual prayers; but unlike the Evangelicals, they, as well as women, were required to be in a state of ritual purity during *ṣalāt* and when inside the mosque. Moreover, they did not sing or eat during worship (Lebbai: 84-145, 213-16). Like the church, the mosque was an image-free building painted white and with a pulpit; yet unlike the church, it had no altar and no priestly rituals. They, too, heard a weekly sermon expounding scripture, but their scripture was the Qur'an revealed to Muhammad in untranslatable Arabic, a total of 77,934 words, which they memorized, and some of which they recited during *ṣalāt* (Al Fārūqī: 100). Those Arabic sounds, when correctly pronounced, turned their minds to God. They, too, knew Adam, Abraham, Moses, and Jesus; but from their standpoint, Ziegenbalg and his Bible distorted the teachings of those prophets. Moreover, Ziegenbalg altogether ignored Muhammad, whom they believed was 'honored above all Prophets, above all Angels and above all Allah's creation' (Lebbai: 10).

Perhaps the church reminded them more of the nearby court of a Muslim mystic or Sufi. Men and women went together to see the Sufi master, and sometimes they sang while worshiping (Ziegenbalg 1717: 32-37). As Ziegenbalg did, the Sufi nurtured individual piety and spiritual growth, and his own life was meant to be a model for others. Yet, while the Pietist talked of the experience of faith in God, the Sufi master talked of the experience of God directly. Ziegenbalg waited to see God in the next life, but the Sufi longed to see him in this life now. Ziegenbalg wanted to be a model of faith and repentance for his congregation, but the Sufi's disciples looked to their master as an embodiment of holiness, for as Ziegenbalg described him:

> His Dress was Mahometan; he had on his Head a green silken Turbant, with a black silken Scarf about his Body. He was besides loaden with Gold, Silver, Pearls, and other precious Ornaments hanging about him. A Scymeter lay on his left Side. His Bed was all of pure red, black, and green Velvet. Whilst we thus conversed together, a great many Moors sitting on the Ground near

> us, listened with much Attention to what we said. All the Moors of both Sexes, very reverently kissed his Feet both when they came, and when they went, and behaved themselves so respectfully as if he had been a Piece of a Deity. (Ziegenbalg 1717: 34-35)

As we noted, Ziegenbalg had no better knowledge of Islam, or respect for it, than most Europeans of his time. During his first two visits to the Sufi master's court, he refused to remove his shoes even though he thereby offended everyone. On his second visit, Ziegenbalg reported, the Sufi told him 'that even the King of Tanjour himself, did not only take off his Shoes in his Presence, but prostrating himself on the Ground, did not rise till he bade him.' In response Ziegenbalg told him that he was too proud and needed to practice humility. Not surprisingly, the third time Ziegenbalg visited, he was not admitted at all. But from his point of view, the lack of welcome merely illustrated the 'intolerable and silly Pride' of Muslims (Ziegenbalg 1717: 32-37).

Muslims told him that they venerated Muhammad as the greatest prophet, but, more than that, as the intimate friend of God, as a unique man whose life was for them the model of piety and faithfulness. He was, after all, the man God had chosen to reveal fully the preexistent and eternal Book that others, such as the Jews and Christians, had distorted, as the Qur'an explained *(Sura* 5: *Māida).* Nevertheless, Ziegenbalg insisted that Christians knew more about Muhammad than did Muslims. Not only was the Prophet morally corrupt, he told them, but it was he who had corrupted divine revelation. Attributing the Qur'an to Muhammad's authorship, he said it

> . . . is partly taken out of the Writings of our holy Bible, and partly out of the Books of Pagans, mix'd with many of his own Extravagancies, as may be clearly seen by any discerning Reader: Therefore Mahomet gave the World no new Law; but dismembered, mangled, and corrupted the Laws of Moses, and the Gospel of Jesus Christ. (Ziegenbalg 1719: 227)

His openly hostile attitude toward the Prophet provoked at least one public disturbance during his career, and a predictable response from Muslim intellectuals.

They told him that Muslims have a better understanding of Jesus than Christians, because Christians turned Jesus into a god and are therefore polytheists. As one man explained,

> For tho' Jesus Christ was adored as God by some of his own Disciples and heedless Followers; yet he himself preach'd against the Plurality of Gods:

> And when he came to hear, that some of his Disciples adored him, calling him the Son of God, he abandon'd them to themselves, and retir'd into the Wilderness. . . . Therefore Mahomet was sent into the World to destroy the Worship of many Gods, both among the Heathens and Christians. (Ziegenbalg 1719: 302-3)

The Muslims even wondered if Christians, both Catholic and Protestant, were not idolaters like the 'pagan' Malabarians, with the exception perhaps of the Pietists. Ziegenbalg and Pluetschau had gone out of their way not to use the crucifix in the New Jerusalem Church or on liturgical garments to avoid any idea of idolatry. But the absence of any image, even the cross or crucifix, made it unclear to Muslims whether the missionaries belonged to the same religion as the Danish Zion Church, where such images could be found. As that same Muslim told Ziegenbalg,

> ". . . I don't altogether disapprove of your Religion; and was mightily pleas'd to see no Idols of Images in your Church, as among the Portugueze [Catholics]; who symbolize almost in every thing with the Heathens, in the Number of Idols and Graven Images. I was likewise in the Danish Church, where all the Hearers are White Men; and there also I saw some Images: Pray, are your Religions different?" (Ziegenbalg 1919: 304)

The Muslims venerated Jesus and his virgin mother as the Qur'an presented them. According to *Sura* 4 *(Nisāa):* 157-59, Jesus was not killed on the cross, but God did raise him up, and on the Day of Judgment he will be a witness against those 'People of the Book' who deny him, namely, the Jews. In other words, the heart of Evangelical faith, which is the atoning death and resurrection of Jesus Christ, is a complete delusion, although Jesus as a prophet must be believed. As Lebbai Mapillai 'Alim wrote in the nineteenth century, toward the end of the world the prophet Isa (Jesus) would return, and

> invoke the people to embrace Islam. . . . His appearance and his being called 'Prophet' is similar to the Moon being called 'Moon' even when it is merely present in the sky during the day when the Sun [Muhammad] shines in all its splendour and glory. After a time he too will die, and be buried beside the grave of our beloved Prophet. . . . (Lebbai: 11)

The Tranquebar Muslims, feeling politically and economically secure, believed Islam to be the future of the world. As Ziegenbalg wrote to Europe,

> The Mahometan-Moors are far greater Enemies to the Christian Religion, than the Heathens themselves. They often visit me, as I do them; but they will seldom listen to any Reason, firmly believing their own Religion to be of the greatest Extent of all, as having possessed no less than almost Three Parts of the Universe. This is the Reason, that when they write a Letter to a Christian, they cut off three Corners of the Letter, leaving but one entire, to intimate thereby, that the Christians possess but one, and they, the other three Parts of the World. (Ziegenbalg 1717: 32)

In addition to their own doctrine of Jesus, which denied the Christian doctrine, and their sense of being the religious 'wave of the future', Muslims were discouraged from taking the missionaries seriously by the communal sanctions they faced if they converted to any other religion. According to Muslim law, apostasy dissolved the apostate's marriage, invalidated the marriages he arranged for his daughters, made the meat he slaughtered inedible, and prevented him from receiving an inheritance or passing one on (Lebbai: 408). No Muslim became a Protestant in Ziegenbalg's time, and few at any time in the eighteenth century.

CHAPTER 5

'Pagans'

Let us now consider the Malabarian 'pagans' or 'heathens' who watched from the doors and windows of the newly built church. In 1709, when Ziegenbalg answered the European question, 'By what Means do the Malabarians get their Livelihood?' he gave a rather full picture of 'pagan' society by describing secular occupations. He expressed deep suspicion of the renunciant ascetics (whom he called *faqīrs*), who followed none of them:

> Some of the Malabarians maintain themselves by Trade and Commerce; others by the Plow; others again by Handycraft Work, and other Labour and Business of that Nature. In such Sea-port Towns as Tranquebar, Trade is far greater, and everything more plentiful, than in any other Parts of the Country. Those that can and will Work, find Employment enough to get a Livelihood. There are no Beggars to be seen among them except the Faquiers, who pretend, that for the better serving of the Gods, they have denied all their Friends and Relations, their Houses and Estates, their Wives and Children; and such have some Rice given them wherever they come.
>
> There are many rich and great Men among the Malabarians; but for the generality they are poor, or of midling Circumstances. The chief Handycraft Trades among them are, Linnen-Weavers, Shoe-makers, Taylors, Knitters of Stockings, Dyers, Painters, Masons, Carpenters, Joiners, Potters, Goldsmiths, Brasiers, Ironmongers, etc. and some work in Chalk and Lime-Houses, in Brickilns, and Glass-Houses, where Glass-Bracelets are made.
>
> There are Physicians, Surgeons, Barbers, Exchangers of Money, etc. I may truly say; the Malabarians are as expert and ready in their several

> Trades and Arts as any Nation in Europe, and are able to imitate almost everything that cometh to their Hands, and relateth to their Profession.
>
> Their Women maintain themselves by Spinning of Wool, grinding of Rice; by selling of Cheese, Milk, Butter and Fish; by baking Cakes, fetching and carrying of Water; by putting themselves out to Service, etc. (Ziegenbalg 1717: 21-22)

A spokesman for the Malabarian literati would have organized that same description somewhat differently. For example, we may turn to the *Sattiya Sūttiram* ('Scripture of Truth') written by Dandapani Swami (1839-98), a Saiva Velalan of Tirunelveli in the southern part of what by then was Madras Presidency. He was devoted to Murugan, the son of Siva, known also as Kartikkeya, Skanda, and Subrahmanya. In order to make Saiva views of society clear to fellow Tamil-speakers in the colonial context of the late ninteenth century, Dandapani Swami articulated ancient Tamil traditions traceable to such fifth- and sixth-century texts as the *Tirukkuṛal,* the *Tolkāppiyam,* and the *Cilappatikāram.* He also drew upon the ritual traditions of the Saiva Agamas. In the twentieth century Ti. Ce. Murugadasa Aiya wrote a gloss *(urai)* on *Sattiya Sūttiram.* It will guide the following discussion.

Dandapani Swami's 'Scripture of Truth'

Dandapani Swami discussed 12 topics in this Tamil work, entitled *Sattiya Sūttiram (Satya Sūtra),* arranged in sets of ten verses each. He began with the nature of the divine *(teyvam, deva).* It is, he said, a single unity (1.1). He then turned to the guru as the person who manifests the divine (2.1), and to the practice of ascetic discipline, which he called *tapas* (3.1). In the most general sense, he said, *tapas* is the self-disciplined performance of one's 'work' *(toḻil)* in order to attain a higher realm after death. Under that broad umbrella, the Swami then described the nature of people in society by noting what their 'work' was.

He taught an ancient south Indian revision of the 'holistic' class and caste ideology that claims revealed knowledge (Veda) as its basis. The Sanskrit narratives of Valmiki's *Rāmāyaṇa* and Vyasa's *Mahābhārata* illustrate that ideology, and the Sanskrit 'System of Order Taught by Manu' *(Māṇavadharmaśāstra),* commonly known as the 'Laws of Manu', prescribes it systematically. It is part of a larger concept of the right order of everything *(dharma)* that constitutes the 'moving universe' *(jagat)* of space and time.

Dharma, or universal order, is a single but complex and all-pervasive linking together of what Europeans of the Enlightenment were separating into the human, natural, and divine. According to Dharma, changes in time, the cosmos, nature, human society, and an individual's life unfold as an organic whole. Anyone who lives contrary to order *(adharma)* threatens both himself and the larger whole; but in the end Dharma always prevails.

The 'Laws of Manu' (Books 1 and 10) describes four ritual classes *(varṇa)* of people that constitute civilization. They are not thought to be arbitrary, but to be as 'natural' as the sun, moon, and weather. The four civilized classes function, however, because an unnamed fifth class of uncivilized or 'alien' peoples enables them to do so. The hierarchical pattern of those four-plus-one classes, based on the symbolism of the human body, is well known. The Brahmins, as priests and scholars, are the body's head; the Kshatriyas, as ruling warriors, are its arms; the Vaishyas, as farmers and merchants, are its abdomen and thighs; and the Sudras, as servants of the other three, are its feet. The feet, however, walk upon the uncivilized fifth class; it consists of people who are ritually polluting to the other four: scavengers, corpse-burners, hunters, tribals, and barbarians.

That social hierarchy also defines access to the sacred words *(mantra)* that constitute revealed knowledge (Veda). By birth, only male Brahmins, Kshatriyas, and Vaishyas are eligible to receive consecration *(dīkṣā)* into vedic knowledge and to use vedic mantras. Women, Sudras, and everyone else are theoretically excluded. But as our discussion of Dandapani Swami's 'Scripture of Truth' will show, that ideal system of Manu, conceived in the ancient north, never fit the social realities of the ancient south.

The Swami described people according to the tradition that people are born with a 'nature' *(taṉmai)* that expresses itself as their 'work' *(toḻil)*. As with the 'Laws of Manu', he began with the Brahmin *(antaṇaṉ)* who follows the Veda.[1] The ideal Brahmin's nature, he said, is to consider the souls or spirits *(uyir)* of all people as equal to his own (4.1), which leads to a life of cooling compassion (4.2). That mode of life, generally, is a prerequisite for attaining emancipation from death and birth *(mutti, mukti)* (4.7).

Interestingly, the use of intention or attitude to define 'Brahminness' leaves open the possibility that someone born a Sudra may have the same intention or attitude, and therefore by 'nature' be brahminic. That possibility theoretically cuts across all the classes *(varṇa)* to modify the application of

1. The word for Brahmin, *antaṇaṉ*, may be glossed as 'one possessing a beautiful *(am)* nature *(taṉmai)*', or 'one possessing the "end" *(anta)* of Veda' (Vedānta), i.e., knowledge of the *Upaniṣads*. It is synonymous with *pārppār* or 'seer', which describes the acharya as an adept in visualization *(dhyāna)*, and suggests the king's acharya, who used the consecrations *(dīkṣā)* prescribed in the Agamas to purify the king for vedic rites.

what otherwise appears to be a rigid system of social categories. A common explanation for such a person — for example, a Sudra whose nature is that of a Brahmin — would be the doctrine of rebirth: a Brahmin had died and, for some karmic reason, was reborn a Sudra, but had retained his previous nature. Rebirth explained why that person's body did not fit the nature he or she should have, and why he or she should be treated differently from others of the same caste. Modification of general rules would depend on specific social and ritual contexts, a fact 'The Laws of Manu' (chap. 10) itself recognized.[2] India's context-specific practice of caste *(jāti, kula)* would elude efforts by European scholars and colonial administrators to organize it into a clearly defined system based on consistently applied universal principles. In a case we will examine later, their effort evoked at least one well-argued response from Tanjore Evangelicals.

In his discussion of the next three classes, Dandapani Swami continued to follow the *varṇa* sequence of the 'Laws of Manu', but with a significant difference. None of the classes was genuinely Kshatriya or Vaishya, nor had they ever been, which the examples drawn from Tamil literature in the gloss demonstrated. When he turned to the ruler, the Swami called him king *(aracar)*, but not Kshatriya. The king's nature, he said, is to possess truth, political skill, and compassion, and be like a mother toward the people of the world (5.1). The warrior *(maṛavaṉ)* under his command, no doubt, would have a fiercer nature.

The Swami then turned to two classes that appear similar to the Vaishyas and Sudras of 'The Laws of Manu'; but as we will see, ancient Tamil tradition viewed them as deriving from a single indigenous class. One class comprised the merchants *(Vaṇikar)*, known by the caste title Cetti; it is in Tamil a form of *setti* or *śreṣthin*, which typically denotes Vaishyas throughout India. The nature of Cettis, the Swami said, is take and give, which is demeaning, except for the fact that the god Murugan himself was said to have been born a Cetti in Madurai (6.1), and he acts as a Cetti: he takes devotion *(patti, bhakti)* and gives emancipation *(vīṭu)* (6.2).[3]

The fourth class comprised the Velalans, of which there are many

2. The *Marapiyal* section of the *Tolkāppiyam* revealed some of those variations. It noted that the Brahmin *(antaṇaṉ)* and Velalan do not bear arms, while the ruler and merchant do. The Velalan may do so, however, when commanded by the king. The Brahmin, moreover, may rule in place of the king, and the king may perform certain vedic rites. Petty kings may possess warrior insignia, but members of the 'lower' (fifth) class may not, even if they are like petty kings (Ilakkuvanar: 256-58).

3. The reference to Murugan or Skanda as a Cetti is in *Tevāram* 742.10 *(Tamil Lexicon: cetti).*

branches doing various kinds of 'work.' But cultivation is primary (7.1-2). We will return to them shortly.

The Swami then went on to the fifth class, which resembled Manu's fifth class of 'aliens.' The 'people of the fifth' *(pañcamar),* he said, include anyone whose nature is to kill souls and eat meat (8.1). That, of course, would include most Europeans, some Velalans, and probably all warriors. Nevertheless, the Swami assumed that the paradigm for such 'polluted' peoples lived in the *cēri,* the forest, and the hills. But, he also said, any Pancamar who becomes a vegetarian and adopts an auspicious style of life may be classified among people of higher status (8.4), and he referred to three 'untouchable' saints to illustrate his point (8.5): the Saiva Nayanars named Nandanar and Tirunilakanta Yalppanar, and the Vaishnava Alvar named Tiruppan. In fact, he said, anyone who gives up any experience of killing, eating meat, lying, and other such evil acts, even if born among the 'fifth', is superior to one born to a high family committed to that good path as a goal (8.7). One's behaviour *(o̲lukkam)* can change one's nature *(ta̲nmai).*

After Dandapani Swami had described the 'civilized' and 'uncivilized' classes that make up the human world, he discussed their worship. He recognized four aspects to it. One was ritual action *(karumam, karma),* a subset of 'work' *(to̲lil).* In all cases, he said, it is essential to abstain from killing animals in worship (9.1). Another aspect was the proper service of divinity *(upāca̲nai, upāsanā).* Although divinity is both with and without form, the highest form of worship is visualization *(dhyāna)* of deity *(teyvam)* with form *(rūpam),* together with the repetition of *mantras (mantiram cepippatu)* (10.1-3). The third aspect is true knowledge or wisdom *(jñānam).* Wisdom is to live according to the belief that God *(kaṭavūḷ)* is a transcendent being completely pervading the world he envelopes (11.1).

The fourth aspect of worship is public ceremony or practice *(jñayam, ñyāya)* at a temple. Here the Swami made an important observation about the effect of human action on gods and demons. If pure worship is performed, he said, even a demon *(pēy)* is divinity *(teyvam).* But if animal sacrifice is performed, even divinity is a demon (12.1). That means that pure and impure ritual acts convey power not only by expressing the nature of the performer, but also by affecting the nature of the recipient. Behaviour shapes identity, just as identity shapes behaviour.

Let us now turn to Dandapani Swami's discussion of the Velalans and Pancamans in greater detail, for they contributed the majority of Evangelical Christians in the eighteenth century.

The Velalans, Dandapani Swami explained in the *Sattiya Sūttiram,* and Murugadasa Aiya amplified in its gloss, differ according to region, language, and function.[4] They have differing titles, for example Mudaliar, Pillai, and Cettiyar (the last is merely a different form of Cetti). They provide subsistence for ascetics, Brahmins, and rulers, and their fundamental and ancient duty has been to worship God *(kaṭavūḷ)* when rain is required (7.1-5).

Presumably, that 'fundamental and ancient duty' derived from Velalan responsibility for producing an abundance *(vēḷāṇmai)* of food, especially the rice paddy that sustained society. Rice paddy is an ancient paradigm for food *(aṇṇam)*, and food is an ancient metaphor for matter *(prakṛiti)* in Saiva and Vaishnava thought and ritual. Velalan 'work' in producing it was therefore thought to be essential to the whole of society, and Dharma depended on it (*Sattiya Sūttiram* 7.3-4, 7). In the terms of the metaphor used in vedic tradition, the body cannot function soundly without the feet, and society cannot function soundly without Velalans (*Sattiya Sūttiram* 7.6). We may thus gloss 'Velalan' to mean, 'he who produces abundance [*vēḷāṇmai*] by means of sacrifice [*vēḷvu*] motivated by desire [*vēḷ*].' Velalans, in other words, formed a wide-ranging class of castes whose nature desired to express itself by generating agricultural abundance.

That work obligated Velalans to serve specific deities, whom we may consider briefly. In times of drought, Velalans were responsible for worshiping the gods for rain (*Sattiya Sūttiram* 7.5), and a caste in the ancient Pandya realm is known as 'the Velalans who saved the dark rain clouds' *(Kārkaṭṭavēḷālar)* (Thurston and Rangachari: 7:378-80). As traditionally understood, the water that sustains the rice paddy comes from the ocean that surrounds the subcontinent on three sides. By absorbing ocean water, clouds turn it into rain, which feeds the rivers, ponds, and storage tanks. The lord of the ocean, and of the watery realm under the earth, is Varuna. He rules *asuras,* 'the forces of darkness' (or anti-gods), who are half-brothers to *devas,* 'the forces of light' (or gods). The *asuras* reside in the dark waters under the earth with the *nāgas,* who are multiheaded snakes or cobras; the *devas* reside above earth in heaven. The God of gods, by whatever name (e.g., Siva or Narayana), transcends the whole while also pervading it.

Among Varuna's subjects on earth are the demons who eat humans, the *rākṣasas.* They are lower-status kinsmen of the *asuras,* and their kingdom is Lanka to the south. Subordinate to them are the demons who eat corpses, the *piśācas.* Half-brothers to the *rākṣasas* are beings who possess people and affect their fertility and prosperity, the *yaksas.* They are ruled by Kubera, the lord of wealth, who dwells in the Himalayas to the north. In the north lies the source of human prosperity, and in the south lies the source of death. Varuna in the west

4. For a history of the Velalans, see Ganesh.

rules over all those 'dark' beings affecting human well-being and death — the *asuras, rākṣasas, piśācas, yakṣas,* and *nāgas.* In classical Tamil poetry, Varuna signified directional west and the seashore (Ramanujan: 237; Sutherland: 54-65).

An ancient Tamil grammar, *Tolkāppiyam,* identified the Velalan with the *asura* ruler Varuna in the same way it identified the Brahmin with the *deva* Brahma, the king with the Kshatriya Krishna, and the merchant with the *yakṣa* Kubera (Irakavaiyaṅkār: 175). But since Kubera is a dependent of Varuna, that suggests that the merchant is a dependent of the Velalan; or, more precisely, merchants are a subset of Velalans who are motivated to distribute food rather than to produce it. The status of merchants was ambivalent. To the degree that they were removed from food production — and thus from killing — they were ritually more 'pure' than those Velalans who actually tilled the soil. But the desire to 'take' as well as to 'give' could easily balance in favor of the former and turn desire into greed *(ulōpam, lobha),* a common stereotype for merchants throughout India, Dandapani Swami observed (*Sattiya Sūttiram* 6.3). Greed would make such merchants less 'pure' than those Velalans motivated primarily to 'give' through production.

The 'Civilized' and the 'Alien' in Ancient Tamil Literature

Dandapani Swami's teachings had a long career in the courts of Tanjore and other Tamil kingdoms, as a brief discussion of selected ancient texts reveals. An influential account of the origins of 'uncivilized' and 'civilized' peoples is the story of King Prithu, which appears in the *Bhāgavata Purāṇa* (4.14-15), a Sanskrit text addressed to the learned elite whose influence may be discerned in early Tamil poems (Hudson 1994b).

According to the story, 'uncivilized' and 'civilized' peoples originated from a single body of 'Inordinate Desire' (Vena) churned by seers *(ṛishi).* Vena had been born in the line of the seer Anga and had received the unction that endowed him with brilliant conquering power *(tejas)* from the divine protectors of the world (4.14.23). But Vena carried his divine identity to an extreme: He demanded that he, rather than Narayana as Hari, the Person of the Sacrifice *(Yajñapuruṣa),* be the object of sacrificial worship (4.13.33; 14.4-6; 25-28). The seers therefore killed him with the *mantra 'hūm.'* But in the absence of a 'lord of earth' *(bhūpati),* robbery and murder arose, and plunder pushed society toward ruin. A ruler was needed, and to gain him from the proper Anga lineage, the seers churned Vena's corpse as if it were milk.

From the thighs of the corpse arose a servile man, black-skinned and short, who asked the seers what he should do. They said, 'Kneel down' *(niṣīda),* so he was known as Nishada, the progenitor of the Naishadas, the people who live in the forests and hills. They inherited the defiled dregs *(kalmaṣa)* of Vena's nature (4.14.43-46). The seers then churned the arms of the corpse, producing protective portions of Narayana in his mode as God Vishnu and Goddess Lakshmi. Those portions became Prithu and Arci, the first king and queen. After their consecration, Prithu created civilization for the non-Naishada people by 'milking' plants *(oṣadhi)* from the Goddess Earth in the form of a cow with Manu as her calf. Following that model, all other beings 'milked' out their needs from analogous 'cows' with 'calves', and civilized society began (4.15-19).

Three facts are notable in the story. First of all, the nature of 'wild' Naishadas is to humble themselves before people 'tamed' by civilization, because they carry the defilement of a cruel and arrogant nature. Secondly, Goddess Earth took the form of a cow to be a nourishing mother for the civilized. Anyone, therefore, who killed or ate cows would be slaying or cannibalizing his or her own 'mother.' Categorically, such people would be Naishadas. Thirdly, in his first and only act of milking Goddess Earth as cow, with Manu as her calf, the paradigmatic king produced *oṣadhi,* plants that die after ripening. Cultivation of such plants, especially of grain, is essential to royal rule and civilization, which means that cultivators are of inestimable value to both. In ancient Tamil society, the cultivators were the Velalans.

The fifth-century courtly narrative 'The Anklet's Sovereignty' *(Cilappatikāram),* illustrates ideas that develop the Prithu story. The civilized realm is represented by the *ūr,* in this case the ancient walled city of Madurai, the Pandya capital. At its center stood the temple of Siva, the 'God whose matted hair was crowned with laburnum.' Siva's consort was herself the 'Great Goddess Madurai' (*Patikam:* 39-43).[5]

In the story, after the ancient *ūr* was set ablaze, four protecting gods *(kaṭavūḷ)* left the city to the flames. They protected the four types of people living inside Madurai's walls, each ruling over beings *(bhūta)* whom the people worshiped according to their 'work.' The descriptions of those gods depict the ideal nature of the class they protected.[6]

The first god is 'the overlord god of the chief beings', who resembles an idealized Brahmin (22.16-36). Shining with the white light of a pearl necklace, he faultlessly lives the ritual life of the three vedic fires as established by

5. For Madurai as the Goddess, see Hudson 1993.

6. Ilankovayikal 1985: chap. 22: sts. 17, 34-36, 51-61, 62-76, 85-88, 97-102. My reading, which is interested in cultic details, differs from the interpretations of Parthasarathy in Ilankovayikal 1993: 195-96 and of Venkatacami in Ilankovayikal 1996: 458-61. In the *Purāṇas,* Rudra Siva is known as the Bhuta chief (Mani: 145), but none of these gods resembles him.

Brahma in the Veda. He represents the Brahmin teacher-priest *(ācan, ācārya)*, 'a great scholar and interpreter of Dharma' for the king, who appears as the scene opens (22.8; also 28.222).

Next is 'the god of rare conquering power of kingly beings', who resembles an idealized ruler (22.37-61). He represents the Pandya king who has just died. He is a victorious and righteous warrior, shining with the luster of red coral, and his fame compares to that of the 'The Tall One' *(Neṭiyōṉ)*, who grew and spread in the four directions (22.58-61). 'The Tall One' refers to Narayana's appearance on earth as a Brahmin dwarf, Vamana, who swelled up to become the huge Trivikrama, a story of particular significance to ancient Tamil kingship.[7]

As the story is told in the *Bhāgavata Purāṇa* (8.15-23), Vamana the dwarf went to the horse sacrifice sponsored by Bali. He was an *asura* king who had emerged from the underworld, had pushed the *devas* out of heaven, and now ruled the world. In the sacred context of the horse sacrifice, Bali spoke the words of a ritual gift *(dāna):* he promised to give the Brahmin dwarf the amount of land the dwarf could measure with three of his own strides. Instantly, Vamana swelled up to become 'The Tall One' *(Neṭiyōṉ)*, and in two steps measured out the cosmos. With no place left for Vamana's third step, Bali had failed to be true to his word, the highest duty of a king. But the *asura* king Bali, though of a 'dark' nature, was nevertheless devoted to Narayana. He immediately took refuge in him as the dwarf who took three strides to measure out the universe (Trivikrama) and thereby conquered him. In response Narayana gave Bali an underworld kingdom in the realm called Sutala, and promised to protect him there with his personal presence. King Bali, ruling in the 'dark' underworld under Narayana's protection, represents the Sudra king ruling under the protection of his Brahmin acharya. Through *mantra* rites, Narayana's brilliant conquering power *(tejas)* manifests itself on behalf of the Sudra king's rule.

Returning to 'The Anklet's Sovereignty', the third god represents both cultivators and merchants (22.63-88). He is greenish-gold in color, and is dressed like the king, except for the crown. He lives a faultless life based on growing food, and in one hand he holds a plow and in the other a pair of scales; he sells what he produces to the world at large. That god shines with the light of Siva, who wears the moon in his matted hair. That means that he

7. 'The Tall One' *(Neṭiyōṉ)* appears at the beginning of part 3 of *Cilappatikāram* (25.21-22) to describe the tall mountains from which the Periyar River flows in the Western Ghats: 'The Periyar transversed the great mountain as does the necklace on the chest of Netiyon.'

resembles Kubera, because Kubera dwells in Siva's presence on Mount Kailasa and receives moonlight from his hair (Sutherland: 67).

The fourth god represents cowherds *(āyar)* who sing and dance (22.101-2). He has a body dark as sapphire and wears a brightly colored cloth. He is pleased with pounded paddy *(aval)*, which is prepared for dancing (or trembling), enjoys many songs, and receives sacrifices in the noisy city, where he is called 'Leader of Beings' *(Bhūtat-talaivaṉ)*. This god resembles Krishna, whose skin is dark like a sapphire and who wears a yellow cloth (16.45-51). The cowherds living inside Madurai's wall sang and danced for him, for his white-skinned elder brother Balarama, and for his cowherd wife Pinnai (chap. 17). Their songs expressed ideas of the Prithu story: that the consecrated Tamil king is a mode of Krishna or Vishnu, who themselves manifest Narayana (17.*uḷvari vāḻttu* ff.).

Three Types of 'Sudras' Dwelling in the *Ūr*

When we compare the descriptions of Tamil society by Dandapani Swami, by the *Tolkāppiyam*, and by the *Cilappatikāram*, we find a pattern of social thought different from the prescriptions of the 'Laws of Manu.' In contrast to Manu's four distinct ritual classes of civilization *(varṇa)*, plus a generalized uncivilized 'fifth', the ancient Tamil descriptions present only two *varṇas*, both living inside the ritual boundaries of the *ūr*. There were the Brahmins, and there were all the others, whom 'The Laws of Manu' classified as Sudras. The Sudras, however, were of three types: those who ruled, those who cultivated and distributed, and those who tended cattle.

Not mentioned in those descriptions are the people of 'the fifth' implied by 'The Laws of Manu' and discussed in the 'Scripture of Truth' as the Pancamar. In ancient times they would have comprised tribal groups and hunters in the mountains and forests, and the vassals *(kuṭimai)* and praedial slaves *(aṭimai)*, who were compelled to live in their own settlements *(cēri)* outside the bounded realm of the *ūr* (Pfaffenberger: 38-42).

In 'The Anklet's Sovereignty', they appear twice, first as fierce Eyinans living in a village fenced by thorns at the wild edge of the Pandya realm. The Eyinans are described as warriors *(maṛavar)* who plunder travellers, eat meat, drink liquor, and offer human sacrifices to the goddess Aiyai. She speaks to them by possessing a virgin, and is herself depicted as an extension of the Great Goddess Madurai (*Cilappaktikāram* 12). They appear secondly as Kuravans, mountain people living in small huts who, for seven generations, have been slaves or vassals *(aṭi)* of the Cera king (15.56-57). They worship the six-faced Murugan or Skanda, perform rites of possession, and believe that Murugan's second wife Valli belongs to their own Kurava clan (24.4.17).

As in 'The Laws of Manu', people living in the *ūr* did not count the Pancamar, 'people of the fifth', as part of civilization. It was obvious to them that their nature was polluted by sin *(kalmaṣa)* and that therefore their work was to perform the ritually polluting tasks that allowed those in the *ūr* to live with the purity civilization requires.

The Brahmins in the Tamil texts, we may assume, were primarily those of the Saiva and Vaishnava Agamas, who early on had initiated the non-Aryan Tamilians into the vedic rites, and were teaching priests or acharyas to the rulers.[8] Leaving them aside, everyone else — the rulers, agriculturists, merchants, and dancing and singing cowherds — living inside the city walls were much alike, but divided according to work. Ritually speaking, they were all Sudras in the classification of Manu. To some degree, they were all 'Velalans' in the sense that they sought the abundance that comes through work and sacrifice motivated by desire. Let us consider them more closely.

The coral red ruler, likened to God Narayana in the form of 'The Tall One', represented those few 'Velalan' lineages that provided kings; they ruled through the brilliant conquering power generated by the vedic and agamic rites they sponsored under the guidance of their Brahmin acharyas.[9] They were Dravida kings, the 'Laws of Manu' said, who had once been Kshatriyas, but had sunk to the condition of Sudras (10.20-22; 10.43-44). But they were not alone in that status. According to the *Bhāgavata Purāṇa* (12.1), the sign of the present and degenerate age (Kali Yuga) is that almost all rulers are Sudras.

The greenish-gold figure without a crown, Kubera as farmer and merchant, represented an elite whose color not only signified the wealth generated by the young chartreuse paddy but also their status as lighter-skinned aristocrats; they administered that wealth indoors away from the sun. The plow and scales held in each hand signified civil divisions between lineages of the 'right hand' (plow) and lineages of the 'left hand' (scales). Each set inter-

8. For a discussion of the spread of the Agamas of the Bhagavatas to South India, see Hudson 1994b: 113-40.

9. Those rites appear to have been of the Agama followed by Bhagavata acharyas in the early Tamil courts. Once consecrated, the king ruled as an 'Indra among men' *(Narendra)*. But since that same consecration had made him, like Bali, a 'slave' of Narayana, the God of gods who rules Indra himself, he simultaneously represented Narayana to his realm; specifically, he represented the forms Narayana took as 'The Tall One', Vishnu, and Krishna. For that reason, ancient Tamil tradition likened the Tamil kings to a form of Narayana (*Cilappatikāram* 11.29-31). For an exploration of the evidence for early Bhagavata presence in Tamil courts see Hudson 1994, 1993, 1995a, and 1997.

married within itself to form 'castes' *(jāti, kulam).* Those civil distinctions between the 'right' and the 'left', which eventually appeared in inscriptions, were socially and politically important during the eighteenth and nineteenth centuries (B. Stein: chap. 5).

The plow signified the fields, their sowing, and the oxen that pulled the plow. The honored right hand held it presumably because the entire society depended on the plants the plow produced. The dependent left hand held the scales, for it signified the merchants who distributed the produce of those plants. Nevertheless, they were two sides of a single social body, an aristocracy attentive to Kubera, the lord of wealth, whose vehicle, tellingly, is a human.[10]

The last type of 'Velalan' living inside the *ūr* dealt directly with the Master of Beings through song and dance, the latter perhaps involving rites of possession or 'trembling' *(cāmiyāṭutal).* Like that of Krishna, their skin color was like black gem, for they worked in the sun, herding cattle and transforming milk into butter and ghee. Perhaps as part of their work during the day outside the *ūr,* they also supervised the vassals and praedial slaves who planted and transplanted, and built dikes. As masters of song and dance, and probably of trance and possession, they may have been crucial to sacrificial rites addressed to resident beings *(bhūtas)* responsible for the fertility of cattle and fields. Ziegenbalg encountered cultic sites for a number of such local beings as he walked through the Tranquebar colony in the early eighteenth century.

Velalans as 'Sudras' Dwelling in the *Ūr*

Among those functionally different 'Sudras' dwelling inside the *ūr,* those represented by the 'right' and 'left' hands of the greenish-gold Kubera figure became typical Velalans in later centuries, some of whose members taught Ziegenbalg. They divided themselves into variously ranked castes and lineages identified with specific regions and villages as their places of origin. From the vedic ritual point of view, they were all Sudras, but we now see that the ritual category of Sudra did not mean that socially they were not powerful, wealthy, prestigious, aristocratic, or learned. Prestigious Sudra kings also

10. Regarding the meaning of 'right' and 'left', the following may be noted. The Tamil word for 'right' *(valam)* means 'power' (as in *bala*); and the emblem of the avatar of 'power', Krishna's elder brother Baladeva or Balarama, is the plow. The word for 'left' *(iṭam)* includes the meanings 'wealth' and 'prosperity', signified by the pair of scales. Kubera, the lord of wealth who rides humans as his vehicle *(naravāhana),* dwells in the Himalayas of the north; in the typical east-facing position for sacrifice, the worshiper's left side is toward the north and toward Kubera.

appear in the *Mahābhārata.* Tamil kings, along with other southern kings, attended Yudhisthira's royal consecration (2.31). Moreover, like those Tamil kings, the great and tragic figure of Karna, a Kshatriya who had 'fallen' to the level of a Sudra, had been made the Sudra king of Anga.

What being Sudra meant, according to Veda and Agama, was what being female meant: that by birth alone one was not qualified to be 'reborn' through vedic consecration into the use of vedic *mantras* for ritual purposes. Yet, if one's 'impure' Sudra or female body had first been purified through the rites of Agama, then, in certain ritual contexts, Sudras and women could function as the 'twice-born' equivalents of the Vaishya ritual class *(varṇa).*

The Velala Saiva reformer of the nineteenth century, Arumuga Navalar of Jaffna, clarified that idea for Tamil schoolchildren in an essay entitled 'Varna' in his 'Children's Primer: Book Four' *(Palapāṭam: Nānkām Puttakam).* He published it in 1850-51. Sudras, he wrote, are qualified to recite such teachings as epic History *(Itihāsa)* and Ancient Lore *(Purāṇa),* and to hear the meaning of Veda. Among the five major sacrifices *(pañca-mahā-yājña)* expected of householders, they are qualified to perform four: the sacrifice to *devas,* to ancestors, to beings *(bhūta),* and to humans. But they are not qualified to perform the sacrifice to *brahman,* for it is the study of vedic *mantras* (Kane: 2:1.696-704). They are also qualified to give ritual gifts *(dāna).*

He then explained that Sudras fall into two types: the 'Pure Sudra' *(sat-śūdra)* and the 'Impure Sudra' *(asat-śūdra).* Those who do not consume liquor and meat, and keep the religious conduct prescribed by the texts, are the 'Pure Sudras.' The others are 'Impure Sudras.' In ritual, he said, 'Pure Sudras' are equivalent to Vaishyas. Dandapani Swami's teachings were similar.

Sudras, Arumuga Navalar also said, may become 'twice-born.' They receive the sacred thread of *upanāyaṇa* at any age during agamic consecrations. In contrast, the other three ritual classes *(varṇa)* receive it at ages stipulated by Veda. Prior to his thread investiture a Brahmin is ritually a Sudra, and if after receiving the thread he does not recite Veda, he is disqualified for any vedic rite and, for ritual purposes, he becomes a Sudra again (Arumuga Navalar 1969: 75-83). Furthermore, as Navalar noted in a comment on 'The Path of the Saiva Religion' (*Caivacamayaneṛi* 1.3), those among all four *varṇas* who become twice-born by means of agamic consecration have the authority to recite Agama texts, which are the basis for temple worship. Indeed, males among all four *varṇas* (except for 'Impure Sudras') may become teacher-priests or acharyas (Ārumuga Nāvalār 1911: 13).

In other words, a person may be born with a 'nature', but that 'nature' is not necessarily unchangeable. One's behaviour may modify one's 'nature' and, with it, one's 'work.' A story about Arumuga Navalar's ancestor, Jnanaprakasa the Sage *(Muni),* illustrates the idea (Hudson 1998: 40-41). Jnanaprakasa was born into a line of the Pandya Velalans who had 'saved the dark rain clouds' *(Kārkaṭṭavēḷālar)* that had settled in Jaffna. When the Portuguese annexed the Jaffna kingdom in 1619, the story says, its new 'barbarian' rulers required each house to supply a cow to feed the Portuguese officer in residence. When Jnanaprakasa's turn came — anxious about the sin of giving a cow to be killed and eaten — he fled during the night. He reached the Tanjore kingdom and went to the Siva temple at Chidambaram, where he bathed in its pond *(kuḷam)* for 45 days, ate pepper and pure water, and at the sanctum worshiped the Goddess as 'The Mother Beloved of Siva.'

He then left Chidambaram, walked northward, and came to Gauda, which is Bengal. While there, he encountered a Brahmin renouncer *(sannyāsi)* teaching logic, grammar, vedic ritual theory *(mīmāmsa),* and other subjects to some boys. He was also teaching them to chant the *mantras* of Veda. Jnanaprakasa went there regularly, stood respectfully at a distance, listened, and memorized what he heard. Yet because it was forbidden for a Brahmin *sannyāsi* to talk with a Sudra, the story says, the teacher never spoke to him. One day, however, when the teacher examined his pupils, they could not answer any questions. So, probably out of frustration, the teacher summoned Jnanaprakasa and told him to repeat everything he had heard from the day he had arrived. To everyone's astonishment, he did. The Brahmin then told Jnanaprakasa the Sudra, 'you alone are a Brahmin', and took him as his student. He taught him logic, grammar, and other texts, and, after he finished the sequence, told him to return and work in the Tamil country.

Accordingly, Jnanaprakasa returned to the Tanjore kingdom. At the monastery at Tiruvannamalai, he received the ochre robe of a *sādhu* and studied Saiva Siddhanta. Then he moved to Chidambaram, where he wrote commentaries in Sanskrit on Sanskrit texts, translated Tamil works into Sanskrit, and wrote a Tamil gloss on *Śivajñānasiddhiyār.* He also built a pond *(kuḷam)* in Chidambaram, which is known today by his name, Jnanaprakasa Muni. Beside it a small temple houses a festival icon of his Velalan descendent, Arumuga Navalar (Hudson 1998: 41-43).

That story makes clear that an internal nature does not always match the external body housing it, and that Sudras may also be 'Brahminical.' Stories about the nonhuman analogues of Sudras discussed earlier make the same point. *Asuras, rākṣasas, yakṣas,* and *nāgas* may also be purified. As we noted, the *asura* king Bali rules in Sutala under earth under the protection of Narayana as Trivikrama. The *rākṣasa* king Vibhishana rules in Lanka under Narayana's protection as Rama. And the poisonous *nāga* named Adisesha is so pure that he serves as Narayana's own couch and throne.

The story of the *asura* king Bali instructively illustrates the Sudra king. In Kerala he is believed to rise up from the underworld of Sutala in the autumnal 'nighttime' of the year to be honored by the people (Hospital: chap. 7). That ancient rite of honoring a devout *asura* king protected by Narayana in the form of the dwarf parallels the rite of honoring a Sudra king protected by Narayana in the form of his acharya. As noted earlier, Vamana the dwarf represents the Brahmin acharya in the court of the Sudra king (Hudson 1999). The Bali story, moreover, may be related to a story about Velalan origins, which probably appeared during Nayaka rule in the fifteenth to seventeenth centuries, after Vijayanagara had subdued the Chola and Pandya dynasties. The story explains why castes represented by the plow of the right hand were opposed to castes represented by the scales of the left hand. It also explains how Velalans remained crucial to Tamil kingship even though, under Nayaka rule, they no longer provided the kings.

According to the story (as told by Thurston and Rangachari: 7:363-66), while God Siva and Goddess Parvati were at erotic play on Mount Kailasa, the artisan of the gods, Visvakarman, intruded on their privacy. Visvakarman is the progenitor of the 'left hand' artisan Kammalans. The couple was angered and told Visvakarman that, on the bank of the Ganga River, Goddess Earth *(Bhūmidevī)* would give birth to a being to oppose him. Visvakarman found out where that birth would take place, vowed he would slay his enemy with one blow, and flew to the Ganga to wait anxiously.

One day the ground began to crack, and, just as a human child emerges from the womb headfirst, the being that was his enemy began to rise out of Goddess Earth, his crown suddenly visible. Thinking the crown to be his head, Visvakarman chopped it off with one sword stroke. The being then emerged fully, garlanded with flowers, holding a golden plow, but without a crown. Visvakarman seized him violently. But Brahma, Vishnu, Siva, and the gods of the eight directions suddenly appeared and stopped him. Visvakarman had not killed the being with one blow as he had promised, they said, and therefore he had to let his enemy live. Moreover, they made Visvakarman agree that his five Kammalan sons (silversmiths, carpenters, ironsmiths, stonecutters, and braziers) would be subservient to the 'Son of Goddess Earth' *(Bhūmīputra)*.

Next, the gods named the son of Goddess Earth 'Protector of Earth', 'Descendent of Ganga', and 'Protector of the Plough.' But because he had lost his crown, they did not allow him to rule. Instead, he and his descendents were to till the ground, and one of their members would have the privilege of placing the crown on the king's head at his coronation. As in agamic consecration, they then invested the son of Goddess Earth with the thread that signified his qualification for vedic rites *(yajñopavītam, pūnūṛkaliyāṇam).* Afterwards they married him to two wives. One wife was the daughter of Indra, king of gods, and the other was the daughter of Kubera, the *yakṣa* lord of wealth. Then God Siva and God Yama each gave him a white bull to plough the ground; from that came the Telugu name of his descendents, Vellal Warus, meaning 'those that plow with white bulls' (Thurston and Rangachari: 7:364). In Tamil, the name is Velalan.

The marriage of Goddess Earth's son to Indra's daughter aligned him with political authority. They produced 54 sons. His marriage to Kubera's daughter aligned him with the wealth of cultivators and merchants. They produced 52 sons. Those 106 sons then married the 106 daughters of Kubera's son, Nala. Through those alignments, Indra's 'work' of ruling had been subsumed by Kubera's larger 'work' of generating wealth, but authority to rule under the king locally remained. Those 106 sons made the following agreement with their *yakṣa* father-in-law, Nala: 35 of them would plow the ground, 35 would trade, and 35 would breed and feed cattle. Those divisions match the 'Velalan' divisions of cultivators, merchants, and cowherds in 'The Anklet's Sovereignty.' But one son remained. He would not join any of those three groups, so they called him the 'Alien' Vellal Warus.

The 105 brothers produced 12,000 children, who intermarried and lived together as a single caste, although they maintained their different occupations. The 'alien' brother gave birth to 2,500 children, who formed a separate caste, but the account does not name their 'work.' Presumably, they also lived in the *ūr* and were not the 'aliens' of the *cēri.*

'Pariahs' as 'Aliens' in the *Cēri* and the Wild

Having considered the groups placed by tradition within the ritual boundaries of civilization, let us now turn to the people that it placed outside the *ūr* in the *cēri* and in the forest and hills. The 'Laws of Manu' (10.45) called those people 'aliens' *(dasyu).* Dandapani Swami, in the 'Scripture of Truth', called them 'the people of the fifth [class]' *(pañcamar)* and explained that they consist of those people whose nature is to kill souls and to eat flesh (*Sattiya Sūttiram* 8.1-10). Their nature, presumably, resembles that of the demonic *rākṣasas.* Their duty, he said, is to do whatever the ruler commands, and to announce events to people, usually with the drum called *paṛai.* From *paṛai* comes the caste name Paraiyan and its European derivative, 'pariah.' Yet, he also explained, there is no reason to fault them for serving people of the other four groups, and they are to be respected.

In fact, the Swami continued, those of this class who do not eat flesh are to be counted among the higher-status people, because purity inside purifies the outside. Implied is the agamic consecration that purifies the grossly physical body and gives 'true being' *(sat)* to the 'unclean' and to Sudras and women. The 'Sudras of true being' *(sat-śūdra)* have a ritual status analogous to that of the 'twice-born' Vaishya class described in 'The Laws of Manu.' It is possible, therefore, that a Pancaman could become a Sat-Sudra.

In any case, continued the Swami, no person anywhere is to kill intentionally, even if the Veda requires it for sacrifices. According to the acharyas of Agama, he asserted, even if Veda itself appeared and spoke, and even if Brahma, Vishnu, and Siva appeared and spoke, still people of high-status castes are not allowed the sin of eating flesh. No one with a compassionate mind, he said, can bear the tormented thrashing of a victim being killed.

The primary advantage of human birth, he went on, is worshiping God, which is done by imagining his form in visualization, by reciting mantras, and by controlling the breath. Wisdom is to believe in and follow God, who encompasses the world and exists within it. Social status does not derive from birth, but from conduct arising from wisdom. The Brahmin who ruins his conduct falls to the level of the fifth class; a member of the fifth class who is outstanding in conduct is superior to a 'fallen' Brahmin.

Each of the many religions *(samayam)* has its god, he explained, and its god may be called the 'guru' of that religion. Once a person has become one with the soul of the 'guru' god, that person receives the great joy of emancipation, a joy that comes from wisdom. Still, he said, the evil of eating flesh is not a wisdom that all people are ready to receive. That is no fault of theirs; rather, people receive the divine grace for which they are qualified.

Behaviour, however, may modify one's qualification for divine grace by modifying one's nature. As an example, the Swami discussed the case of demons and gods. According to common wisdom, he said, when 'pure' vegetarian rites are used to worship a demon *(pēy)*, they will turn it into a god *(teyvam)*. On the other hand, when souls are sacrificed in the worship of a god, those rites turn it into a demon. The reason, he explained, is that God is love *(anpu)*. The body is the abode of the soul, and the soul is the abode of God; being love within the soul, God does not desire its affliction or slaughter. To be close to God within the soul, therefore, one should not kill animals or eat them.

Yet, we may add, some Velalans customarily did eat sheep, goats, and fish, though not beef. Therefore, we may spell out what the Swami implied, making a distinction between those who slaughter animals for meat and those who eat that meat. Those who slaughter animals will also eat them, but those who eat them, like many urbanized people today, will not slaughter them — their 'nature' will not allow it. According to Agama, however, it is best to do neither.[11]

In sum, Dandapani Swami followed ancient Tamil tradition in adapting the classical *varṇa* model as found in vedic-based Sanskrit literature, so that his five classes do not in fact correspond in ritual status to the pattern of four classes plus the fifth that they follow. In *varṇa* terms, his description contains only three classes: the Brahmins, the Sudras, and the Pancamar. The rulers of Tamil society may have been Kshatriya by nature, but they functioned through Sudra bodies; the aristocrats had Sudra bodies too, but their nature was Vaishya.

Obviously, by the eighteenth century, whatever the word 'Sudra' may have connoted in the northern kingdoms of India, in the southern kingdoms its meaning included castes whose functions would classify them in the north as Vaishyas. Moreover, as W. Francis reported regarding the Velalans, 'By general consent, the first place in social esteem among the Tamil Sudra castes is awarded to them' (Thurston and Rangachari: 7:373).

Nevertheless, when the British East India Company formed the Presidency of Madras at the beginning of the nineteenth century and began to classify castes according to the 'Laws of Manu', the connotation of the word 'Sudra' changed in southern India. The dignity it implied gave way to the connotation of servility. When the Municipal Commissioners of Madras listed Velalans as Sudras in the British census of 1871, some Velalans in Madras sent a petition of protest, arguing that they should be classified as Vaishyas:

> . . . it is impossible to imagine that the Vellalas, a race of agriculturists and traders, should have had to render menial service to the three higher

11. A story in the *Nārāyaṇīya* section of the *Śānti Parvan* of the *Mahābhārata* illustrates agamic teaching about non-killing. It is about King Vasu, also called Uparichara, who followed the Satvata or Pancaratra Agama. According to the story, the seers, through whom the *mantras* of Veda had been revealed, said that the word *ajas,* when denoting an offering, means only seeds or vegetables. The gods, who received those offerings as their food, said that it meant goats. In that dispute, the righteous king Vasu sided with the gods. After King Vasu died and ascended to heaven, the seers angrily cursed him to fall into a hole in the earth. The gods, now repentant, used the ghee of the offerings, called *Vasudhāra* ('support of Vasu'), to sustain him in that hole until he had fulfilled the curse. The *Vasudhāra* offerings are made on the side of a wall; after a horizontal red line with seven spots is created, ghee is poured from those spots to run down the wall, creating vertical lines. Eating the ghee dripping into his hole, King Vasu remained faithful to Narayana through daily worship with *mantras.* The kite birth Garuda finally came and carried him back to heaven (Ganguli: 126-29).

> classes. For the very idea of service is, as it needs must be, revolting to the Vellala, whose profession teaches him perfect independence, and dependence, if it be, upon the sovereign alone for the protection of his proper interests. Hence a Vellala cannot be of the Sudra or servile class. (Thurston and Rangachari: 7:366-67)

Leaving aside the question of what 'Sudra' connotes, W. Francis, in the Madras Census Report of 1901, described the Velalans in a way that helps our understanding them in the eighteenth century (Thurston and Rangachari: 7:372-76). They were divided into four main divisions identified by region, he said. They did not intermarry, and were themselves divided into endogamous groups linked to specific places (an important fact to be discussed later). The Velalans of the ancient Pallava region of Tondaimandalam bore the caste names Mudali, Reddi, and Nainar (the last two denoting Telugu-speaking origins). Those of the ancient Chola region around Tanjore bore the caste name Pillai, as did those of the ancient Pandya region around Madurai. Those of the ancient Kongu country around Coimbatore bore the caste name Kavandan (Kavuntan or Goundar) and included Kannada-speakers *(Tamil Lexicon: kavuntan).*

According to Francis, members of those four divisions generally followed the same customs, which denoted high ritual and social status. Most were either cultivators or merchants, as ancient tradition prescribed. Brahmins performed the weddings for all except those of ancient Kongu. All practiced cremation rather than burial of the dead, and observed 15 days of pollution and a sixteenth day of ceremonial purification.

In matters of religion *(samayam),* Francis said, they were divided between Saivas and Vaishnavas, who nevertheless intermarried. Each of the four divisions had Saiva Velalan priests *(paṇḍāram),* who officiated at funerals and certain temple ceremonies. For example, the Choliya *paṇḍārams* of the Tanjore region included householders and renunciants; the latter were monks *(sādhu),* some of whom managed Saiva temples, or were abbots *(maṭhāthipati)* of monasteries *(maṭha).* They bore the title 'Master' *(Tampirāṉ).* Saiva monasteries contained libraries of palm leaf books, and in the Tanjore kingdom, where monastic leaders were often learned in the Saiva Agamas and Puranas, some were important creative centers for Tamil literature.

A noted Tampiran, for example, was born the year Ziegenbalg and Pluetschau landed at Tranquebar. He was Tayumanar Pillai (1706-44),[12] the

12. Zvelebil (1973: 221) gave his dates as 1706-44. According to Irāmanātaṉ Piḷḷai (1975: 36), however, Tayumanavar died in 1662.

son of a Saiva Velalan who served as the chief accountant for a Nayaka ruler in Tirucirappalli, near Tanjore. Before he was married, Tayumanar Pillai practiced yoga and experienced a vision of Siva as 'the silent teacher', which he described in a poem, 'Worship of the Silent Teacher' *(Mauṉakuru vaṇakkam).* When his wife died soon after their first child's birth, Tayumanar Pillai renounced the householder life and became Tayumanar Atikal. Eventually he led the 'Monastery of the Silent Teacher' *(Mauṉakuru Maṭam)* in Tirucirappalli and, 'as a real giant of Tamil religious and philsophical poetry' (Zvelebil: 221), composed 56 Tamil works of Saiva Siddhanta devotion and theology.

In some temples and monasteries, a Sudra like Tayumanar Atikal had greater authority and status than a Brahmin priest who served the icons or was a musician (Thurston and Rangachari: 6:48-50). A telling example in the late nineteenth century was the Smartha Brahmin student of Tamil literature, U. V. Swaminathaiyar (1855-1942). He was a devoted disciple of the Velalan scholar Minakshi Sundaram Pillai (1815-76), the 'Great Scholar' *(Mahā Vidvān)* of the Saiva Tiruvavatuturai monastery near Tanjore, which was led by Velalans. That Brahmin's devotion to his Sudra guru *(guru bhakti)* led him to write his biography, one of the earliest in the Tamil language (Hudson 1981).

If *paṇḍarāms* had received agamic consecration, Francis explained, they wore the sacred thread, while other Velalans wore it only at funerals. All Velalans performed the monthly memorial rites of *śrāddha* and the annual memorial rites of Mahalaya, the dark half of the lunar month Bhadrapada. Customarily, they would eat only with other Velalans, or with Brahmins, and abstained from alcohol.

In the Tamil-speaking region, where public behaviour denoted identity, the Velalans sustained a lifestyle that placed them ritually and socially second only to the Brahmins. The Kshatriya and Vaishya ritual classes known by the 'Laws of Manu' did not exist. Sudras played their roles.

As we noted earlier, and will return to again, Malabarians believed that one's nature is subject to change; behaviour not only expresses one's nature, but it may also change it. Consequently, castes and families guarded their customary behaviour *(oḻukkam)* and customs *(vaḻakkam)* carefully. Or, in order to change their nature and therefore their 'work', they changed their behaviour and customs gradually. It was thus possible, over the years, for lower-status castes to transform themselves into 'Velalans', though others might not recognize them as such. A Tamil maxim put the matter of change succinctly: a 'Thief' *(Kaḷḷaṉ)* may become a 'Warrior' *(Maṟavaṉ);* a 'Warrior', through respectable behaviour, may become a 'Landowner' *(Akamuṭaiyaṉ);* and a 'Landowner', by slow degrees, may become a Velalan (Thurston and Rangachari: 7:377; 1:6-7).

With change in 'nature' and 'work' possible, any alteration of custom by an individual, a family, a lineage, or a caste was a serious matter. Indeed, according to the concept of Dharma, it could even affect the cosmos. With that background, let us now return to the 'pagans' of Tranquebar and Tanjore, who were watching the two German Pietists in their newly built New Jerusalem Church.

CHAPTER 6

'Pagan' Thought in Tranquebar and Tanjore

In Ziegenbalg's time, Tranquebar town possessed five large temples, and numerous large and small temples dotted the colony. Ziegenbalg called them 'pagodas' and counted a total of 51 (Ziegenbalg 1926: 124). In contrast to the Evangelical church and the Muslim mosque, which each religion considered a place for people to meet and worship God, who dwells in no particular place, the temple was considered a particular place where God resides in a specific material form *(mūrti)*. The temple was a *kōyil,* 'house of the king,' the same term used for a royal palace. Siva, or Narayana, or the Goddess, or minor members of their families and courts, lived there in a 'body' made of wood, plaster, paint, or stone called an *arcā* or icon.

The large temples had the servants any palace required. Ziegenbalg named 13 in a list that moves hierarchically, beginning with the office with the most encompassing authority in palace affairs. First was the temple director. He had either built the temple or supervised it. As we noted in the previous chapter, he was often a Velalan, that is, a Sudra. Second was the Brahmin priest who supervised other Brahmin priests as the personal servants of the resident deity. Third was the Brahmin cook who prepared the daily food for the deity and the temple servants. Fourth was the Brahmin who lit the temple lamps and put them out. Fifth was the man who kept the temple rooms clean, who could be a Pandaram. Sixth was the man who brought flowers from the temple garden; he could be either a Brahmin, a Pandaram, or an Anti. Seventh was the man who ground sandalwood and saffron into paste for the rites, eighth was the man who safeguarded the treasury, ninth was the washerman, and tenth was a servant for minor tasks.

The 'slaves of God', the *devadāsis,* women who sang and danced, were the eleventh. Ziegenbalg said that they had to learn to read and write and become minimally conversant in poetry, so the most sophisticated and refined girls with faultless bodies were chosen for that position. But they were not allowed to marry. In fact, he said, they were really nothing but common whores *(Huhren),* whom Europeans called 'dance whores' *(Tantzhuhren).* Musicians who played instruments for the daily worship, during festivals, and in processions were the twelfth. The man who kept everything in the temple in good repair, finally, was the thirteenth (Ziegenbalg 1926: 131-32).

Ziegenbalg described the temple rites as 'sacrifice' *(Opffer).* In the large temples, the common sacrifice was *pūjā,* and Brahmin priests conducted it. He described it as a daily sequence of rites beginning with the unction *(abhiṣeka)* of the deity followed by a bath and a vegetarian meal shared with the priests and other temple servants. In the morning and afternoon, little music accompanied those rites, but when they were performed at night, *devadāsis* sang and danced before the icon accompanied by instrumental music loud enough to be heard in the streets outside (Ziegenbalg 1926: 96). Devotees could enter the 'palace' during those ceremonies to see their enthroned 'King' or 'Queen', be seen by him or her in return, offer gifts, and verbalize their petitions and praises. In the eighteenth century, traffic in and out of such temples was limited to men and women of requisite purity; devotees in polluted bodies, such as 'aliens' and menstruating women, could worship only outside the temple boundaries.

Those ceremonies conducted by Brahmins were strictly vegetarian *(caiva).* In smaller temples for lesser deities, however, animal sacrifices called *bali* were conducted by non-Brahmins. Ziegenbalg described those deities as fierce and like devils — for example, Virabhadra had 1,000 heads and 2,000 arms. But goddesses ruled over them, and he named them Bhadrakali, Durga, Mariamman, and Pirattiyar, who, he said, are 'gods of the village' *(grāmadevatā).* They received sacrificed pigs, but, most commonly, goats and cocks.

As an example, he described a festival for the goddess Mariamman that fell in April. During it, village leaders or watchmen (*talaiyāren* [*talaiyāri*]), whom he called 'soldiers', offered the goddess more than 100 goats and even more cocks. One by one, a *talaiyār* chopped off animal heads in front of the goddess, and then the men either ate the meat themselves or sent it to friends. In the meantime their wives gathered in large numbers near Mariamman's temple and cooked rice. Some they offered to her, some they tossed onto the ground before her, and the remainder they ate that night to the accompaniment of storytelling and dancing *(Gauckel-Spiel und Tantzarten)* (Ziegenbalg 1926: 97-98).

Besides *pūjā* and *bali,* Ziegenbalg described rites people performed at the end of their worship to protect its auspicious conclusion *(tiruvantik-kāppu).* They rang bells and waved lighted lamps before the deity, and circumambulated the icon clockwise. They also burned incense and sang hymns of praise describing the deity's deeds and works (Ziegenbalg 1926: 97). But the best sacrifice, he said, was called *ekkiyam (yajña)* or *ōmam (homa).* Both names refer originally to rites of the fire prescribed by Veda, but Ziegenbalg described rites prescribed by Agama.[1] He was probably never allowed to see a performance, and described them from books.

Only Brahmins and Sudra priests called Pandaram and Anti (all of whom were Saivas) could perform the fire sacrifice, he said, but that was only partially true. The same type of rites were available to Vaishnava priests and ascetics, and to non-priestly and non-Brahmin householders in both the Saiva and Vaishnava religions. Few householders practiced them, however, even though they could receive the requisite consecration *(dīkṣā)* from an acharya, because the rites required greater ritual purity and took more time out of a day than most householders could afford. The worshiper began early in the morning by gathering twigs. He then performed an elaborate liturgy in his house during which he established a fire pit, placed the twigs in it one by one, set them ablaze with a burning cloth soaked in oil, and placed substances into the fire. He used posture *(āsana),* hand gesture *(mudrā),* external divinization of the body *(nyāsa),* internal purification of the body through breath control *(prānāyāma),* recitation of sacred sounds *(mantra),* and carefully constructed visions *(dhyāna).* Done correctly, it took hours, required considerable control of body, mind, and speech, and purified the worshiper in body and mind. But Ziegenbalg, true to his Evangelical disdain for any ritual efforts to save oneself from sin, especially when the efforts were complex, thought the liturgy was more like sorcery than sacrifice (Ziegenbalg 1926: 97-99).

Agama had governed the 'pagan' religious life of the 'civilized' *ūr* in the Tanjore kingdom, including Tranquebar, for more than a millennium. Chola kings had patronized the Agama of Saiva Siddhanta when their rule began in the eleventh century. Then Nayakas patronized the Vaishnava Agama of the Pancaratra and Vaikhanasa schools after Vijayanagara rule began in the fourteenth century. Then again, the Saiva Agama was patronized by the

1. For examples of Agamas in English translation, in these cases Vaishnava, see Agama: 1940, 1965, 1972. For studies of Saiva Agama rituals, see Davis 1991 and Diehl.

Maratha Bhonsala ('Bhonsle') clan after it seized Tanjore kingdom from the Nayakas in the late seventeenth century.

Yet those Agamas had an even earlier history in the region; their ideas and practices were so pervasive that most liturgies performed in the *ūr* related to them in some manner. In the sixth to ninth centuries, worship according to the Saiva Agama produced *bhakti* poets called Nayanar or 'Masters.' Saiva acharyas, who canonized their Tamil poems as the 'Songs of God' *(Tevāram),* instituted their recitation during temple liturgies by Saiva Velalans called 'Reciters' *(Ōtuvār).* Similarly, in the seventh to ninth centuries, the rites of the Pancaratra Agama produced *bhakti* poets called Alvar, also meaning 'Masters.' Vaishnava acharyas canonized their Tamil poems as the 'Four Thousand Divine Verses' *(Nālāyira-divya-prabandham),* and had Brahmin specialists recite them during temple worship.

By the eighteenth century the Saivas and the Vaishnavas, who believed themselves to dwell at the center of Dharma, yet had long had a tradition of mutual angatonism, could identify each other easily. In most of 'Malabar,' the Siva religion *(śivasamayam)* dominated numerically. Those who had received consecration from an acharya, whom Ziegenbalg called 'Siva bhaktas' *(Śivapattikārar),* wore the emblem of Siva on their body in the form of ash made from cow dung, which they smeared on their foreheads and limbs. They believed it to be purifying. Moreover, it showed that they had been consecrated into the knowledge and use of the '*mantra* of five syllables' *(pañcākṣara-mantra), Namo Śivāya,* which literally means 'Veneration to Siva.' That *mantra,* however, is believed to house God in a body of sound, which means that the devotee consecrated into its use carries Siva in his or her consciousness as a 'temple', and is therefore expected to live a life of ritual purity.

Similarly, the minority initiates of the Vishnu religion *(Viṣṇusamayam)* wore the emblems of Narayana or Vishnu on their body. They called the design the 'Name' *(Nāma)* of God. Earth brought from the Mughal region, Ziegenbalg reported, was mixed with colors and applied to the forehead and limbs. In addition, he also reported, 'Vishnu bhaktas' *(Viṣṇupattikārar)* had images of the Wheel and Conch branded into the skin of their right and left shoulders respectively (Ziegenbalg 1926: 24). As is done today, an acharya had burned in those marks during the rites of the 'Five Sacraments' *(Pañca-saṃskāra)* (Rangachari: 34-37). They stamped the bearer as Narayana's protected 'slave,' someone now qualified to employ the religion's *mantra* of eight syllables *(aṣṭākṣara), Om Namo Nārāyaṇāya,* which literally means, 'Om, Veneration to Narayana.' Such initiates were also 'walking temples' for God and expected to maintain a life of ritual purity.

The importance of the acharya, and of the *mantras* and rites he initiated the devotees into, is illustrated vividly by Vijayaraghava, the last Nayaka who ruled Tanjore before the Maratha Bhonsala dynasty took over. Vijayaraghava reigned for nearly 40 years (1634-73) and, under the guidance of his acharya, became famous for his personal devotion to Krishna housed southeast of Tanjore in the temple at Raja Mannarkuti.[2] The temple had been developed under Chola rule in the twelfth century, and the Tanjore Nayakas had been devoted to it, but Vijayaraghava's extravagant patronage built most of what we find today; his sculpted image now stands in the temple's main hall (Tondiman: 154).

According to T. M. Bhaskar Tondiman, the temple marks the place where Krishna revealed 32 of his 'plays' *(līlā)* to two sages. Krishna's kingdom had been in the north, on an island in the western sea called Dvaraka; this lavish temple was therefore known as the 'southern Dvaraka.' It faces east. To reach the sanctum, Vijayaraghava would have passed through gateways in five concentric walls, each wall enclosing separate shrines. Sixteen gateways rise above the five walls to various heights; the tallest is the entrance gate on the east, which rises 152 feet. In front of it, a figure of Garuda, Krishna's kite bird servant, stands at the top of a pillar, 54 feet tall, facing west in devout veneration of his master. As Tanjore's ruler, Vijayaraghava would have imitated Garuda in his own devoted service of Krishna.

When Vijayaraghava reached the sanctum *(garbhagṛiha)* at the temple center, no doubt in the midst of a richly sensuous and elaborate *pūjā,* he would have seen two icons. One is a large standing immovable icon, probably stone, which depicts Narayana in the formation *(vyūha)* known as Vasudeva. He has four arms, two of which hold the characteristic Wheel in the right hand and the Conch in the left hand. The king himself no doubt bore those same emblems branded into his own shoulders. The rite of 'infusion' *(pratiṣṭha),* which long ago placed Vasudeva's presence into that icon to make it his material body, was believed to have been performed by God Brahma himself, for the temple exemplified the type Ziegenbalg described as 'built by the gods' *(devabhūyatiṣṭha)* (Ziegenbalg 1926: 124). But it was not the majestic Vasudeva who drew the king to the temple.

In front of Vasudeva stands a smaller movable image *(utsava mūrti)* that depicts Vasudeva's birth on earth as Krishna the 'Royal Cowherd' *(Rājagopālan).* Krishna is depicted with two arms and as standing at ease with his weight on his right leg. He holds a cowherd staff in his right hand, and drapes his left arm around the shoulders of Satyabhama, one of his eight

2. Rao, Shulman, and Subrahmanyam 1992: 2. They discuss Vijayaraghava in detail (e.g., 305-13).

principal wives. It was him that Vijayaraghava had come to see, for he loved Rajagopalan intensely, and patronized his palace lavishly. That icon of Krishna ruling in the guise of a cowherd, we may say, represented the ritual fact of Vijayaraghava's own rule, for as a Nayakan he was a 'Kshatriya' nature in a 'Sudra' body.

The theme of Krishna the cowherd ruling in Dvaraka was lavishly repeated in the temple's rectangular pond of water known as a 'tank for floats' *(teppakkuḷam)*. Built of hewn rock, and inset with stairways leading down into the water, it covers 23 acres, ample room to paddle the 'Royal Cowherd' around during festivals celebrating his kingly leisure. At the center of the *teppakkuḷam* stands a small temple, and inside it resides another icon of Krishna, the 'Cowherd with Flute' *(Veṇugopālan)*. Satyabhama is with him, as is his chief queen, Rukmini; all three are relaxing, it appears, on an island in the cooling waters of a wooded park (Tondiman: 147-55).

As noted, Vijayaraghava, like all the Nayakas, was a Sudra king. Not only was that status not denied; it was openly celebrated. According to Rao, Shulman, and Subrahmanyam (chap. 3), the Telugu-speaking Nayakas had descended from aggressive traders, who were Sudras of the 'left hand' with entrepreneurial and martial qualities and skills. But in becoming rulers, they had moved, so to speak, toward the 'right hand.' Poets of the Nayaka period constantly praised their rulers' Sudra origins, noting, for example, that since the Nayakas had been born from the feet of God Hari, as had the Ganga River, the Nayakas were brothers to the purifying Ganges River (Rao et al.: 74-75). Moreover, their rule was god-like. In their daily activities and in poetic depictions of their daily activities, they imitated the rites of *pūjā*, even while they sponsored those liturgies for the 'Royal Cowherd' at Raja Mannarkuti. Vijayaraghava in particular sponsored lavish rituals. He celebrated the Panguni festival of March-April, when the temple's huge chariots called *ratha* or *tēr* were processed. To observe the Margali rites of December-January, he rose before sunrise each morning of the month, worshiped Rajagopalan for five hours, lived as an ascetic, and ate in strict purity.

The ritual basis for Vijayaraghava's daily life, whether imitating *pūjā*, sponsoring *pūjā*, or performing *pūjā*, would have been his earlier consecration as Krishna's slave through the 'Five Sacraments.' No doubt he bore the scar of the Wheel on his right shoulder and of the Conch on his left. He was Vasudeva Krishna's property. Theologically, he ruled Tanjore as Rajagopalan's slave, which meant that the 'Royal Cowherd' ruled the kingdom through him. Assuming that Vijayaraghava truly believed that, it is not surprising that he served Rajagopalan and his acharya with lavish piety.

The first of Vijayaraghava's acharyas of whom we have information was

Kumara Tatacharya (d. 1658). The king's behaviour toward him revealed a sense of profound dependence. During the annual 'worship of the guru' *(guru pūjā)*, Kumara Tatacharya was carried through the streets of Tanjore in a richly decorated palanquin. His slippers, which represent the acharya's feet at whom the king had taken refuge in the 'Five Sacraments,' were carried in another palanquin. Vijayaraghava, the 'slave,' walked in front of both, perfuming them with incense (Sathianathaier: 58-88). When Kumara Tatacharya died, Vijayaraghava mourned lavishly as for a father. After he had been shaved from head to foot in the rites of mourning, he and his queen traveled southward to Rameshvaram to worship the deity named Ramanangur. There, in a rite called 'the weight of the scales' *(tulābhāram)*, the royal couple gave the deity their collective weight in gold. According to Tanjore custom, Velalan Chettis would have weighed him.[3] When they returned, the king gave more gold to Rajagopalan at Mannarkuti.

In 1664 the Nayaka of Madurai defeated Vijayaraghava, whereupon he performed the ceremony of 'the golden womb' *(hiraṇyagarbha)*. He apparently sought thorough purification. He was placed inside a cow made from metal, and, after various rites, emerged as a 'newborn' from it and was placed into the arms of his acharya's wife. She was now his 'mother', just as her husband, the acharya, was his 'father.' He must have been the acharya who had taken Kumara Tatacharya's place, perhaps his son. During that same period, Vijayaraghava visited the temple of Sri Rangam daily, starting the 30-mile journey early enough to worship there by sunrise (Sathianathaier: 81).

That devotion to the acharya in the Tanjore court continued even during its rule by Saiva Maratha kings. The missionary C. F. Schwartz reported in 1772 that when he visited Tuljaji (r. 1765-88),

> the Great Bramin [sic] (whom we might call the court-chaplain) joined us. The King prostrated himself on his face before him. Not far off was an elevated seat furnished with a mattress and a cushion to recline upon. The Bramin went and seated himself while the king stood before him with folded arms as before a god. (Paul 1961: 33)

3. The rite of *tulābhāram*, performed after unction by an acharya, suggests the famous story of the Ikshvaku king named Sibi, who gave himself totally to a hawk in order to protect a dove that had taken refuge in him. That story and the ritual combine the symbolism of the plow and scales held by the Velalan in *Cilappatikāram* 22: the king's body is placed in the scales and weighed against gold produced by the fertility of the plow. In Tanjore, the Vellalan Chettis had the right to weigh the king (Thurston and Rangachari: 7:202-4, 367).

Agamic rites conducted by acharyas, it was believed, could be applied to the practical matters of ruling. When the Jesuit John De Brito, for example, was imprisoned by the Maravan ruler Ranganathadevan, priests performed a three-day sequence of mantraic rites to kill him, and when that failed, they performed a five-day sequence, which also failed (Farnum: 139). However, as noted earlier, De Brito did end up without head, hands, or feet, hanging on a post in public.

Such royal behaviour, even if exceptional, dramatically exemplified the ideas of Agama for the kingdom. Central to those ideas is the concept of the *maṇḍala,* a design whose sacred center expands outward into peripheries bounded by a wilderness. The *maṇḍala* mapped the world, kingdoms, capital cities, temples, ritual arenas, and relations of peoples to one another. Drawing upon another nineteenth-century description by a Saiva Velalan, we may understand the *maṇḍala* mapping of socioreligious groups this way (Sabhāpati Nāvālār: 1-6).

At the *maṇḍala*'s center stands the Light that is wisdom or knowledge *(jñāna),* identified as Siva or Narayana, depending on the Agama. Around that center of Light circles and squares expand concentrically outward toward Darkness to form the realm of Dharma. Outside of Dharma is the wilderness of delusion, the dark realm of ignorance *(ajñāna)* where, in European terms, the 'heathen' live. To Malabarian 'pagans', all traditions that accept Veda are truly civilized and exist within Dharma's realm. Within that realm, however, only those that also accept Agama are in, or near, the center of Light.

Although Saivas and Vaishnavas followed Agama, their Agamas differed and they disagreed about who was in the center of Light. Their conflict was ancient and at times fierce. Ziegenbalg wrote that Saivas said in their books that kings should expel from the land whoever smears earth rather than ashes on their body and brands their arms with the discus and conch, which of course meant the Vaishnavas (Ziegenbalg 1926: 24). On the other hand, some Vaishnavas taught that Narayana's devotees should never set foot inside a Siva temple. Still, both religions agreed that anyone who rejects Veda is outside Dharma, is uncivilized, and is in the realm of darkness. In the eighteenth century, the acharyas knew who lived in the realm of 'heathen' darkness outside the boundaries of Dharma. They were the flesh-eating and demon-worshiping 'aliens', the anti-vedic Buddhists and Jainas, and the 'barbarian' Muslims, Catholics, and Evangelicals.

Evangelical Rites in a 'Pagan' Context

Any Saiva or Vaishnava participating in that agamic world of thought would have understood Ziegenbalg's proclamation of Christ as the form of God's love *(anpu)*, yet must have thought it odd that he would be present as an icon for only a few minutes and then in bread and wine. In their temple, God was present throughout the day and in anthropomorphic forms that stimulate devotion. Ziegenbalg's use of food must also have seemed both familiar and strange. God embodied in iconic form in his palace receives 'pure' food and distributes 'pure' food through his serving priests, so the transaction of food between God and communicants over which Ziegenbalg presided in the Holy Supper was not unfamiliar. Yet he used polluting wine, and the interpretation he gave it and the bread he served was even worse. To think of eating the flesh and blood of a human, even if 'under the form of bread and wine' as the 'Augsburg Confession' stated, must have been repulsive to anyone who gave it literal thought (Pelikan: 4:185-86, 333-34). The 'Gospel according to John' had addressed the problem explicitly in 6:35-65. It even noted that after Jesus said, 'He who eats my flesh and drinks my blood abides in me, and I in him' (6:56), some of his disciples responded, 'This is a hard saying; who can listen to it?' (6:60). Yet the feast of the Lord's Supper, in which Christ's body and blood were eaten, was so important to the New Jerusalem liturgy that anyone who wanted to eat those sacred elements had to give notice eight days in advance, and then each day receive an hour of instruction and admonition (Lehmann 1956b: 61).

Nevertheless, in agamic terms the symbols of the Lord's Supper evoked the bloody and polluting 'pariah' rites of darkness.[4] The thoughtful 'pagan' observer must have found it strange that the familiar doctrines of God, love, grace, and purification from sin should be taught through such a mixture of the clean and unclean, and with such defiled imagery. Standing at the boundary of the church, he would have seen a curious mixture of 'heathen darkness' and wisdom.

Still, he would no doubt have noticed that those sitting within the sacred arena did maintain the distinction between Velalans and 'aliens' or 'pariahs', the former sitting on mats and the latter sitting directly on the floor. He probably noted it in the distribution of the bread and wine, too, although that is less certain. Despite the report by some later missionaries that caste distinc-

4. Similar comments about Bible accounts were made by Dubois: 28-34 and by Hough: 117-22. For a discussion of the comparison of biblical temple rites to agamic Hindu rites, see Hudson 1994a: 55-84.

tions were not made in the rite of the Supper, if one cup of wine was used, Velalans were most likely served before 'pariahs.' Perhaps even two cups were used, one for each group, for in Germany two full cups were consecrated during the rites of the Supper. If two were similarly consecrated in the Tranquebar context, the Velalans would have drunk from one and the 'pariahs' from the other, as was in fact the practice in 1777. Censorship in Germany of missionary reports from Tranquebar may have eliminated information about the practice.[5] In any case, Malabarian Evangelicals made efforts to sustain such caste distinctions throughout that century and the next.

During Ziegenbalg's time, the congregation's self-consciousness about observing caste distinctions in the sacred context was unambiguous. It revealed itself, interestingly, the first time missionaries reported its members sitting together without observing such distinctions, which was during Ziegenbalg's funeral in 1719. Arno Lehmann, working in the twentieth century with archives in Germany, viewed that funeral event as 'A splendid example of what the Church was able to achieve already in 1719, something that in Hindu circles had not been considered a possibility' (Lehmann 1956b: 64). Yet, in fact, it reveals quite the opposite.

According to the categories of Dharma, funeral rites are polluting, and everyone who participates in them is polluted. Moreover, insofar as all the baptized members of Ziegenbalg's congregation viewed themselves as forming one 'family' headed by him, they understood themselves as all polluted by virtue of the 'kinship' code they customarily used to identify their relationships to those with whom they shared close bonds. In such a funereal situation, there is no purity to preserve, and everyone who is polluted may intermingle without regard to caste distinctions. The unity that Lehmann applauded in the context was the social unity of people who shared the temporarily unclean ritual status of 'pariahs'; accordingly, their behaviour revealed a conscious break with their normal adherence to social distinctions based on the opposition of the 'pure' to the 'impure.' We will return to that type of behaviour later.

Most of the high-status people Ziegenbalg talked with at length, and corresponded with, appear to have been Saivas. To them it was not strange to

5. Lehmann 1956b: 65. Arno Lehmann discussed the fact that the Halle authorities 'had a large pair of editorial scissors to cut out everything from the reports which seemed strange to the readers, or might diminish the flow of gifts for Missions. Prof. Francke said very plainly: "Unpleasant things I leave out of all diaries on publication"' (62). Lehmann then added, 'We do not find any helpful statement by Ziegenbalg, Pluetschau, or Gruendler, about the order of distributing the Sacrament and about the question whether one or two cups were used in Tranquebar at that time.'

think that God had revealed himself and his way of life through a series of disciples and their books, as Ziegenbalg taught. The idea of salvation through divine grace was not new either, nor the fact of resurrection, because both were attested to in the lives of their saints, the Nayanar. They also believed that Siva takes on human form, so that doctrine, too, was sensible. What may not have been appealing to them, however, is the doctrine that God was born through a woman's body, which is what the Vaishnavas taught and Saivas disdained. But responses by Vaishnavas to Ziegenbalg were fewer than those by Saivas. Perhaps as a religious minority that relied more on Brahmins for leadership than did the Saivas, for whom there were many Velalan priests and monks, Ziegenbalg found them less accessible.

When Ziegenbalg wrote to people, almost all of whom were Brahmins and Velalans, he often asked, 'What do the Tamilians think about the Christian Religion and Law?' (Grafe: 51). One of his 99 respondents wrote back,

> Christianity is being despised by us for the following reasons:
> because Christians slaughter cows and eat them,
> because they do not wash after eating themselves,
> because they drink strong drinks,
> because they do not do many works, when someone has died, in order to help the soul of the deceased to reach the place of bliss,
> because they do not do many works of joy at weddings.

That seemingly random sequence, which a European reader would likely have found amusingly incoherent, in fact articulated a coherent and serious statement of Dharma by describing significant infringements threatening to the social *mandala.*

First of all, European and Eurasian Christians slaughtered cattle and ate them, as did the 'pariahs.' The cow, whose special status goes back at least to vedic rites, and has always been hard for Europeans to understand or take seriously, represents all the ideal qualities of the mother. Out of love for her offspring, whom she licks clean at birth, she pours out food from her own body. Her milk is a crucial ingredient in worship, so that the cow with her calf represents the 'mother' of all the beings sustained by the rites of Veda and Agama. As we noted in Chapter 5, according to the *Bhāgavata Purāṇa* (4.18), when the first king, Prithu, began civilization, the Goddess Earth herself became a cow and poured out plants when Prithu milked her. As the purest of animals, cattle were used to embody the divine in Saiva temple rites, and, as noted, Vaishnava rites in 1664 enabled the Nayaka of Tanjore to be reborn through a metal cow.

Secondly, Europeans perpetuated their 'pariah-like' pollution because they did not use water to remove the pollution of urination and defecation. In traditional India, water is the only relevant purifying agent. Thirdly, as was common 'pariah' custom, they also drank alcohol and lost their self-control, which the drunkenness and debauchery common to Europeans of the trading companies revealed. In other words, the respondent was saying, Christianity is dangerous because it creates unclean people who live chaotic lives. Like the 'pariah' or 'alien,' Christianity signifies sin and disorder *(toṣam)* (Pfaffenberger: 135-46).

He was also saying, fourthly, that Christians weakened the family, which is the social heart of Dharma. The Pietist Lutherans, for example, buried the dead with a ceremony and left it at that. Neither fasting nor feasting, they did nothing to assist the soul to reach its rebirth, and thereby invited disaster from the 'ghost' *(preta)* unsatisfied by required ritual feedings. Fifthly, they likewise conducted simple weddings and did not spend generously on feasts for families, caste members, friends, and fellow villagers. In other words, they left the social ties that bind kin, caste, and village into a social whole in a weakened state, which made the present and future family socially vulnerable. By injuring the past and future of the very lineages on which they themselves depended, Evangelicals appeared to be ignorant and ungrateful.

Ziegenbalg asked his correspondents another question: 'Why do the Tamilians refuse to embrace the Christian religion?' One man responded,

> There are many castes among men, which have been created by the Lord. Now because we see that Christians do not observe such distinctions of castes, but bring everybody to one level, and although there is a big difference between the male and the female sex, they gather them all without distinction into one congregation, we do not like to embrace such a religion. (Grafe: 53)

Despite the fact that members of Ziegenbalg's congregation did sustain fundamental caste distinctions, people knew that for the most part the converts had stepped outside the *maṇḍala* of Dharma into 'heathen darkness.' The price many of them paid was high because once they had been 'reborn' through baptism into that 'darkness,' they were in the realm of the polluted; and their families, in order to protect themselves, in theory should have cut them off from all social, economic, kinship, and ritual relationships. That was one reason the mission had to support its members and had established Charity Schools. No matter how positively those respondents may have felt toward the Evangelical message — which shared much in common with the *bhakti* generated by Agama — they did not think such a break with Dharma necessary. '[We] believed,' one man wrote, 'that God will give us salvation, if we in this life go by what we discern as true in your law, although outwardly we do not convert to your Church' (Grafe: 54).

A quick glance at four of the 99 'pagan' responses Ziegenbalg received to his written questions will open their thoughts more deeply. One response offered a Saiva definition of 'heathen.' The word *ajñāna,* which Ziegenbalg had used to translate 'heathen,' this respondent applied to Christians. Anyone who does not wear the ashes of Siva, does not rely on Siva's five-syllable *mantra* for ritual purposes, does not make offerings and fast, and is without mercy, love, humility, and patience — that person is a heathen (Grafe: 60).

Another response provided a theological version of the multiplex concept of Dharma. Just as God created different communities and nations with different modes of dress, laws, and customs, so he created different religions, and he wants to be worshiped in different ways. That means that to remove many religions in favor of one, as the Christians and the Muslims wanted, is not only unnecessary, but it will lessen God's own pleasure. If truly seen, this whole moving universe of enormous complexity manifests the joyful play of God.

A third response sought to clarify Ziegenbalg's misunderstanding about polytheism. God is the Supreme Being, the writer said, and he has no bodily shape and cannot be compared to anything else. He creates the various *devas* or gods for his purposes, but ultimately they are forms of himself that he will reabsorb one day. Many ignorant people worship as *devas* beings that are not *devas* at all, but are actually lies, while others worship beings so low in the hierarchy of gods that they appear to be demons. Those ignorant modes of worship, he said, are what Ziegenbalg erroneously had taken to represent all of Tamilian worship, and so he attacked it as gross idolatry. When properly understood, he maintained, those who follow 'polytheistic' Agama are no less monotheistic than the Christians and the Muslims.

Finally, some respondents told Ziegenbalg that although it is important to observe temple rites and to maintain purity, it is more important to cultivate personal devotion to God. Faith in God, love for God, and faithfulness to God are the essential elements of religion, they said, and at times they may take precedence over temple worship and purity. That approach is perhaps characteristic of those who had broken with the normal householder life, an example of which were the renunciant 'faqīrs' of whom Ziegenbalg had initially been suspicious. A later nineteenth-century example was Dandapani Swami discussed in the previous chapter.

All the written responses Ziegenbalg received came from the Tamil elite, the Brahmins and the Velalans of leisure and learning. We know little of what unsophisticated people without leisure thought, or what those at the bottom of the social hierarchy like the 'pariahs' thought. We have, in fact, no direct information from those whom the people of the *ūr* considered 'aliens' regarding their views of themselves in the eighteenth century, or their views of people living in the *ūr*. Most of the information we have comes from the literati. We do know, however, that some Malabarian 'pagans' of the *ūr* and of the *cēri* found Ziegenbalg's message persuasive and became Christians. However, most did not. Ziegenbalg, of course, attributed that fact to the devil's power to keep people blind to the otherwise obvious truth.

CHAPTER 7

Patterns in Development

Leaving aside Ziegenbalg's devil, what patterns in Evangelical developments among the Malabarians of eighteenth-century Tranquebar and Tanjore emerge from the materials available to us? I have identified four to discuss in this chapter: the Roman Catholics who preceded the Pietists, the soldiers who spread Evangelical thought and worship, the expansion of cultic sites to the southern region of Tirunelveli, and the emergence of a distinctive Velalan Protestant culture. Let us begin with the Roman Catholics.

Roman Catholic Predecessors

Protestant beginnings depended significantly on Catholic predecessors. That, of course, repeats the history of sixteenth-century Europe, when Martin Luther, John Calvin, Huldreich Zwingli, and others sought to reform what was already there. It also follows the pattern of seventeenth-century Jaffna, where the Dutch East India Company transformed Portuguese Catholic churches into those of the Reformed Church of Holland. When Ziegenbalg and Pluetschau arrived in Tranquebar at the beginning of the eighteenth century, they began by using Catholic literature in Portuguese and Tamil; and Roman Catholic 'Portuguese' and Malabarians formed a significant portion of their earliest converts. Some former Catholics, notably Rajanayakam in Tanjore, spread their message elsewhere.

By the beginning of the eighteenth century, the Catholic presence in India was well established. Although the Catholic center lay in Portuguese Goa on the west coast, there was a pan-India ecclesiastical network. The Portuguese had appointed two archbishops, one at Goa and one at Cranganore in what is now Kerala, and two bishops, one at Cochin south of Cranganore and one at San Thome, on the coast just south of Madras. The Pope had stationed three other bishops, one at Bombay, one at Virapoly, and one at Pondicherry, the last a French colony north of Tranquebar. By 1787, about 100,000 Roman Catholics lived up and down the Coromandel coast (Spear: 112-14).

As in Europe, Roman Catholics provided Malabarian Evangelicals with a model of a 'heathenized' Christianity to protest. In 1815 the French Catholic missionary J. A. Dubois, using 'Hindu' with its original geographical meaning, described the way 'Hindoo Christians' celebrated the saints, an approach he found personally embarrassing but other Catholic missionaries approved:

> Their processions in the streets, always performed in the night time, have indeed been to me at all times a subject of shame. Accompanied with hundreds of tom-toms, (small drums,) trumpets, and all the discordant noisy music of the country; with numberless torches, and fire-works: the statue of the saint placed on a car is charged with garlands of flowers, and other gaudy ornaments, according to the taste of the country, — the car slowly dragged by a multitude shouting all along the march — the congregation surrounding the car all in confusion, several among them dancing, or playing with small sticks, or with naked swords: some wrestling, some playing the fool; all shouting, or conversing with each other, without any one exhibiting the least sign of respect or devotion. Such is the mode in which the Hindoo Christians in the inland country celebrate their festivals. They are celebrated, however, with a little more decency on the coast. They are all exceedingly pleased with such a mode of worship, and any thing short of such pageantry, such confusion and disorder, would not be liked by them. (Dubois: 69-70)

Compared to those Catholic rites, Protestant worship was simple — indeed, Dubois judged it too simple 'in its worship to attract the attention of the Hindoo: as it has no show, no pomp, no outward ceremonies capable of making a strong impression on the senses' of a 'quite sensual people' (Dubois: 18). Catholic worship, which Protestants judged idolatrous, he reported,

> has a *Pooga* or sacrifice; (the mass is termed by the Hindoos *Pooga,* literally, sacrifice;)[1] it has processions, images, statues, *tirtan* or holy-water, fasts,

1. As noted in Ziegenbalg's description of *pūjā* discussed in the previous chapter, the word does not designate sacrifice in the sense of the object offered being destroyed, as

> *tittys* or feasts, and prayers for the dead, invocation of saints, etc., all which practices bear more or less resemblance to those in use among the Hindoos. (Dubois: 18)

Evangelical Malabarians also saw in the Catholics a heresy that did not allow its people to read the Bible, which for Evangelicals was God's 'Word' speaking directly to any person who read it with faith, a 'Word' that would create faith in those who read it. The Bible was therefore to be translated, read aloud, preached from, printed, and disseminated. Roman Catholics believed, however, that the Bible could be understood correctly only within the context of the Church Tradition that had created it. It was to that Tradition based on the figure of Jesus in Scripture and conveyed by the Church that people were to be converted, so that they then could understand the 'Word.' Dubois summarized that Catholic view when he observed that many Protestants

> entertained the unfounded idea that the reading of the holy scriptures is forbidden to the catholics. This is one of the many calumnies spread against them, to render them odious to the other sects. So far from this being the case, the study of the holy writ is strongly recommended, and forms a leading feature of education in every seminary. What is required of the catholics on the subject is, that they shall not presume to interpret the text of the scriptures in a sense different from that of the church, or give it a meaning according to their own private judgment. (Dubois: 27-28)

He in turn criticized Protestant missionaries for disseminating the 'naked text of the Bible' to the 'unprepared minds of the prejudiced Hindoos.' That, he said, is like curing a person with severely sore eyes by having him stare at the sun 'at the risk of rendering him altogether blind, or at least of being altogether dazzled and confounded by an excess of light' (Dubois: 31).

That differing approach to Scripture and Tradition remained throughout the century. While Pietist Malabarians were encouraged to engage directly with Scripture themselves, Dubois judged that among the 7,000 or 8,000 Catholics under his religious authority, only four would be capable of understanding the meaning of the Bible and would find any use in 'the reading of the naked text' (Dubois: 125). He therefore composed a short cate-

in an offering in a fire (which is *yajña* or *yāga*), but rites of waking, bathing, feeding, entertaining, and putting to bed addressed to deity in the form of an icon *(arcā)*. Dubois may have been thinking of the 'sacrifice of the Mass', which is indeed a meal that enacts a bloody sacrifice; but that type of 'sacrifice' is more like a *bali*, also discussed in the previous chapter, where the victim is eaten.

chism of 10 to 12 pages explaining 'the principal truths of the Christian religion', which even then 'the great majority' did not understand (Dubois: 125). In his judgment, the method of the earliest Catholic missionaries had been best. They got a hearing, he said,

> not by circulating amongst the natives spurious, and almost unintelligible versions of our sacred book . . . ; it was chiefly by scrupulously conforming themselves to the usages and customs of the country; it was by becoming Hindoos in their habits and manner of living, that they insinuated themselves amongst these people. (Dubois: 130)

Then, from their most talented converts, they trained catechists to gain the confidence of ordinary people, and gradually brought them to the missionaries, 'who finished the work' (Dubois: 131-32). Yet the catechists were not trained in Scripture. Instead, they were trained in 'several religious tracts explanatory of the Creed and of the Ten Commandments', and in others 'containing some plain and short proofs of the existence of the only true God, and explanation of his divine attributes, and a refutation of the idolatry prevailing in the country' (Dubois: 131). The Catholic approach was not unlike that of the Dutch Reformed Church in Jaffna discussed in Chapter 1.

Evangelical Soldiers

Once the mission had been established in Tranquebar, the Evangelical message spread first through the Malabarians, and through soldiers who were both Malabarian and European. 'The progress of the church in India', Stephen Neill observed, 'was at all times linked to the mobility of Christians, and especially of Christian soldiers in the armies of the Company and of the local rulers' (Neill 1985: 53). That pattern persisted throughout the century.

There were others besides Rajanayakan, his brother, and fellow soldiers who were instrumental in founding the congregation in Tanjore. A German captain in the service of the Tanjore king, Pratap Singh (r. 1741-65) — perhaps the same German officer who had assisted Rajanayakan during a siege — obtained permission in 1755 for a missionary to come to Tanjore to serve the Lord's Supper (Paul 1961: 28-29). A door for the Tranquebar missionaries had now opened.

In 1762 the German Pietist missionary C. F. Schwartz visited Tanjore and then went on to the English garrison at Tiruchirapalli where, we recall, the Saiva poet and mystic Tayumanar Atikal had led the monastery of the 'Silent Teacher.' It was a fortified center up the Kaveri River near Uraiyur and was important to the 'ruler of the Carnatic', the Nawab of Arcot, who was a Muslim (Neill 1985: 47-48). There, for nearly 15 years, Schwartz served the needs of Malabarian and European Protestants, of Eurasians, and of others. He was both the Chaplain to the English garrison and a missionary sponsored by the Church of England's Society for Promoting Christian Knowledge. In Tiruchirapalli, he employed five Indian catechists, built a large church for Europeans, Malabarians, and 'Portuguese', and at the same time remained involved in Tanjore.

Schwartz's persistent involvement in Tanjore proved crucial to Protestant developments as British influence in its court increased. An English garrison stationed in Vallam, seven miles outside the capital, included a small number of European and Malabarian Protestants. Schwartz sent them a catechist who was a former 'pagan' Velalan. He had converted with considerable opposition from his family, and had taken the name Sattianadan (Satyanathan). The Vallam congregation thereafter grew at Tanjore's expense. When the government of the British East India Company at Fort St. George in Madras decided to help the Nawab of Arcot dethrone Tuljaji of Tanjore (r. 1765-88) and annex his realm, the British army attacked Tanjore. Its small Protestant church was destroyed in 1773, and the congregation shifted to Vallam (Paul 1961: 34).

Three years later, however, the Company's Court of Directors in London overruled the Madras Government's action and restored Tuljaji to the throne. The Company in Madras then stationed an English Political Resident at the Tanjore court and garrisoned English troops inside the fortified town. Schwartz thereafter moved from Trichy back to Tanjore and revived the Tanjore Evangelical congregation (Paul 1961: 34-35). In that same year, 1776, a British major built a mud-and-thatch church for the congregation, which by now consisted of garrison soldiers, Malabarians, and others.

Two years later, in 1778, the British sent Schwartz as their emissary to Haidar 'Ali Khan, in Mysore. As a general, Haidar 'Ali had taken control of the kingdom of Mysore from its Vaishnava ruler, Krishnaraja II. Taking advantage of Mughal weakness, Haider 'Ali and his son and heir Tipu Sultan Fath 'Ali Khan (r. 1782-99) expanded their realm, which brought them into conflict with the expanding interests of the British East India Company at Madras. Between 1767 and 1799, father and son fought four wars with the British and attacked Madras twice (Davis 1997: 149).

Inevitably, the British at Tanjore were pulled into those conflicts, and they sent Schwartz to Mysore to mediate. His diplomacy gained him the respect of both sides. He then used his enhanced political influence, together with money Haidar 'Ali had given him, to establish an English orphan school in Tanjore, to help rebuild the church in brick, and to build another church less than a mile outside the fort's walls (Neill 1985: 49-51; Lamb: 17-18).

But that prosperity ended, for in 1779 Haider 'Ali invaded the Tanjore kingdom and three years of war and famine began. Starving refugees fled the villages and crowded into Tanjore town and fort, leading Schwartz to report: 'A vigorous and strong man is scarcely to be met with; in outward appearance, men are like wandering skeletons' (Lamb: 18). Jointly, Tuljaji and the Company asked Schwartz to administer famine relief; and out of his own respect for Schwartz, Haider 'Ali, their enemy, allowed him to pass through his own camps to do so.

By the end of his reign in 1787, Tuljaji felt enough affinity for Schwartz to ask him to become guardian of the ten-year-old boy he had adopted to inherit the throne. His name was Serfoji. 'This is not my son', Tuljaji had told Schwartz before he died, 'but yours; into your hand I deliver him' (Neill 1985: 55). Tuljaji had also given Schwartz his income from a village to support his school and orphanage. Nevertheless, Tuljaji's brother, Amir Singh, usurped the throne, and Tuljaji's surviving heir remained a threat to his claim to it. Schwartz was left protecting Serfoji and his widowed mothers from Amir Singh, while mediating between him and the Company.

In the meantime, members of the low-status Kallan caste, whom Schwartz had helped to convert from 'pagan thieves and henchmen' to 'Christian cultivators', faced violent opposition from others. In their view, the prosperity of the Protestant Kallans derived from their disruption of caste Dharma. Still, in 1793, Schwartz was able to persuade the Protestant Kallans to contravene their own martial customs and not retaliate with violence (Lamb: 35).

That same year, 1793, out of fear for the safety of his royal ward and his widowed mothers, Schwartz moved them from Tanjore to Madras. Serfoji studied there with missionaries. Five years later, after Schwartz had died, the Company installed Serfoji on the Tanjore throne, where he reigned for 35 years (1798-1833). To commemorate Serfoji's well-known esteem for Schwartz, a marble sculpture depicting his visit to the deathbed of his guru was erected inside the church within the Tanjore fort (Lamb: 43; plate facing 40). Notably, the 'guru' was an Evangelical and the 'disciple' a Saiva.

One result of that 'guru-disciple' relationship was continuing access by Evangelical Velalans to the 'pagan' court of Tanjore. When Serfoji studied under Schwartz, he had come to know another student, a Velalan named Vedanayagam Pillai. As we will see, their respect for one another continued even after Vedanayagam Pillai became a schoolmaster in Tanjore and became famous among Tamil Protestants as 'Vedanayagam Sastri, the Evangelical

Poet' (Manasseh: 23). Various other Evangelical Velalans held positions in Serfoji's court, including his 'pursebearer', who accompanied him on his pilgrimage to Benares in 1821 (Hough: 200-201).

Those court connections enabled and encouraged Velalans in the Tanjore congregation to sustain their ancient identity as aristocratic 'Sons of Earth' belonging to the righthand plow. That, of course, implied that the 'pariahs' in the congregation sustained their ancient identity as 'aliens.' Custom aligned both groups of Evangelicals with the same 'right hand', and they worshiped together, but separately. They did indeed sit as a single congregation, but on separate mats.

Expansion to the South

Once again, the Evangelicals spread by means of the military. In 1765 the Company's alliance with the Nawab of Arcot had led the Tanjore contingent to station an English garrison of Indian soldiers or sepoys far to the south in a fort called Palayankottai. It stood on the Tambraparni River, near the temple town of Tirunelveli (Neill 1985: 53-54). By 1771 a Malabarian Lutheran named Savarimuttu was living there, and an English sergeant married to an Indian had baptized a young 'pagan' accountant. In 1778 Schwartz visited. He did so because a European officer wanted to get married, and because by now there was a congregation of about 50 soldiers with their families and others, and instruction and baptism were needed. From his Pietist point of view, it was not enough that converts knew the 'five principal articles' of Luther's 'Small Catechism': the Lord's Prayer, the Creed, the Ten Commandments, the words of Baptism, and the words of the Eucharist (Packiamuthu: 2 n. 2). His concern was with true piety, as his baptism of a Brahmin widow illustrated. Her story, studied by David Packiamuthu in 1993, stands at the heart of Protestant developments along the Tambraparni River.[2]

Schwartz had known the Brahmin woman years earlier in Tanjore and had already refused to baptize her. Her name appears to have been Kohila, and she came from a 'royal' Maratha Brahmin family. Her husband, likewise a Maratha Brahmin, had held a position in the Tanjore court. But when he died, and she became a Brahmin widow, Kohila played her new role in a way that excluded her from her family. She did not follow her caste Dharma. For reasons that remain obscure, she became the concubine of an English officer

2. In 1915 A. Madhaviah related her story in a Tamil novel that David Packiamuthu translated as *Clarinda: A Historical Novel* (Tirunelveli: Nanbar Vattam, 1992).

stationed in Tanjore named Lyttleton. While living with him, she asked Schwartz for instruction and baptism, but he refused on the basis that she was living in a 'sinful state.' Nevertheless, Lyttleton, who suffered seriously from gout, taught her English, the Bible, and the chief doctrines of Christianity. She in turn took care of him in his illness. When he was transferred to Palaiyankottai as part of the English garrison, she went with him. Lyttleton died in Palaiyankottai and left her all his property. Kohila was once again a 'widow', but no longer an 'adulterous sinner.' Therefore, after Schwartz arrived in Palaiyankottai, she went to him again to ask for teaching and baptism, and this time he agreed. Kohila took the baptismal name 'Clarindal' or 'Clarinda' (Packiamuthu: 4-5; Devapackiam: 87-92).

Due to her royal family and her husband's service in the Tanjore court, people knew Clarinda as 'Royal Clarinda' *(Rāsa Clarinda),* an allusion also to the status of 'Col. Lyttleton' in the British military. Now an esteemed and propertied member of the Protestant congregation, she began to use her new wealth to support it. With the aid of several English officers, she led the construction of a small church inside the fort walls, which was popularly known as 'the temple of the Brahmin woman' *(pappattiyammal koyil).* It also served as the Company's 'official' church, and the Commanding Officer required all his officers to worship there with the Indian Christians (Devapackiam: 91). Nevertheless, the two groups were buried in separate cemeteries (Hough: 297).

Among Protestants, it appears, distinctions between the faithful were acceptable, even after death. People could, in good faith, disagree over which distinctions were valid, but the assumption that there are social distinctions that should be articulated seems to have been unquestioned. In this case, the distinction between the European rulers and the Indians they ruled prevailed in a cemetery open to the public. Where, one wonders, would Clarinda's adopted son, Henry Lyttleton, have been buried? Was he among the rulers or the ruled?

A baptismal register of 1780 tells us that all the official members of the congregation were Malabarians. No European is listed. Forty people are named, with Clarindal at the top. Packiamuthu noted, however, that the list we have may be the one revised four years later (Packiamuthu: 5). It does not give the caste identity of 18 members, but among the remaining 22, it lists 13 different social identities, most of them of low status, including carpenter, beggar, Vadugu, Paraiyar, washerman, Iluvar, Svalakkarar, Chetti, horsekeeper, Pallar, Maravar, and Panikar (Devapackiam: Appen. 7). Two members were former concubines of the same English officer, one of whom had a child. Seven Velalans were also listed. Six of them belonged to a single family headed by a man named Devasagayam Pillai. He was a Tamil poet from Tirunelveli who had once been a Catholic catechist. We will discuss him and his son, Vedanayagam Pillai, in the following chapters.

In 1783 Clarinda took her adopted son, Henry Lyttleton, to Tanjore for Schwartz to educate and, while there, solicited support for the Palaiyankottai congregation. The Pietist missionaries in Tranquebar responded by dispatching a catechist named Visuvasi, then working in Ramnad, to Palaiyankottai, but he proved to be useless. After that, Schwartz sent his catechist, Gnanaprakasam. He and Clarinda began to spread the Evangelical message outside the fort, starting with a village in the southern part of the Tirunelveli region named Terivilai. It had been mortgaged to Clarinda. In Terivilai, Gnanaprakasam baptized nine Shanans (whose 'work' was with palmyra trees) and 16 Paraiyans (whose 'work' was as slaves); Clarinda paid for a small prayer house, for a catechist's residence, and for the salary of a catechist named Maria Savari, presumably a former Catholic.

Although Terivilai can no longer be located, it is possible, as David Packiamuthu suggested, that Clarinda and Gnanaprakasam's work there was the root of the Shanan movement to Protestant Christianity that began in 1797 (Packiamuthu: 6-7). Within three decades, Protestant Christianity was well established among the Shanan people, who came to be known as Nadars. By 1824, as James Hough reported, about 4,000 Protestants, mostly Shanans, lived in 63 villages in the Tirunelveli District of Madras Presidency. One village of 300, and another of 400, were entirely Protestant; each had a church, a boys' and a girls' school, a native pastor, a catechist, and two schoolmasters (Hough: 192-93).

Returning to Palaiyankottai, in 1785 the congregation had completed building Clarinda's church and Schwartz came from Tanjore to dedicate it. A Velalan pastor named Rayappan occasionally visited to administer the sacraments, and the master of a newly established school offered boys an 'English' or a 'Malabar' curriculum. By this time there were 150 people in the congregation, 80 of whom were qualified to participate in the Lord's Supper (Neill 1985: 54). The summary of a letter Schwartz wrote in 1785, however, stated that there were 120 members:

> Some of them are merchants of an inferior sort, some artificers, some washermen, some farmers, and a few soldiers of the natives, called sepoys, all having their respective employments, and none, as far as he [Schwartz] knew, living upon the charity of others, much less of the Church. (Paul 1961: 39)

Subsequently, Schwartz transferred the Velalan catechist Sattianadan from Tanjore to Palaiyankottai. In 1790 Sattianadan received Lutheran ordination

The severely plain interior of the small church that 'royal Clarinda' built at the end of the eighteenth century in Palaiyankottai follows the custom begun by Evangelical missionaries in the New Jerusalem Church constructed in Tranquebar in 1707. Except for the cross and necessary ritual implements, all symbols inside the room that might be interpreted by observers watching the rites from the doors and windows as 'heathen' images were eliminated. The single chair is for the leader; all other worshipers in Palaiyankottai, as elsewhere, sat on mats on the floor in the traditional manner, men on one side and women on the other. [The photo was taken by D. Hudson in 1993.]

and served as pastor in Palaiyankottai, and as the 'First Superintending Missionary of the Tirunelveli Church' (Packiamuthu: 7).

The 'temple of the Brahmin woman' now stood at the center of a Protestant expansion out from the Company's fortress, east and west along the Tambraparni River, and north and south along the Bay of Bengal. By 1829 missions of the Church of England owned the land of the Protestant enclave inside the fort, which consisted of Clarinda's church, small houses or 'huts' placed around for Indians, a bungalow for a European missionary, and a schoolhouse (Caldwell 1881b: 232-33). A new 'official' church would replace 'the temple of the Brahmin woman' in 1856.

Inevitably, the early diffusion of Evangelical thought and practice by means of British military and East India Company networks had its consequences. For one, in contrast to the 'Moors' and the 'pagans', but like the Catholics, it aligned the Tamil-speaking Protestants with European powers institutionally, theologically, liturgically, and in some cases economically. To their sorrow, that was the way the local overlords or 'Poligars' *(Pāḷaiyakāraṉ)* in the region viewed them. As an 1802 mission report stated, the Poligars fought the British in Tirunvelveli and 'plundered, confined, and tortured the Christians, destroyed some of their chapels, and burned the books they found in them.'[3]

That Poligar view of Christian alignment with the ruling Europeans coincided in some cases with the view of Protestants themselves. In 1814, the Evangelical poet Vedanayagam Sastri in Tanjore revealed that view in his long Tamil poem called *Śāstirakkumi.* He used five stanzas (20.141-45) to prescribe the way the customary wedding pendant, called *tāli,* should be designed for Christian women. The center of the pendant, he said, should bear the two signs of 'your God's suffering': the sign of the cross on one side and the cup of the Eucharist on the other. But he also understood the cross to signify personal and political victory:

> . . . since the emblem of the auspicous consecration you received is the sign of the Cross, where else but in the sign of the Cross is now your victory? (141)
>
> . . . the Europeans brought the banner of the Cross and conquered the whole country, for only in the sign of the Cross is there absolute victory. (143)[4]

3. The S.P.C.K. report of 1802 was cited by Caldwell (1881a: 199), but without giving his source.

4. Vedanayaga Sastri 1969: 24-25. Details regarding the *tāli* as described in the poem were clarified by Priscilla Christodoss.

The cross, signifying victorious Protestants aligned with victorious and ruling Europeans, was to be placed at the symbolic center of Malabarian society: on the wedding pendant of the woman who, as daughter, wife, and mother, represented the past, present, and future of the Malabarian home and family.

Another consequence of military and Company alliance was that, in a version of Christianity that believed itself to have reformed the Church according to the first- and second-century practices as recorded in the New Testament, the antimilitary and anti-imperial voice of that early period was virtually silent among the Malabarians. Continuation of the fourth century 'Constantinian' accommodation to the state by the Catholics and by the 'magisterial reformers' Luther, Calvin, and Zwingli had left rejection of the state and its violent enforcement of power and authority to the 'radical reformers', the Anabapists and Moravians (J. Dillenberger and C. Welch: 62-67). The only foothold they had obtained along the Coromandel Coast was the Moravian mission in Tranquebar discussed earlier, which lasted about half of the eighteenth century.

A Velalan Protestant Culture

During the eighteenth century, the Evangelical converts and their descendents in Tranquebar, Tanjore, and Tirunelveli created their own understandings of Protestant Christianity. Despite the intentions of the missionaries, they applied Pietist doctrine to the contexts of their lives in their own ways, keeping in mind the 'pagan' and 'Moorish' gaze metaphorically focussed on them at the windows and doors during worship.[5] They participated through language, family, caste, and custom one way or another in the larger society signified by the temples, mosques, and palaces around them. At the same time, as the Danish and British forts and churches stated, the story of Jesus

5. Alan F. Segal summarized studies of conversions and drew these conclusions that are useful to keep in mind. '(1) A convert is usually someone who identifies, at least retrospectively, a lack in the world, finding a remedy in the new reality promulgated by the new group. . . . (2) The central aspect of the conversion is a decision to reconstruct reality so that (3) the new group the subject enters supports that reality by its self-evident assumptions. (4) Finally, the talents and attitudes that the convert brings into the movement are greatly affected by the previous socialization, no matter how strongly the subject affirms the conversion or denies the past. Though conversion is one of the sources of a particular person's commitment to a religious group, it is not the only one. Conversion necessarily involves strong emotional commitments, but conversion itself is not enough to preserve the commitment to the group after initial entrance to the group, unless the other social mechanisms of commitment act in concert with it' (Segal: 75).

was preached to them most authoritatively by Europeans from a different civilization. Yet, as the case of Tranquebar illustrated, the Europeans to whom they listened were themselves at odds with the fort and its church, and critical of its seemingly debauched and impious way of life. Their own New Jerusalem Church demonstrated by its doorway emblem that they shared the religion of Denmark's king, but they did not aspire to the culture of his Company. Somehow, Malabarian Christians worshiping at that church had to locate themselves somewhere between the 'Dharma' of Tanjore and the 'Dharma' of Denmark, and they searched for that cultural 'place' throughout the century.

Initially, they found it in the sacred setting of the Lord's Supper as celebrated by Ziegenbalg. Let us recall the matter of seating in the New Jerusalem church. Modes of dress implied modes of sitting, and within that sacred context both dress and placement signified distinctive social identities. Those who wore European clothes sat on benches and stools, which would include the missionaries and Eurasians and sepoys in uniform. Those who wore indigenous clothes sat on mats, which would have been the high-status Velalans; or they sat directly on the floor, which would have been the low-status 'pariahs.'

By conducting the Lord's Supper in that setting, the missionaries conveyed to the congregation and to the onlookers — even if they did not intend to do so — that the social order articulated by their seating arrangement expressed an acceptable Evangelical notion of community. Similarly, the rites of the temple expressed the hierarchy of Dharma, and the rites of mosque expressed the equality of the Muslim path of life or Shari'a. From the point of view of those Evangelicals, faith in God's love as expressed in the story of Jesus Christ expressed itself as a cultic or 'spiritual' unity that was socially pluralistic. At the Lord's Table they sat together separately.

The missionaries explicitly affirmed that interpretation. When they rebuilt the New Jerusalem Church in 1718, they designed it in the shape of a cross, apparently so that worshipers could sit separately in its sections according to the division between the Velalans and the 'pariahs' (Lehmann 1956b: 50, 64). Missionaries reported in 1727 that 'pariahs and sudras sit in the church separated by one yard. But in the distribution of the Sacrament, no difference was made' (Lehmann 1956b: 64). Between 1743 and 1746 they built a church in Porayar, an important Muslim town an hour-and-a-half walk from Tranquebar town. They built it to serve Evangelicals living in Tranquebar and in various villages, and again designed it as a cross to facilitate the social pluralism of Christian unity. In the south wing behind the altar sat the Velalan ('sudra') women. Opposite them in the north wing sat the Velalan men. In the east wing sat the 'pariah' women. And in the west wing sat the 'pariah' men (Lehmann 1956b: 129). Moreover, according to a letter of 1732, in the mission school at Tranquebar the Velalan and 'pariah' children sat, learned, ate, and slept separately (Lehmann 1956b: 128).

The liturgical practice of Evangelicals sitting together separately had begun in 1707 with the New Jerusalem Church in Tranquebar, and it continued in all the Evangelical congregations into the nineteenth century, when 'new missionaries' made it a subject of controversy. Seating, however, represented other contested issues, which we shall examine in Chapters 8 and 9. But first let us consider developments in Tanjore that led to the controversy with the 'new missionaries', at the center of which was C. F. Schwartz's ardent disciple, Vedanayagam Pillai.

CHAPTER 8

Vedanayagam Pillai, the Sastri (1774-1864)

Vedanayagam Sastri's story, his son Noah Gnanadickam tells us, begins with Sastri's father, Arunacalam Pillai (1735-99). In this chapter we will follow Noah Gnanadickam's discussion of his grandfather, published in 1899, supplementing it with the later, and at times more detailed, accounts by D. V. Devanesan, published in 1945 and revised in 1955, and by Dayamani Manasseh in 1975. All three authors drew upon family memory, and their accounts contain the narrative details that a lineage preserves as important to its understanding of itself. That family memory will be our guide.

The Father

Arunacalam Pillai was born in the town of Tirunelveli in a family belonging to the Saiva Velalan lineage discussed earlier as 'Protectors of Dark Rain Clouds' *(Kārkaṭṭavēḷāḷar)*. When he reached his early twenties, his father set him up with a money-changing shop in town on the main thoroughfare called King's Road. His son was a pious Saiva, and he wanted to prevent him from becoming an ascetic *sādhu*. At the shop, Arunacalam expressed his piety by bringing rice to give to the poor. A Catholic catechist named Jnanendra Kaniyan noted his charity and praised him for it. But he also urged him to learn about the 'true God.' Arunacalam became interested in the catechist's ideas and asked him to take him to his guru, who worked 40 miles away in the village of Kamanayakkanpatti. The guru was a European Catholic priest known in Tamil as Adattuman Vedapotagam Guru, 'Adattuman, teacher *(guru)* of revelation's *(veda)* awakening *(bodhaka)*.

When Arunacalam Pillai went to meet the Catholic priest, he dressed as a pious Saiva should in the emblems of Siva: *rudrākṣa* beads around his neck and head, and ash smeared on his body. Adattuman Vedapotagam Guru saw him at the church entrance, decided he was 'demonic', and refused to meet him. Nevertheless, Aruncalam did not leave, and the catechist urged the priest to take his interest seriously; he had, after all, walked 40 miles to get there. The priest eventually relented, sat down with Arunacalam inside the church, and taught him the basics of Catholic doctrine.

Surprisingly, when the priest finished, Arunacalam said he believed and asked for consecration *(dīkṣā)*. Neither priest nor catechist took him seriously until Arunacalam asked for a pot of fire, dropped his *rudrākṣa* beads in it, and rubbed off his ashes. On the spot, Vedapotagam Guru gave him Catholic instruction. Arunacalam memorized the doctrines, scriptural texts, and prayers. The priest then baptized him as his own 'spiritual son' with the Christian name Devasagayam, 'Help of God.' He was 25 years old.

Devasagayam Pillai eventually convinced his father of Catholic doctrine, and he, with Devasagayam's brothers and sisters, received baptism. Yet their new faith did not take root quickly. Devasagayam generated a serious family division when he knocked down the 21 altars they kept in their garden for demons *(pēy)*, but nevertheless they kept to their new religious commitment.

Vedapotagam Guru began to teach Devasagayam Latin, intending to qualify him to become a 'guru', probably meaning priest. During the qualifying examination that followed, Devasagayam answered all the questions correctly, but the examiners decided that the new Catholic should not begin at the level of 'guru' because that ordination could be given only from the third generation as a Christian. Instead, Noah Gnanadickam reported, they dressed him in a long cloak *(angi)* and appointed him 'Dominie Catechist' as second to the 'guru' (Gnanadickam: 7).

'Dominie Catechist' apparently denoted ordination to the noncelibate Minor Orders, which included Porter or Door-Keeper, Lector, Exorcist, and Acolyte. If traditional rites had been followed, as explained by S. Rajamanickam, the bishop would have dedicted him to that status during a Mass by cutting his hair at the front, back, close to the ears, and on the top of his head in the rite of tonsure. Next the bishop would have given him his long cloak or surplice. Then he would have given him the implements of his office: the keys of the church, a book for teaching, a book of rites to exorcise those among the baptized and catechumens who were possessed, the candles and candlesticks to light the church, and the cruets to serve wine and water for the 'Eucharist of the Blood of Christ' (Jeyeraj 1998: 118-20).

Devasagayam Pillai worked in that public role as Roman Catholic cleric for ten years as a bachelor. In 1770, when he was 35, however, his 'spiritual father' arranged for him to marry Jnanappu Ammal, the daughter of a Catholic Velalan named Saverirayan Cetti. Four years later they had their first child, a son. To honor Devasagayam's 'spiritual father', they baptized him with the name Vedapotagam ('revelation's awakening'); but in daily life they called him Vedanayagam ('revelation's eminence').

Vedanayagam's mother died when he was seven years old; she had been visiting her parents at the time. By now he had two sisters, Susaiyammal and Pakkiyammal. When the widowed Devasagayam returned to his work as 'Dominie Catechist', he left his son and two daughters with their maternal grandparents. Two years later he married Mariyamuttu Ammal, and they lived in Tirunelveli with Vedanayagam, leaving his two sisters with their grandparents. In the meantime Vedapotaga Guru had been replaced by another European priest named Devarthanatha Guru ('teacher [*guru*] of the Lord [*nātha*] who is the meaning [*artha*] of God [*deva*]'). He, it turned out, was the occasion for Devasagayam's move from the Catholics in Tirunelveli to the Evangelicals in Palaiyankottai.

No doubt many factors led to the break, including, perhaps, Devasagayam Pillai's own interest in Evangelical teachings and his continuing loyalty to his 'spiritual father' whom the new priest had replaced. But the immediate cause was the new priest's behaviour regarding the wearing of a beard. A beard signified a celibate *sādhu,* or *sannyāsi.* In Malabarian terms, the European Catholic priest was a *sādhu,* and he wore a beard, as did a *sādhu* friend of Devasagayam Pillai known as Nonti Jnani, 'the lame *sannyāsi*', a Catholic whose nickname also means 'the cripple who possesses wisdom.' The European priest resented the fact that Nonti Jnani wore a beard, and, in a personal confrontation with him, angrily insisted that only he had the right to wear it, and that the lame *sādhu* was not to appear in his presence bearded. He then forcefully cut off Nonti Jnani's beard, an act of physical coercion inconsistent in Velalan Catholic culture with the role of a *sādhu* Catholic priest.

Nonti Jnani told Devasagayam Pillai about the encounter, and he responded angrily that not even the 'heretical' Evangelicals would behave that way. Word of his statement reached Devarthanatha Guru. He decided that the 'Dominie Catechist' had gone too far; that he had in fact gone over to the 'heretics.' He announced in church that Devasagayam Pillai had been cast out of the congregation and, according to custom, no one was to give him water or fire.

Devasagayam Pillai then turned to the Evangelicals in Palaiyankottai. He and Nonti Jnani went to 'royal Clarinda' and recounted the incident. In a manner typical of Protestants, Clarinda replied that Roman priests do not practice what they preach and keep Scripture separate from their conduct. Moreover, they forget to rely on the fruits of the Saviour's merit and instead worship the Mother Mary and the Saints. She urged Devasagayam to leave the Roman priests and teach for her, and offered to support him if he did. He agreed.

Devasagayam Pillai, the Catholic 'Dominie Catechist', now had to learn Protestant thought and practice. He began to study with the catechist named Jnanapprakasa, reading a Tamil work called 'The Axe of the Heretics' *(Patitar Koṭāli).* Shortly thereafter, in 1785, Clarinda sent him to Tanjore to study with C. F. Schwartz. Four months later Devasagayam returned to Palaiyankottai. Then, in that same year, Schwartz went to Palaiyankottai, and when he left, he took Devasagayam's son with him to be his student in Tanjore. In the meantime Devasagayam continued working in Palaiyankottai. He preached to Christians and non-Christians, warning them of the coming Kingdom of God. He composed songs from biblical texts, copied the Gospels, and worked at convincing his family in Tirunelveli, whom he had previously persuaded to become Catholics, that they should now become Protestants.

The Son

Vedanayagam Pillai was now 12 years old and a student in Tanjore. He had begun studying at the age of five, but after his mother died, and while he and his sisters were living with their maternal grandparents, he lost that discipline. At loose ends, he spent more time wandering with cows and cowherds than studying, 'the bull belonging to Devasagayan of Tirunelveli', as he later described himself (*Cepamālai* 1.1.11). He was nine when his father and his new stepmother took him to live with them in Tirunelveli, and they sent him to study with a Hindu teacher in a village near Cokkampatti. He studied writing and arithmetic there, and had a vision.

One morning, while he was sitting outside, he saw a man on a tall cross very near him in the sky, slowly moving from his right to his left. The cross looked like wood and not like a cloud formation. A fellow student appeared and slapped him for sitting there without studying, but Vedanayagam pointed to the vision and said, 'Look, look, our Lord is going by.' The vision lasted about 15 minutes. He told his grandmother, who said it was a sign that something special would happen in his life.

Vedanayagam so often left his studies to play that his teacher finally refused to school him any further. Devasagayam thenceforth took up the task. The potential for tension to develop between father and son in that situation is easy to imagine. Like a 'young bull', the son is more accustomed to playing than studying. The father, now forced to 'tame him', adds daily tutoring to his already demanding work life. A stepmother has replaced a deceased mother. The sisters are away, living with the mother's parents. In such a situation, strains could easily develop in the already charged relationship between father and eldest son in a Malabarian family. We have no information about the matter, but those imagined factors may help to explain why, three years later at age 12, Vedanayagam was willing to leave home with Schwartz for Tanjore, and why Devasagayam was willing to let him go.

Shortly after Schwartz and Vedanayagam had reached Tanjore in January of 1786, the Maratha king Tuljaji died. Schwartz immediately assumed responsibility for his young heir Serfoji, who was now vulnerable to intra-family struggles for the throne. Serfoji at age ten was Vedanayagam's junior by two years and a student with him in Schwartz's school. They became friends.

Schwartz gave Vedanayagam a place to live in his own residence, where other boys lived as disciples. Schwartz emulated the Pietist ideals of Francke in Halle by including orphans, the poor, and others in his household, but he also adapted those ideals to Tanjore culture. Like Ziegenbalg and Pluetschau early in the century, Schwartz kept only high-caste servants to cook and prepare food so that, without question, Velalan boys like Vedanayagam Pillai could be faithful to their caste status while under his scholarly care. Vedanayagam, however, became more than Schwartz's student; he became his 'son', one of three who would play important roles in the development of Tanjore Evangelical culture over the next five decades.

As Indira V. Peterson, whose research underlies much of the following discussion, noted in her study of Tanjore culture during this period, Schwartz put into reality the idea of an English medium 'Provincial School' that the British Resident had promulgated in 1784 (Peterson 1998: 6). But Schwartz permeated it with Pietist educational goals and the Halle curriculum. Besides teaching in English, Tamil, and Persian, he included an important 'hands on' approach to natural science as 'a direct way of knowing God through working with real-life objects for real-life purposes.'

The director of the school was a second 'son' of Schwartz named John Caspar Kohlhoff (1771-1844), three years Vedanayagam's senior. J. C. Kohlhoff had been born in Tranquebar to the German missionary J. B. Kohlhoff, but his own language was Tamil rather than German. Schwartz had taught him 'Christianity, English, German and some country languages.' Schwartz presided over his ordination in 1787, during which the 16-year-old gave a graceful 'Malabar sermon.'[1] J. C. Kohlhoff remained a friend, colleague, and 'protector' to Vedanayagam until his death in 1844. In a later work Vedanayagam remembered him affectionately as an 'outstanding guru' full of love for him when he first arrived in Tanjore (Vedanayagam Sastri 1964: *Payiram* 7; Manasseh: 49).

Raja Tuljaji had supported the school generously, and his own adopted heir, Serfoji, had attended it with Vedanayagam before Schwartz took him away to Madras for protection in 1793. Serfoji was Schwartz's third 'son.' He and Vedanayagam shared a lively interest in the latest knowledge about astronomy, biology, and geography, and both became poets. In 1798 the prince ascended the Tanjore throne as Serfoji II, and he ruled under the administrative authority of the British East India Company until his death in 1832. He was crucial to Vedanayagam's career at a time of crisis, and important to his literary creativity, as we will see below. Both men used modern scientific findings in their poems, but in ways that revealed the differences between a Saiva and a Pietist at the turn of the nineteenth century (Peterson 1993, 1996).

In sum, when Vedanayagam Pillai moved from Tirunelveli to Tanjore in January of 1786, he entered a rich educational milieu permeated by Evangelical piety and modern scientific thought, where he played the role of 'son' and disciple to his 59-year-old Pietist 'father' and guru. A cycle of prayer, study, work, and service to the guru constituted his daily life; sometimes he studied with other boys in the school, sometimes alone with Schwartz. The newly emerging worldview of the 'Enlightenment' as Pietist education transmitted it influenced him, as it did the Saiva, Serfoji, and the newly ordained 'Malabarian German', Kohlhoff. All three 'sons' of 'father' Schwartz shared a lifelong devotion to him, but Vedanayagam in particular felt a disciple's devotion to him. It shaped his self-understanding as poet and musician in important ways until his own death at age 91.

Schwartz, it seems, may have anticipated Vedanayagam's poetic and musical career, for the first book he gave him to study was a book of songs. As if to make that point himself, Vedanayagam wrote in 1820 that no matter how much praise he received from his poems and dance-dramas, his greatest glory was that the Lord had made 'Vedanayam of Nelai Town' known as the disciple of 'Schwartz Aiyar of expansive and prosperous Tanjore' (*Jñāṉavuḷā:* 660; Manasseh: 85-86).

Two years after he had arrived in Tanjore, Vedanayagam's father and

1. Peterson 1998: 15, citing M. E. Gibbs, *The Anglican Church in India: 1600-1970* (Delhi: ISPCK, 1972), 18.

This portrait depicts Serfoji II after his 1798 enthronement on the Tanjore throne. He sits in a royal posture of ease while holding the royal sword casually in his left hand. Painted in the Tanjore Maratha style, the portrait addresses his Saiva court in Tanjore. It suggests Serfoji's rule as the instrumental devotee or 'slave' of Siva through royal themes used also in liturgies for Siva at the Brihadesvara Temple he patronized, for example, the stool on which his feet rest and the mirror held before him by a flying attendant. [Photo taken from Devanesan]

stepmother moved there. His father continued to catechize and preach. Schwartz soon realized, however, that, for reasons unexplained, their presence would disrupt the boy's studies, so he sent Vedanayagam to Tranquebar to study in the Pietist school for catechists. In such matters, it appears, the guru's authority superceded the father's.

Between the years 1789 and1792, Vedanayagam Pillai studied in Tranquebar with Germans, possibly with August Friedrich Caemmerer (1767-1837) and Johann Peter Rottler (1749-1980), but notably with Christoph Samuel John (1747-1813). C. S. John was viewed in Halle as excessive in his emphasis on natural history and 'secular studies' (Peterson 1996: 12, 14). Besides theology, Vedanayagam studied astronomy, anatomy, and mathematics; they all appeared in his later poems in a manner both new to Tamil poetry yet consistent with it. His creative aspirations apparently never moved beyond the Tamil language, for in the complex linguistic and cultural setting of Tranquebar and Tanjore, he did not become linguistically cosmopolitan. Although he studied the Gospels in German, Vedanayagam was never accomplished in the language, and, as examples below will show, he never mastered English.

Early Poems

Vedanayagam Pillai returned from Tranquebar to Tanjore at age 18, and Schwartz sent him out with a catechist named Jnanamuttu and others to spread the gospel in surrounding villages. They went to Vallam, Putuppatti, Putalur, and Cittirakkuti; and further south to regions such as Ramanathapuram and Uttarakocamankai (Manasseh: 32). Dayamani Manasseh reported from Vedanayagam's later poetic autobiography that, in that period, he used the songs he had been composing since the age of 16. They are now found in his later works, for example, in 'The Garland for God' *(Parāparaṉ Mālai)* of 1794 and in 'The *Kummi* of Wisdom' *(Jñānakkummi)* of 1796.[2] Quietly, Vedanayagam Pillai had begun a career of poetry and music that would last 64 years and would produce more than 120 works in Tamil based on the Christian Bible.

In 1794, when Vedanayagam was 20 years old, Schwartz made him headmaster of the 'school of Scripture' or 'seminary' *(śāstrapaḷḷi)* he had established in Tanjore. He held that position for 35 years. He was so successful as headmaster and teacher that Schwartz said he no longer had to send stu-

2. Manasseh: 32, 45. His poetic autobiography is contained in *Tarumanūṟṟerivu.*

dents to Tranquebar to study. Both European and Malabarian pastors sent their children to him. Five of his students became ordained, and 70 became teachers, catechists, or government workers. In addition to teaching in the classroom, Vedanayagam occasionally taught Tamil to Europeans and composed texts for teachers and catechists. His two-part *Parāparaṉ Mālai* of 1794, Manasseh said, was used in the Tamil curriculum to replace poems to God Murugan *(Katirkāma Mālai)* and to the Goddess *(Ambikai Mālai)*.[3]

Despite his good fortune as headmaster, 'lost fatherhood' was a theme dominating his career's first five years. In 1795, when he was 21, his two 'fathers', Devasagayam and Schwartz, arranged a marriage for him with his father's-sister's-daughter, Viyakammal. But in the next year, before he could father a child, she died. Two years after that, in February of 1798, 'father' Schwartz died. During the next year Devasagayam died while on a preaching trip to Jaffna. The only 'father' remaining to him now was the one of faith, the 'Messiah' born in Bethlehem.

Widowed, childless, and without father or guru, Vedanayagam Pillai nevertheless continued to participate creatively in the musical and poetic 'renaissance' then taking place under the patronage of the Tanjore Marathas and local poligar rulers (Peterson 1993). In the year his wife died (1796), his compositions seem to have been especially influenced by the Bible's 'Song of Solomon.' According to Manasseh, 'The *Antati* of Wisdom' *(Jñāna Antāti)*, was based on that work (Manasseh: 45-46). Its 101 stanzas are in the traditional 'end is the beginning' *(antāti)* form: the last words or their rhymes are the first words of the next stanza, and the last stanza ends the way the first begins to form an unbroken verbal garland of sound (Vedanayaga Sastri 1964: 353-64).

In the same year he produced the '*Kummi* of Wisdom' *(Jñāṉakkummi)*, which he revised in 1831. It followed the *kummi* genre of a joyful song designed for clapping girls dancing during festivals and other joyful occasions. Vedanayagam may have been inspired by the famous Saiva devotional poem called *Jñāṉakkummi*, as a former Saiva Velalan monk named Arumugam Tampiran had been. In 1837, after Arumugam Tampiran had become the Protestant Christian named Wesley Abraham, the Church Mission Press in Madras published his *Jñāṉakkummi* as *G'nana-kummi: On Creation — Idolatry — Salvation by Christ — Heavenly Bliss; and the Pains of Hell* (Gaur: 1b). But Sastri's *Jñāṉakkummi* was quite different, as the preface to an old edition (now minus its title page and date) made clear:

3. Manasseh: 33. Other works included *Jñāṉa Ettappāṭṭu, Jñāṉavaḻi, Ātiyāṉantam, Aṛivāṉantam, Paramanītip Purāṇam,* and *Kāla Vittiyācamālai.*

The **Gnanakummy** [*Jñāṉakkummi*] is a kind of poem which the Christian congregations may sing to the praise of God both during their feast days and during any other joyful occasions. It is written in a mystic manner similar to the Song of Solomon, representing King Jesus having married the daughter of Zion, the Church.

It is divided into five parts.

In the first part, the Daughter of Zion sings the glorious procession of Jesus the king when entering Jerusalem.

The second part describes the Wise Virgins going to meet the bridegroom.

The third part is called **Nattiaykummy** [*Nāṭyakkummi*]. In this first is shewn the beauty of the virgins of the Church, and then is given an historical account of the wonderful incarnation of Jesus the king.

The fourth part is called **Vivahakummy** [*Vivāhakummi*]. In this is shewn the glory of the marriage of the lamb of God. Though all of this part is not taken from the Scriptures, yet it is not contrary thereto.

The fifth part is called **Chitragnanakummy** [*Citrajñāṉakkummi*].

The fourth part formed at first a part of the third: but the whole of the Gnanakummy having been corrected in 1831 by the Author who composed it in 1796, the verses that were not taken directly from the Word of God were seperated [sic] from it and placed after it as the fourth part. [Vedanayagam Sastri, n.d.]

More significantly, perhaps, in this period he adapted the *kuṛavañci* dance-drama to Evangelical themes and concerns by composing the 'Bethlehem *Kuṛavañci*' of 1800, which he revised again in 1820. As Indira V. Peterson explained, the *kuṛavañci* plot consists of three themes. A lovelorn lady is anxious about her lover; a fortune-telling woman who is a bird catcher *(Kuṛavañci* or *Kuṛaṭṭi)* arrives and divines her future; a bird catcher man *(Kuṛavaṉ)*, then appears while catching birds and engages in a lusty dialogue with the fortune-teller. The Kuravan's crude passion contrasts with the exalted lady's refined longing (Peterson 1993: 19).

Customarily, an all-female cast of *devadāsis* danced the *kuṛavañci* at festivals and other events, and it was popular especially in regional temple-centers as well as in Tanjore. For example, a dance-drama that honored the Maratha king Shahji (the *Tyagēsar Kuṛavañci*) was performed at the Tyagaraja Siva temple in Tiruvarur near Tanjore. Tiruvarur was the home of Vedanayagam Pillai's contemporary, the great Rama devotee and musician Tyagaraja (1767-1847). A *kuṛavañci* that honored Vedanayagam Pillai's friend Serfoji II (the *Sarabhendra Bhūpala Kuṟavañci*) was performed at Siva's Brihadesvara Temple in Tanjore itself. Serfoji II is himself the attributed author of a Marathi version of the genre (the *Devandra Korabvanji*); Indira Peterson described it as a 'geography of the world as narrated by the wandering soothsayer' but without the major elements of the *kuṟavañci* plot. The most famous of the genre, however, is the *Kuṟṟālak Kuṟavañci* by Tirikuta Racappa Kavirayar. It focused on Siva in his temple at Kurralam in Tirunelveli District, where it was studied in the Tamil school curriculum. Vedanayagam was said to have composed the *Bethlehem Kuṟavañci* to replace it in Christian schools.[4]

He used the *kuṟavañci* genre allegorically to present themes from the Christian Bible as Evangelicals interpreted them. Firstly, in accord with Song of Solomon 5:8, the exalted lady in the *Bethlehem Kuṟavañci* is the virgin daughter of Zion named Devamohini ('A woman infatuated by God'). She represents the Church. Secondly, following Hosea 2:19, the bird-catching Kuravanci is a maiden born at Bethlehem who represents faith. Through the use of Old Testament prophecies, she predicts that the daughter of Zion will become the bride of Christ. Thirdly, Jesus' statement in Matthew 4:18-22 that he will make the fishermen with nets, Peter, Andrew, James, and John, into 'fishers of men' is transposed into 'catchers of birds'; the bird catcher with a net is named Jnanacinkam ('the fowler of wisdom'). He represents the catechist, who ensnares people in the 'net' of the Old and New Testaments in order to give them, like birds, to King Jesus as gifts.

The villain in the *Bethlehem Kuṟavañci* is a thieving bird catcher *(kaḷḷakuṟavaṉ)* who opposes the catechizing bird catcher. Interestingly, he represents not a Saiva, nor a Vaishnava, nor a Muslim, but the Pope of Rome. The perceived enemy of the Evangelicals at this period continued to be other Christians. The thieving bird-catcher Pope tries to gather birds not for Christ, but for himself. Vedanayagam Pillai's grandson E. Vedabothagam wrote an introduction for the 1938 edition of his grandfather's work in which he noted that each of its set-pieces *(taru)* introduced 'the whoredom of Popery' and 'may, in general, excite the hatred of the Papist.' Moreover, he observed,

> In the last verse of almost every song, according to the version of scriptures, the old Romish church was attacked and the Papal aggrandisements were checked and criticised. Then the verses were sung impressing the doctrines prevailing at that ancient period of Papal Supremacy. All these abuses are

4. Reported by E. Vethabothagam in his preface to the work, where he also said that it 'is performed as a Dramatic piece by Kanears about the country' (Vedanayagam Sastri 1938: v).

> now [in 1938] out of date and are out of use. Yet they are retained [in this edition] as they are retained in scriptures, by way of warning and edification as allowed by the present Christian churches.[5]

According to Manasseh, when Vedanayagam Pillai presented *Bethlehem Kuṛavañci* in Tiruchirapalli, some 'Papists' did indeed find offense and plotted to kill him as an apostate (Manasseh: 92-93).

Before Schwartz died, he had turned Vedanayagam over to the care of the 'German Malabarian', J. C. Kohlhoff. Being only three years older, Kohlhoff was more an 'elder brother' than a new 'father', but he did play a parental role in one instance. He arranged his second marriage in 1801. Vedanayagam married his mother's-brother's-daughter from Tirunelveli named Mikkel Muttu, commonly known as Mikkelu Muttammal. She became adept in Tamil poetry through his tutelege.

Vedanayagam Becomes Sastri

Seven years after his second marriage, Vedanayagam Pillai received the first of four honors bestowed on him by Evangelical congregations to celebrate his literary excellence and make it known to others. By this time he had compiled a book on arithmetic for his students in the school, and had composed 52 books in Tamil 'containing the system of Christian doctrine sweetly and metrically' (Devanesan: 24). On February 20, 1808, 'Elders and Members of the Tanjore City Evangelical Congregation' *(Tañcai Nagaram Suvicēsha Sabhai)* signed a document that conferred on him the exalted title 'The Jewel of Scripture and Emperor of the Poets of Great Knowledge' *(Vedasiromaṇi Mahājñāna Kavicakravartti).* With that honor went privileges at church assemblies. He was thereafter to receive the first seating, the first ceremonial offering of betel leaves and areca nut *(tāmbūlam),* and the first ceremonial veneration.

The 50 signatures to the document provide a picture of the elite in the congregation at that time.[6] The signers were all males, and the majority were Velalans. The 30 who signed with the Velalan caste title 'Pillay' (Pillai) included the four identified as 'elder.' Three of the Velalans were employed in the court of the Tanjore king or Maharaja: one as a member of the Court of

5. Vedanayagam Sastri 1938: iii-viii. The second edition of 1964 has omitted those portions, presumably in the interest of ecumenical relations between Protestants and Catholics in contemporary Tamilnadu.

6. The 'Testimonials' of the four honors in English are found in Gnanadickam Sastriar: 100-109, and in English and Tamil in Devanesan: 18-46.

Justice, one as the writer in the Court of Justice, and one as the superintendent of the Maharaja's printing press. Four men were employed by the British Government or its officials: one as the interpreter for Mayavaram District, one as the Post Office writer, and two as translators *(Dubash)* to individuals (Col. Innis and Mr. Edward Borgen). Four were schoolmasters, one of them in English. Aside from one man identified simply as 'of Bengal College' and ten without any role identification at all, the remaining Velalans worked for the Evangelical mission. Four of them were catechists, two were mission doctors, one was a mission writer, one was a mission orderly *(Peon)*, and three were servants to clergymen (the Reverends Horst, Kohlhoff, and Pohle).

Among the other 20 signatories, one appears to have been Eurasian (William Pearson, 'son of the late Captain Pearson'). The remaining 19 probably belonged to the lower-status castes that were grouped together in the congregation as 'of the right hand' *(Valaṅkaimattār)*. They used no caste names in their signatures. Fourteen of those men were catechists, four were schoolmasters, and one was servant to the Rev. Mr. Kohlhoff.

We do not know how many women and children, or other men, made up the congregation at the time, but the pattern is clear. Men ran the congregation, four Velalans held the office of elder, and Velalans dominated both in numbers and in occupational prestige. Non-Velalans were either catechists, schoolteachers, or servants. Everyone, no matter what their caste, was employed by the Maharajah of Tanjore, or by the British Government, or by the Protestant missions. No merchant, soldier, farmer, landowner, fisherman, leatherworker, blacksmith, or field hand is mentioned, even though some of those occupations constituted the traditional 'work' of castes represented in the congregation. At the beginning of the nineteenth century, it appears, Evangelicals in Tanjore did not engage in their culturally prescribed 'work' even though they retained their culturally prescribed caste identities.

Perhaps they believed that baptism had changed their 'nature' *(taṉmai)* and therefore their 'work' *(toḻil)*. Schwartz's earlier success in converting Kallans, whose 'work' was to be 'pagan thieves and henchmen', into Kallans whose 'work' was to be 'Christian cultivators' may be interpreted as illustrating that belief. In 1793 he had persuaded the 'Christian cultivators' not to respond to violence violently, as their 'nature' as 'pagan' Kallans would have dictated. Baptism had changed both their 'work' and their 'nature', which reminds us of the process summarized by the Tamil maxim quoted in Chapter 5: A 'Thief' *(Kaḷḷan)* may become a 'Warrior' *(Maṛavan)*; a 'Warrior', through respectable behaviour, may become a 'Landowner' *(Akamuṭaiyaṉ)*; and a 'Landowner', by slow degrees, may become a Velalan (Thurston and Rangachari: 7:377, 1:6-7).

Returning to Vedanayagam Pillai, one month after the Tanjore Congregation honored him he went to Tranquebar to receive another honor. There he introduced a new dance-drama, the 'Drama of the Crippled Hero of Wisdom' *(Jñāṉa Noṇṭi Nāṭakam)*. According to Peterson, the *noṇṭi* genre followed the 'picaresque dramatic monologue by a character, the cripple-hero [*noṇṭi*], who narrates the events that led up to his getting maimed' (Peterson 1993: 11-12). According to Manasseh's summary of Vedanayagam's dance-drama, the *noṇṭi* had been crippled because of his sin; he received forgiveness through Christ's blood on the cross; and at Christ's resurrection his leg grew and he danced (Manasseh: 40-41). It seems likely that the *sādhu* called Jnani Nonti had been in Vedanayagam's mind when he composed the drama. Jnani Nonti had played the crucial role in his father's move from the Catholic to the Evangelical Church, and his nickname literally meant 'the cripple [*noṇṭi*] who possesses wisdom [*jñāṉi*].' If so, the implied 'sin' that had crippled the hero would have been the Catholic's reliance on the merits of the saints; his 'healing' would have resulted from the Evangelical's exclusive reliance on the atoning merit of Jesus' crucifixion and resurrection.

After he had presented 'The Drama of the Crippled Hero of Wisdom', the Tranquebar Evangelical Congregation bestowed the title 'Evangelical King of Poets' *(Cuvicēshakkavirāyar)* on Vedanayagam Pillai, and processed him in honor around the town seated in a palanquin. In contrast to Tanjore, the 'Elders and Members of the Tranquebar Evangelical Congregation' who signed the certificate consisted of only 15 men, but the caste pattern was the same as in the Tanjore congregation. Nine signers were Velalans. Among them, two were head interpreters for the King of Denmark, two were Malabar judges for the King of Denmark, one was a writer to the Company of Pohold, one was listed merely as an elder, and two had no role identification. Among the remaining six without caste titles, one man was listed as an elder, three as schoolmasters, one as a catechist, and one had no role identification.

The next year, the Evangelical Congregation in Vepery, Madras, where the Bible translator J. P. Fabricius had once served, invited Vedanayagam Pillai to receive a third honor. He and his entourage made the long journey by palanquin, oxcart, and foot, and stayed for two months among the 20,000 Christians living in the Presidency capital (Manasseh: 41-43).

The lay leader of the Vepery congregation was a wealthy man named Muttusami Pillai. He had commissioned a palanquin to be given to the poet, and it was placed on the porch of the church that stood on the grounds now occupied by St. Matthew's Church. Over the course of many nights, Vedanayagam Pillai recited many of his poems from that porch, including the *Bethlehem Kuṛavañci*. At the end, on September 19, 1809, the 'Elders and

Members' of the congregation gave him the title 'Poet of Wisdom's Light' *(Jñānatīpak Kavirāyar).* Then they presented the new palanquin to him, placed him in it, and, as their certificate stated, 'with the different sorts of musics [instruments] according to the Malabar custom, carried him through the streets of the town' (Devanesan: 32).

The signatories made clear in their certificate their evaluation of his 52 works composed in various tunes. With those poems, they said, 'even the most famous poets are not able to find any fault', and their plain and elegant verses could not have been composed by anyone 'unless he understands perfectly the contents of the Old and New Testaments.' Because of them, 'we are very much honoured and praised before the pagans, which is a great advantage to our children' (Devanesan: 31). The congregation, it appears, was well aware of the metaphoric gaze of Saivas and Vaishnavas. Vedanayagam Pillai's adept and creative use of Tamil poetry and music to express the Evangelical story and faith, they believed, made them appear as 'Malabarian' as anyone else, which would benefit their children in the future.

Forty men signed the Vepery certificate — more than in Tranquebar, but less than in Tanjore. Among them, 32 may be classed as Velalans: 24 signed with the caste name Pillay (Pillai), five signed as Mudali, one as Mudaliyar, one as Chetty, and one as Kavirayer or poet. None gave his occupation except for two schoolteachers, one in English, and one musician. The remaining eight signatures bore no caste titles. Three were catechists, three were schoolmasters, one was a poet, and one was occupationally unidentified. The only man mentioned as 'Elder' was the first name on the list, Muthusamy Pillay (Muttusami Pillai), the wealthy patron of the palanquin who had invited Vedanayagam. Once again the Velalans appear to have dominated the Evangelical congregation, in numbers, status, and, in the elder's case, money.

It was probably during that two-month stay in Madras that Vedanayagam Pillai received yet another honor, this time from a Muslim, the Nawab of Arcot living at the time in Triplicane. The Nawab met Vedanayagam and heard his poetry. To honor him, he gave him a gift and a tall, conical, red hat *(kulāh)* customarily worn by Muslim teachers (Devanesan: 64-65). From that time on, Vedanayagam Pillai performed his works dressed in white, wearing a broad band around his waist and the tall red hat on his head. In 1849, when he was 77, two missionaries commissioned a portrait of him wearing a felt version of the *kulāh,* for the original had by then worn out.

Vedanayagam Pillai received his final honor in 1815. The Evangelical congregation at Tiruchirapalli, where his 'father' and guru Schwartz had served decades earlier, invited him to perform new compositions. From a wooden stage in a thatched hall *(pantal)* erected on the main road,

Vedanayagam introduced two works. One he had composed two years earlier, a passionate treatment of Jesus' suffering entitled 'Great and Joyous Love' *(Pērinpak Kātal)*, published in Madras in 1853 with the English title *On the Sufferings of Christ* (Murdoch 1870: 27). The other composition was the newly completed '*Kummi* of Scholarly Knowledge' *(Sāstirakkummi)* of 1814. The American Mission Press in Madras published it as *Sāstirakkummi: A Satirical Poem on the Superstitions of the Hindus in 1840* (Murdoch 1870: 21).

In that second work, Vedanayagam again used the *kummi* folkdance genre to address 850 stanzas to a 'Woman of Wisdom' *(Jñānappēṉ)*. She represented the Evangelicals. He criticized practices taught in Saiva and Vaishnava scholarly texts *(śāstra)*, some of which Evangelicals themselves were apparently engaging in. He noted, for example, the study of astrology, the observance of auspicious and inauspicious times for important events, singing songs addressed to gods and demons, and watching the dance-drama *Ciruttoṇḍar Nāṭakam* (*Sāstirakkummi*, 417-23). The last is the story of radical *bhakti* told in the twelfth-century 'Story of the Great Saints' *(Periya Purāṇam)* and written by a Saiva Velalan of the Tanjore Chola court named Cekkilar. The hero is known as 'The Little Devotee' *(Ciruttoṇṭar)*, a Nayanar devoted to Siva who, with his wife, kills, cooks, and serves their only son to a Saiva ascetic, who is Siva in disguise. Siva then restores the son, and because of their great commitment to him through his ascetic followers, takes them all to heaven. Simultaneously horrifying, gripping, and exalting, the story was commonly enacted at temple festivals, but Vedanayagam said it did not conform to righteous conduct *(mārkkam, mārga)* (*Sāstirakkumi*, 423).

By now he was using the word 'Hindu' not in its geographical sense as 'Indian', but in the narrower sense of the devotees of Siva and Vishnu, otherwise called 'heathens':

> O Woman of Wisdom,
> You know that Vedanta,
>   which Hindu castes think is knowledge,
> Is a hindrance,
> And you have thoroughly
>   and completely
> Rejected the 'True Veda'
>   of dissembling subtlety. (*Sāstirakkummi*, 424)

From May 3 to June 18 in that thatched hall in Tiruchirapalli, Vedanayagam Pillai taught Evangelical doctrine by combining singing with the exposition of devotional works in the manner known as 'passing time' *(kālatcēpam)* by the Vaishnavas. But he called it *catur,* meaning 'skillful means' or 'ability', but used to denote an assembly gathered to witness a play or dance. At the conclusion of this particular *catur,* on June 18, 1815, Christian Phole, the German senior missionary sponsored by the Society for Promoting Christian Knowledge and officiating Chaplain, on behalf of the congregation, bestowed on Vedanayagam Pillai the title 'Scholar of Revelation' *(Vedasāstiriyar, Vedaśāstri).* As Manasseh noted, that title approximates the English honor 'Doctor of Divinity'; as their certificate stated, it recognized that 'he excelled in knowledge all the Hindus who are well versed through all-India.' From that day on, Vedanayagam Pillai signed his name Vedanayagam Sastri. Others thenceforth commonly referred to him by the honorific form Sastriyar. We will now refer to him more simply as Sastri.

The Tiruchirapalli certificate revealed that the Evangelicals of the time, like Sastri, were now using 'Hindu' for those religions that acknowledged the revealed status of Veda and Agama, but at the same time, like him, were continuing to use the word 'Christian' to refer to themselves and not to Catholics. They were 'papists.' As the certificate said, Vedanayagam Pillai had been 'converted to Christianity from popery by the Venerable father, the Rev. Mr. Christian Frederick Schwartz . . . and was brought up in the principles of Christianity under his protection and is now under the patronage of the Rev. Mr. John Casper Kohlhoff' (Devanesan: 37).

Twenty men signed that certificate, and their signatures suggest why it was only in this congregation that the honor had been bestowed by a European missionary on behalf of the congregation rather than by Malabarians themselves. No one identified himself as an elder. Five signed as Pillay (Pillai), and only two of them gave their occupations, which were writer and music teacher. The remaining 15 men gave no caste names. Of them, six were butlers, three were catechists, one an English schoolmaster, one a medical writer, one a translator *(Dubāsh),* and three listed no occupations. Unlike the Evangelical congregations in Tanjore, Tranquebar, and Vepery, the Velalans in Tiruchirapalli were numerically a minority, and no one of any caste represented himself as distinguished in learning, status, or property. The lay leadership, it appears, had looked to the senior missionary from Germany sponsored by the British to represent them. The congregation had erected the *pantal* on a busy thoroughfare, had placed a chair on a wooden pedestal they built inside it, and had invited Vedanayam Pillai to sit in it. But it was the Reverend Christian Pohle who had 'invested him with a white gown together with every privilege that can be possibly given and honoured him with the title Veda Sastriar' (Devanesan: 38).

Sastri and His Family

During the years he was receiving those honors, Sastri's family life had been evolving. Since no child had been born to him and Mikkelu Muttammal after their marriage in 1801, they followed custom and adopted a relative, in this case the seventh daughter born to his sister, Arulayi Ammal, and her husband, Viyakappa Pillai. She was a baby of one month born in May of 1811. They named her Jnanadipa Ammal ('Light of Wisdom'). She grew into a woman skilled in Tamil, English, and singing, and assisted her father in his *catur* performances and with his writings. When she was 32, he arranged her marriage to a relative named Daniel Mangalam Pillai.

Important to the spread of Protestant thought, Jnanadipa Ammal translated J. G. Pike's *Persuasives to Early Piety* into Tamil; she called it 'Early Piety' *(Ilamai Bhakti)*. The Madras Tract Society published that powerful Protestant instrument of persuasion in 1853 (Murdoch: 13). Four years later it would prove important to the conversion of another significant Velalan poet of Tirunelveli, H. A. Krishna Pillai (Hudson 1972: 198-99). Together with his brother and other Velalan converts in Palaiyankottai, Krishna Pillai would create a new and energetic period in the history of the congregation that 'Royal Clarinda' had nurtured.

In the year that their adopted baby was born, 1811, Sastri travelled with his family to Jaffna to stay for several months with his friend, the Rev. Christian David. Among other events there, he engaged in a lengthy dispute about the Virgin Mary with a Roman Catholic named Savarimuttu Mudaliyar. His later summary of the discussion explored a crucial division within Christian thought and devotion. Similarly, he recorded a long conversation he had there with a Muslim named Marup Sahib on May 26, 1822. It revealed the differences between two religions followed by Tamil-speaking people, both of which acknowledged the authority of Jesus of Nazareth but disagreed over who he was.[7]

As that invitation to Jaffna indicated, Sastri's fame as a Christian poet had spread, for by 1814 he had already composed 80 works. Four years earlier he had begun a book of songs intended to parallel the European hymnbook for morning and evening worship, and to encourage Tamil speakers to worship in their own cultural style. He called it 'Garland of Prayer' *(Cepamālai, Japamālā)*; 45 years later (1855) he had completed it in two parts. It was later published with the English title *Jepamalei, or Rosary of Songs and Prayers to Be*

7. Sastri's summaries of those conversations were reprinted in Gnanadickam: 47-54).

Sung in the Morning and Evening (Barnett and Pope: 412). As he explained in the preface, one part contains 31 Tamil songs for each day of the month; the other contains 12 songs about the 12 most important events in the Bible. 'If gurus, teachers, catechists, church members, and even children memorize them', he wrote, 'they will be able to respond to any question that arises from Scripture.' Here Sastri used *Vedāgama* to mean Scripture, which combines *Veda* and *Āgama,* the two scriptural sources recognized by Saivas and Vaishnavas, now called Hindus.

He then went on in the preface to defend himself regarding a traditional practice that the men he called the 'new missionaries' were now disparaging. He said that just as King David of Israel and others had customarily put their own name in their songs, he, too, put his name in a final stanza of his songs. That was a Tamil literary custom, a way of signing one's work. Others like the 'new missionaries' accused him of aggrandizing himself, but he said he did it to bring the memory of him before the throne of grace. As a scriptural warrant, he cited God's instruction in the book of Exodus in the Bible. The priests of Israel were told to write the names of the sons of Israel on two onyx stones of the high priest's ephod, and to write the names of the tribes on 12 stones on his breastplate. Aaron was told to wear those names into the sanctum 'to bring them to continual remembrance before the Lord' (Exod. 28:9-29) (Vedanayam Sastri 1963: iii-iv). If there was any self-aggrandizement in that practice, it was as God's dependent devotee. We will return to that issue, and to the 'new missionaries', later.

In 1813 a son was born to Sastri and Mikkelu Muttammal. They named him Jnanasikhamani ('The Crest-Jewel of Wisdom'). He became a Tamil teacher in the Tanjore seminary, taught Tamil to European missionaries, and wrote two books in Tamil. One, 'The Alliance of Two Religions' *(Iru Samayasambandham),* stated the Protestant view that Catholics and 'pagans' were much like; the Madras Religious Tract Society published it in 1850 with the English title *Identity of Popery and Heathenism.* The other book was an attack on Islam entitled 'The Greatness of the Messiah' *(Mecīya Makattuvam);* the Madras Tract Society published it in 1864 with the English title *The Glory of Christ* (Murdoch: 22, 33). Sastri had taught Jnanasikhamani *catur* performance, and he toured villages. Once he performed in the palace of a Maharaja in Malayalam (Kerala), and once in the palace of the Maharaja of Mysore, where he received the title 'Preacher of the Evangelical *Purāṇa*' *(Cuvicēṭa Purāṇa Piracaṅkiyar).* That title, interestingly, placed the Bible not in the category of Scripture *(Vedāgama),* but in the category of 'old stories' *(purāṇa)* that were remembered *(smṛiti),* often with many variations, but not revealed *(śruti).*

In 1814 Sastri began to conduct singing and teaching sessions at home while he continued to compose for the church. In 1819 he wrote a poem to be used in Evangelical weddings entitled 'Wedding Songs of Praise' *(Kaliyāṇa Vaḻttutal).*[8] In 1820 he used the 'procession' or *ulā* genre, which depicts women stricken by love when they see the hero, in 'The Procession of Wisdom' *(Jñāṉavulā).* The hero, of course, is Christ.[9] In 1821 he continued the wedding theme with 'The Content of Scripture' *(Āraṇātintam),* which again uses the biblical theme of bridegroom and bride to depict the relationship of Christ to the Church.

At the same time, Sastri began an annual Lenten practice. To assist Evangelicals in their meditations on the sufferings of Christ, he set up a thatched hall *(pantal)* in front of his house, and conducted a *catur* between 7:30 and 10:30 for 45 nights. To an audience consisting of Christians, Muslims, and Hindus, he expounded in his strong voice the Evangelical version of the Christian story in its fullness, beginning with the creation of the world and ending with the eschatological New Jerusalem. He continued that Lenten practice until his death in 1863.

The Years of Dissension in the Tanjore Congregation

It is hard to know when the years of dissension in Tanjore began for Vedanayagam Sastri. Already in 1824 he had written a 'Dialogue on the Difference of Caste' *(Jātiācārasambhāvanai),* which reveals that the divisive issues that would split the Tanjore congregation five years later had been present for some time. Sastri may have been referring to the Vepery Congregation in Madras when he wrote that new missionaries, led by C. T. E. Rhenius, had tried to force 'all the castes or nations of this country to be of one caste to make them eat and drink together and to have those of higher and lower classes connected with each other in marriage.' But that Vepery controversy soon appeared in Tanjore, and we will discuss it shortly.

Mikkelu Muttammal, in the meantime, began leaving Sastri to spend extended amounts of time with her family in Tirunelveli District. For reasons we do not know, she eventually left and never returned. She died in her birthplace. Once again Sastri was widowed, this time with two children, Jnanadipa Ammal and Jnanasikhamani.

8. It was published along with other wedding songs in 1879 by the Church Mission Press in Palaiyankottai, and was included in a single volume with 'The Kummi of Wisdom' *(Jñāṉakkummi).*

9. *Jñāṉavulā* is published in Vedanayakam Sastri 1964: 229-66.

In 1829, when Sastri was 55, the Rev. T. Brotherton arranged his third marriage. The bride was Varodaya Ammal, daughter of Santa Pillai of Tanjore. She bore him three children and was of great help to him in his old age. Their first child, born in 1830, was a boy they named Noah Gnanadickam *(Jñāṉādhikkam)*. He helped his father with his *catur* presentations and later wrote his biography. Then, in 1832, they received a daughter named Manonmani Ammal, who went on to teach English and Tamil literature in a Wesleyan school in Nagapattinam. And finally, in 1834, they had a son named Eliya Devasikhamani, who became adept in *catur* performances.

In the year of his third marriage, Sastri experienced a personal calamity. Dissension arose in the Tanjore Evangelical Congregation that eventually led the missionaries to expel him and other Velalans. That painful controversy reveals the depth of Sastri's sense of himself as a Malabarian Christian, for he believed that in his views and behaviour, judged by the 'new missionaries' to be divisive of Christian harmony, he was faithfully following the teachings and example of his guru, C. F. Schwartz.

The issue that brought the controversy to the breaking point was the custom of Evangelicals sitting together separately during worship. As we will see, however, that issue about seating represented other issues, among them efforts by the 'new missionaries' to revise the Fabricius translation of the Tamil Bible, to simplify liturgical practices, and to change the music used during worship. All of them would alter the century-old Pietist heritage transmitted from Ziegenbalg through Schwartz. The authority of the 'new missionaries' to enforce their desired changes, specifically of L. P. Haubroe in Tanjore, derived from the fact that Tanjore's Lutheran congregation was now under the jurisdiction of the Church of England, whose ideology was more 'Reformed' than 'Lutheran.'

The first Anglican Archbishop, Thomas Middleton, had been appointed to Calcutta in 1814. Ten years later, in 1826, the second Archbishop, Reginald Heber, went to Tanjore, met Sastri, and purchased his *Cepamālai* and a book of Christian hymns for the British Library (which was lost when he suddenly died in Tiruchirapalli that April). In the following year the Society for the Propagation of the Gospel appointed L. P. Haubroe to Tanjore. We will discuss the issues in detail below, but here we should note the major elements in this difficult period in Sastri's life as summarized by Dayamani Manasseh (Manasseh: 54-81).

In the Tanjore congregation, as had been customary since Ziegenbalg's time in Tranquebar, the high-status castes (primarily Veḷalans) and the low-status castes (primarily those aligned with the 'right hand' called Valangamattar [*Valaṅkaimattār*]) had sat together separately on separate mats. Those in front (the Velalans) received the sacrament of the Lord's Supper first, and those in back (the Valangamattar) afterward. That arrangement allowed the status of the two groups of castes to be articulated within the sacred arena in a traditional Malabarian manner.

In 'pagan' Malabarian terms, it would have been based on the idea of *eccil,* or saliva-polluted food that was considered 'leftovers.' One signal of deference was to eat another's *eccil;* one signal of honor was to avoid doing so. In the context of the Evangelical celebration of the Lord's Supper, one might say, all communing members ate Christ's *eccil* when they drank the consecrated wine and ate the consecrated bread. But as his dependent devotees, they still retained their social distinctions, and by eating and drinking first, the higher-status castes did not eat the *eccil* of lower-status castes. Although in *Sāstirakkummi* (520-30) Vedanayagam Sastri mocked the inconsistency of the Saiva observance of *eccil* pollution, he did not reject the social distinctions it explained.

The newly arrived missionary, L. P. Haubroe, insisted that the customary seating practice had to stop, and that everyone had to sit on one mat and equally. The Velalans would not agree. Considering Sastri to be their leader, Haubroe and other missionaries summoned him and asked him to have his people conform to the new orders. Sastri's reponse was this:

> The church is now at the stage of drinking milk. The time to eat rice will come. As culture and knowledge and understanding of Christ's love develop, these differences will gradually fall away by themselves. Force will not make it happen. (Manasseh: 55)

In that explanation Sastri seemed to agree that 'mature' Christian love would end in the ideals the missionaries desired, but that it would have to come through organic growth in culture, knowledge, and love from within the devotees over time. Possibly he meant that the Valangamattar would first have to become like the Velalans in culture and education. Possibly he meant that both groups would have to evolve to an as yet unknown stage in culture and knowledge. We do not know. His view, however, was consistent with the Pietism he had learned from his guru and 'father', C. F. Schwartz.

The missionaries did not agree and, in 1829, the dispute increased. In the next year Haubroe threw many Velalans, including Sastri, out of the church and excluded them from rights to burial in the church cemetery. Sastri himself quit his post as headmaster of the seminary Schwartz had founded. The Velalans now met for worship at his house.

In the meantime, Sastri and others sent documents about the events to the various church sponsors. (We will examine them in detail below.) He also continued writing, and one poem generated by this crisis forcefully expressed his distress. 'Worship of the Fast Day' *(Upavāca Nāliṉ Tevāram),* which is included as song 17 in the *Cepamālai,* consists of 11 stanzas in which worshipers petition God and ask Jesus to sustain them. The first stanza tells God that 'the gurus have become beasts' *(paśu),* and that even in the church there is dissension. The last two stanzas summarize their situation:

> Suspicion envelopes shining Tanjore,
> And we of Schwartz Aiyar's congregations
> Fade with sorrow,
> We wither,
> We see no mercy,
> For they are not thinking
>   of You,
>   of Your house,
>   of Your children,
>   nor of us.
> Sustain us, Lord Jesus. (10)
>
> Graciously console us,
> Remove our calamity,
>   but without scandal
>   to any high caste,
> Make the whole congregation flourish,
> Listen to Vedanayagam's song,
>   our petition,
> Forgive everything in love.
> Sustain us each day, Lord Jesus. (11) (Vedanayagam Sastri 1863: 91-93)

In the first stanza, the beastlike 'new missionaries' act only from a narrow, self-serving point of view. In their thoughtlessness they ignore God, the church, the 'children' *(piḷḷai)* or congregation, and those they have excluded. Yet Sastri's use of the word *piḷḷai* for 'children' alluded to the Pillai caste title used by the Velalans in the congregation and suggested particular injury to them. In the second stanza the excluded Velalans identify themselves with Schwartz as the founder of the congregation, aligning themselves with the Pietist religious culture he had transmitted, which the 'new missionaries' were now disrupting. The poem pleads for a flourishing and unified congregation as it had been before, without Velalans experiencing any shame or scandal.

This portrait of Vedanayagam Sastri, age 77, is by an Indian painter commissioned by two missionaries in 1849. The painting addresses a Malabarian audience and depicts the dress Sastri wore during his public *catur* teaching performances. The tall felt hat he wears here replaced the original *kulah* hat of Muslim poets, which had been given to him years before by the Nawab of Arcot in Triplicane, Madras, to honor his poetic skills. The book he holds in his left hand may be the Bible, or an edition of his own poems. The fingers of his right hand form the liturgical gesture *(mudrā)* that denotes the act of teaching. The portrait depicts Sastri's own identification of himself as 'the general and Evangelical Poet to the Congregations.' [Photo taken from Devanesan]

Sastri also wrote about this calamity in the final version of the *Sāstirakkummi* (762-77). Addressing the Tanjore Evangelicals represented by the 'Woman of Wisdom', he reviewed his biography. The Lord himself had taught him, made him a disciple of Schwartz in 1785, gave him song and then Scripture, and made him an 'Emperor of Poetry' and a 'Sastri of All Scriptural Lore' *(Vedapurāṇa)*. He had him compose 80 poems that contain the essence of religious practice *(Āgama)*, made him useful, as a scholar, 'to all your sons in the schools, the congregation, the church' (769), and employed his songs of wisdom in 'your baptisms, weddings, and your other happy occasions' (779). Then, drawing an analogy between himself and the prophets who had suffered opposition in ancient Israel, he said:

Where is one who has done as much?
Where is one who sang
The revealed Scripture *(Vedāgamam)?*
If you respect him,
Why have you brought him grief,
O Woman of Wisdom? (771)

Alas, today you have come
To like that person [Haubroe], you say,
But yesterday,
Who performed all your weddings,
O Woman of Wisdom? (772)

No matter how much good he did,
You disregard it,
And then divisiveness
Within your stubbornness emerges,
O Woman of Wisdom. (773)

'He composed so many poems',
'He enhanced the congregation in so many ways',
Yet you have made
The friend who loved you that way an enemy,
O Woman of Wisdom. (774)

In those days
The Israelites always
Beat and killed

Whomever God sent —
In these days
It's like that too,
O Woman of Wisdom. (775)

The Israelites beat and killed
Every servant of God.
Isn't it astonishing
That you generate scorn
The same way,
O Woman of Wisdom? (776)

Isn't this just what the Lord Jesus had said,
'A seer even in his own village
Is scorned and attacked
In ways seen nowhere else',
O Woman of Wisdom? (777)[10]

Evangelical Sastri and Saiva King

When Serfoji II learned in 1829 of Sastri's difficulties in the Tanjore congregation, he summoned the poet to the court. Since his own enthronement in 1798 they had met periodically, and the king had recognized their friendship generously. Serfoji had given Sastri a plot of land on which to build a house and an annual stipend of 50 gold coins (*vārakaṉ*, worth 3.5 rupees). Now, in this time of distress, he appointed him court poet with a monthly income of 35 rupees. His duties included meeting with the king twice a month, writing a poetic history of the king's Bhonsala lineage of Marathas, composing poems for the court, and singing Evangelical songs or *bhajans* for Serfoji on those days of the month when, for ritual reasons, he was prohibited from reciting Veda.[11] Sastri held that position for three years until Serfoji's death in 1832.

The king gave Sastri a new palanquin to use for travel to and from the court with all its associated honors and requirements. For example, as he was

10. Vedanayagam Sastri 1969: 124-26. In the last stanza, Sastri may have had Matthew 13:57 and 23:34-37 in mind, as well as Romans 11:2-3, where the apostle Paul cites Elijah in 1 Kings 19:10.

11. Days on which Veda was not to be studied included the first lunar days after the new moon and full moon, and the eight, ninth, and twelfth days before and after the full moon.

carried from his own doorway, where a flagpole displayed a cross, until he reached the palace, where the king's flagpole displayed his emblem, a man walked holding a banner. Along the way, in order to maintain the ritual purity of Sastri and the palanquin, the men who carried him on their shoulders would not allow their own shadows to cross the shadows of whatever 'alien' people of the *cēri* they would encounter. When the palanquin reached the palace, a herald would announce in elaborate poetry Sastri's arrival as 'The Emperor of Poets, Vedanayagam the Lion.'

Serfoji's support was crucial to Sastri's continuing career, and the poet made that known in his works. In 1830 he presented before the king a 17-part poem on the biblical story of Noah that he later included in 'Noah's Ark' *(Nōvāviṉ Pēḻai)*. The latter became part 2 of the 'The Drama of Wisdom's Architect' *(Jñāṉat Tacca Nāṭakam)*.[12] He referred to Serfoji's gracious support twice (in parts 10 and 17). In return, Serfoji presented him with 100 gold coins. Yet the king thought that Sastri might be trying to convert him, so he warned him: 'You are receiving a salary. Be careful, do not try to drag anyone onto your Path.' After he had left the court, Sastri interpreted that warning to mean that Serfoji had forbidden him to preach and teach Christian doctrine as long as he was being paid. His conscience was conflicted about the matter, so much so that he went back to the palace to return the 100 gold coins. But the king was away. A court scholar *(paṇḍita)* explained, however, that the king had not meant that he could not preach about his Lord. The scholar turned the gold coins over to a student, and had him escort Schwartz home and leave the money with him (Gnanadickam: 30-31).

The caste issue that led Sastri to rely on the king's support also appeared in his work. Part 4 of 'The Drama of Wisdom's Architect' is entitled 'Only One Caste' *(Orēcāti)*. There he argues that humans are born of Adam and Eve; all people are therefore their children. Caste distinctions derive, he says, from Saiva doctrines and practices, from those who teach and follow the texts of the Vedas and Agamas, and from those who wear such signifiers of status as ash and *rudraksa* beads. According to Sastri's view, prior to the appearance of Veda and Agama caste differences in society existed, but castes were not ranked hierarchically. When the Saiva teachers came to the courts, however, the kings, ministers, and eminent men would ask them, 'Is the Pallan high or is the Paraiyan high? Is the Brahmin high or is the Elder high? Is the Thief high or is the White Man high?' and they would give answers. That, he said, is how Adam's children came to be divided into the inferior and superior lineages that make up the caste system as we know it (*Orējāti* 1-8). In other

12. The *Jñāṉat Tacca Nāṭakam* is published in Vedanayagam Sastri 1964: 285-352.

words, he put the blame for caste hierarchy on Saiva acharyas and on the rulers who acknowledged their authority.

The church, Sastri said, restores the original unity of Adam and Eve's children. The church is one, the gurus are one, the rites of the king's consecration are one, the surety for sins is one, and the cup of goodness is one. Those of any caste who say that their lineage is superior and the other is inferior will be judged severely, for as Jesus said, 'Just as you love yourself, you should love the other' (*Orējāti* 17-20). Sastri went on to discuss the caste complexity of contemporaneous Malabarian society in detail. Given his severe critique of Saivism and of the social order of Dharma that Serfoji was committed to uphold, it is doubtful that he had introduced those parts of 'The Drama of Wisdom's Architect' to his court.

Serfoji and he were former classmates and friends, but the Saiva king and the Evangelical poet had serious differences. In his autobiographical notes Sastri recorded a conversation with Serfoji that lasted over an hour and a half, during which his Evangelical faith and *guru-bhakti* were sorely tested (Gnanadickam: 31-33). After Serfoji had heard him recite *Bethlehem Kuṛavañci,* he asked Sastri to compose a *kuṛavañci* for his own Lord, who was Siva embodied in the *liṅgam* in the sanctum of Tanjore's huge and beautiful Brihadesvara Temple. Sastri refused. He said he could not praise anyone other than God. The king replied, 'Since I pay you a salary, why do you refuse to do what I ask?' Sastri said that he had been raised as a disciple by 'father' Schwartz and was now 56 years old. So far God had protected him. 'I came to you', he said, 'because of the caste division the new missionaries have caused. If I now commit a sin my Creator hates, I will be his enemy.'

The king failed to understand how composing a *kuṛavañci* to Siva would be a sin. Sastri then suggested an analogy: if, after all Serfoji had done for him, he were to go off to another king and serve him, Serfoji would consider him a traitor, would he not? Similarly, by doing something hateful to the teachings of Schwartz, who from the age of 12 until now had given him food and clothes and had established him, he would betray him, would he not? That he would not do.

The king then modified his request. 'If you cannot compose a *kuṛavañci,* let it be. Just compose a single verse of invocation in the name of Pillaiyar.' That god, known also as Ganesa, Ganapati, and Vinayakar, is the son of Siva and Parvati who controls obstacles. Saivas invoke him at the beginning of significant events. Again Sastri said that if he composed even a small song, not to mention a *kuṛavañci,* he would immediately disappear from the Creator's gaze. He would not do it.

The king then made a proposal. 'I will sing a song in honor of your Lord

Jesus. I will compose it according to whatever instructions you give me, and it will be long. After that, you may sing an invocation in the name of our Pillaiyar.' But Sastri replied, 'Great King! No doubt you may sing in the name of the Lord Jesus, but if you do, I still will not sing to Pillaiyar.'

By then Serfoji was annoyed. Turning to his entourage, he said, 'Look at this! I want to listen to songs composed in the name of his master, but if I compose a song in his master's name, he will not compose one in our master's name. How can that be?' Turning back to Sastri, he said, 'It is simple: You must sing. Do not oppose the Maharaja's command.' Sastri had now been pushed to the very root of his Evangelical commitment. He replied that the Maharaja should not think him to be his servant, nor treat him as such. If he thinks he resembles a stable animal, like the elephant supported by a monthly stipend, that is up to him. Or if he wants to dismiss him, that is also up to him. 'Hereafter', Sastri said, 'everyone will hate me and will cause you trouble. Let us stop, for this trial will end only some time in the future.' The king gave in. 'O Vedanayagam Pillai!' he said, 'You need not fear anyone. Continue to sing only to your Lord Jesus.' He kept him as his court poet.

Sastri left his headmaster position in 1830 and never returned to Christian institutional employment. Instead, he supported himself, his family, and the students and singers who lived with him in whatever ways came to hand. His household at times contained as many as 30 people, and over the years it developed into a center of Malabarian learning and devotional practice that complemented the European rites of the Evangelical Congregation. Eventually Sastri and other separated Velalans returned to the Tanjore Congregation, but on what terms is not known.

Sastri's monthly stipend from Serfoji ended when the king died in 1832. Serfoji's son Sivaji, who ruled until his own death in 1855 as the last of Tanjore's Maratha rulers, did not like Christians and no longer invited Sastri to the palace. But Devasikhamani Pillai, a palace officer known as 'Overseer of Learning in the Castle' *(Kalvikkōṭṭai Cirēshtar)*, loved Sastri's songs. Each year he sent him 100 gold coins. Sastri was also paid as a private Tamil teacher to various missionaries, and for a while he earned money assisting Surveyor-General Mackenzie collect vernacular writings about Indian culture and history. In addition, several European missionaries and laymen who valued his songs gave him monthly contributions, supplemented by occasional gifts from a man in Germany.

Sastri's conflict with Haubroe did not prevent him from working with other missionaries to argue against the Saivas. In 1833 a Tamil work he composed with Miron Winslow and entitled *Blind Way (Kuruṭṭuvaḻi)* was published by the Madras Tract Society. The Catalogue of the British Library describes it as 'a Christian controversial tract in which the futility of the four Saiva modes of worship is illustrated by verses from Tamil poets' (Gaur: 411b). It went through 13 editions by 1866. Together with *Sāstirakkummi*, published in 1840 by the American Mission Press in Madras and reprinted frequently, *Blind Way* played a major role in religious disputes among the Tamil-speaking peoples in nineteenth-century India and Sri Lanka. Out of those disputes arose a 'renaissance' in Tamil Saivism and in Tamil literature, inaugurated by the Velalan scholar and Saiva bhakta Arumuga Navalar of Jaffna (1822-79).[13] That subject, however, takes us away from the details of the controversy generated by the 'new missionaries', to which we now turn.

13. For discussions of Arumuga Navalar, see Hudson 1992, 1994a, 1995b, and 1998; and Young and Jebanesan.

CHAPTER 9

'New Missionaries' and the Tanjore Congregation

The dispute within the Tanjore Evangelical Congregation revealed that a coherent idea of 'pluralistic unity' among Protestant Malabarians had developed. A manuscript collection of documents in the British Library, entitled 'The Foolishness of Amending Caste' *(Jātitiruttaliṉ Payittiyam),* explains it.[1] Ideological changes in Europe were now affecting missions in India, and the Evangelical Velalans of Tanjore had found it necessary to explain themselves as best they could in petitions and reports to mission governing bodies. A divisiveness over caste had begun in the Vepery Congregation in Madras, and by 1829 it had appeared in Tanjore. In response, Velalans in the Congregation compiled this collection of Tamil texts.

Vedanayagam Sastri later appended a lengthy English preface to that collection, entitled 'Saditeratoo', which means 'Explaining Caste' [*Jātiteruṭṭu*]). That English preface is itself a collection of six translated pieces that, with one exception, he appears to have written in Tamil at various times.[2] Sastri's open-

1. It is listed by the British Museum, Department of Oriental Printed Books and Manuscripts, as 'Jati-tiruttalin Payittiyam, Etc. (Tamil)', catalogued as OR. 11,742.

2. The title is: '"Saditeratoo." By Vedenayaga Sastree, the Evangelical Poet Tanjore 1829.' The six sections are listed as: (1) 'The Humble Address', written by Vedanayagam Sastri and dated January 18, 1829; (2) The preface of Sastri's work *Jatiyacaracampavinai* ('Dialogue on the Difference of Caste'); (3) A portion of Sastri's *Jnanappattakapan-nirujnayam* ('Twelve Arguments of the Divine Songsters'); (4) A portion of Sastri's *Unkal-velai* ('Your Hour') on the distinctions of caste; (5) A portion of Sastri's *Pandikaip-pirastapam* ('Festival Eulogy'); and (6) The preface and text of *Jatittiruttalinapayittiyam*

ing 'Humble Address' introduces 'Explaining Caste', yet its date of January 18, 1829, places it earlier by a year than at least one of the other pieces included in the collection.

The preface, 'Explaining Caste', summarizes the issues of the collection for 'the most honored Protestant Congregations and their Superiors that are in the Provinces of India.' The writers had in mind the eight principal Evangelical congregations first developed by Germans sponsored by the Danish-Halle mission and the Society for the Promotion of Christian Knowledge. In 1825, however, the Society had turned over its sponsorship of the Lutheran missions to the Society for the Propagation of the Gospel in Foreign Parts. Without consultation, about 20,000 people, mostly Lutherans, at Tranquebar, Tanjore, Tiruchirapalli, Palaiyankottai, Madurai, Ramanathapuram, Cuddalore, and Vepery in Madras had become Anglicans (Hough: 190-91; Lehmann 1956b: 177). In the meantime, the Church Missionary Society also became involved.

London, rather than Halle, was now Protestant mission headquarters, and Luther's Evangelical German message was giving way to Calvin's Reformed French thought as voiced in English. For example, in a letter dated 1820, the Company chaplain James Hough wrote:

> The Church of England, in common with the Kirk of Scotland and all the Reformed Churches of the Continent of Europe, have followed the example of the Church of Christ from its earliest stage, in adopting the Ten Commandments of God which were delivered to Moses at Sinai, and inculcating them as of universal obligation to all that worship the God of Israel. (Hough: 11)

Individual Pietists had once sought the experience of faith within a 'holistic' society, but now religious experience located among discrete individuals within a 'contractual' society was gaining ground. That subtle yet profound shifting from a 'traditional' to a 'modern' worldview produced effects that are still working themselves out in India, and not only among Protestants.

'Explaining Caste' contains four other selections from Sastri's Tamil works, apparently rendered by him into English. His use of the language is deferential, awkward, and often incorrect, yet it conveys passionately held views clearly. Others who were dependent on the mission for their livelihood, Sastri suggested, were afraid to discuss these matters openly, but he was not,

---

('The Foolishness of Amending Caste'), compiled by Velalans in Tanjore under Sastri's leadership, which they had sent to the missionary authorities in 1828.

for his status as 'Learned Scholar' *(Śāstri)* and as 'the general and Evangelical Poet to the Congregations' gave him the freedom to speak. Moreover, he had already resigned as headmaster of the Tanjore seminary. The final selection, which is the preface to 'The Foolishness of Amending Caste', came not from Sastri alone, but collectively from the Evangelical Velalans in Tanjore, although he, too, may be responsible for its English.

In the opening 'Humble Address' of 'Explaining Caste', Sastri explained why he was speaking so openly. 'Junior Missionaries' had come to Madras and Tanjore and were changing customary practices. He was referring to C. T. E. Rhenius, who had arrived in Madras in 1814, and to L. P. Haubroe, who had arrived in Tanjore in 1819. The changes they sought, he claimed, were in fact their ways to cover up Malabarian opposition to them, specifically to the new translations, chiefly by Rhenius, of the Scripture, the prayerbook, and the hymnal.

C. T. E. Rhenius (1790-1837) began his career in Madras, but after six years there spent the remaining 18 years of his life working in the Tirunelveli region with the support of the Church Missionary Society. While in Tirunelveli, he studied Tamil grammar and literature over a 14-year period with the Tamil scholar and poet Tiruparkatalnathan Kavirayar (Kulentiran: 106-8). A generation later that same poet would teach two Sri Vaishnava Velalan brothers who afterward would become Protestants and express their faith in Tamil with considerable insight and influence, H. A Krishna Pillai and E. Muttaiya Pillai of Palaiyankottai.

In the meantime, Rhenius was making his own impact: By the time of Sastri's 'Humble Address', Rhenius's revision of Fabricius's translation of the book of Genesis, which he had begun after only 18 months in India, had been published in 1819 as a specimen for examination. In 1825 his translation of the book of Matthew and his Tamil catechism on baptism and the Lord's Supper had also appeared (Barnett and Pope: 287a). And two years later all four Gospels, along with The Acts of the Apostles, were in print (Murdoch: 23).

Bible Translation

Bible translation into Tamil had been going on, of course, since Ziegenbalg landed in Tranquebar in 1706. These more recent efforts to revise Scripture now came from the British at the Company's headquarters at Fort William in Calcutta. There, in 1804, David Brown, Claudius Buchanan, and William Carey, translators at the Company's College, created the British and Foreign Bible Society. In 1810 the Bible Society in London sent a Tamil printing press to Madras to be used for a new edition of the Bible, and after Rhenius arrived in 1814, he was put in charge of its first project (Hooper: 15-18, 75-76).

A brief review of the history of Tamil Bible translation to this point will shed light on the controversy that concerns us. Ziegenbalg and his successors had already translated and printed the Bible, prayerbook, hymns, catechisms, and various tracts. Their faulty Tamil invited the ridicule of Beschi, the Jesuit famed for his knowledge of Tamil, a ridicule he expressed in a Tamil work of 1728, 'The Explanation of Revelation' *(Veda Vilakkam).* The Tranquebar translations did not satisfy the Protestants of Ceylon either, and a new one was begun there by Philip De Melho (1723-90), whom we first met as the son of a wealthy Protestant Velalan serving on the personal staff of ten Dutch Governors in Colombo (Chitty 1859: 69-76).

Remarkably, De Melho had studied Hebrew, Greek, Latin, Dutch, Portuguese, Tamil, and theology in Colombo. But he turned down an offer of further study in Leiden in favor of an appointment at Colombo as the Native Proponent. In 1744, at the age of 21, De Melho began ministering to Ceylonese; six years later he was the first Ceylonese to receive ordination in the Church of Holland. Then, because he was not pleased with the Tranquebar version of the Bible, he became the first Ceylonese translator of the Tamil New Testament. He began revising it in 1746 so that it would follow more closely the original Koine Greek, and worked at it for 13 years. In the meantime, he moved from Colombo to lead the Protestants in Jaffna, and, while there, his New Testament translation appeared in print in 1759.

At the same time in Madras, a German missionary had been preparing another new translation of the Bible. J. P. Fabricius had arrived in Tranquebar in 1740, but two years later he moved to Madras, where he began to read the Tranquebar translations under the critical guidance of a highly educated 'pagan' named Muttu. Noting their faults, he, too, set out to retranslate Scripture from the original languages, and worked at it for over 20 years. His New Testament was published 13 years after De Melho's version in 1772, and his Old Testament appeared five years later in 1777.[3]

As might be expected, judgments about Fabricius's translation varied. In Tanjore, Vedanayagam Sastri said Fabricius's New Testament and Old Testament translations had created a language that 'could be plainly understood by the learned and unlearned', a 'most agreeable Tamil . . . rejoicing and edify-

3. According to Hooper (73-74), Fabricius's New Testament appeared at Tranquebar in 1773, a metrical version of the Psalms in 1774, and the Old Testament in 1777. According to Neill (1985: 44), Fabricius printed a new version of the Psalms in 1756, and in 1766 began printing the New Testament on a British government press. His complete Old Testament was delayed until 1798, several years after his death.

ing the mind like the joys of the Garden of Eden and the gladness of the city of God.' In Jaffna, however, De Melho thought otherwise. He and his brother-in-law, the clergyman of Colombo and Rector of the Seminary, began to translate the Old Testament from the original Hebrew in the late 1770s. In the meantime, the Fabricius version appeared, and the Dutch Governor wanted De Melho to review it and to annotate its errors. De Melho did and gave the following evaluation:

> The language and style have not been arranged in accordance with the solemnity of such a divine revelation as the Holy Scriptures. The spelling of a great many words is very defective. Foreign words have been introduced, which in Tamil style appear ungraceful and deform the language and disfigure it. Abundant errors have also crept into it, consisting of unnecessary additions of words which are not in the sacred text and inadmissible omissions of those which are in it, bad and incorrect renderings and incompatible interpretations, instead of translations. . . . (Chitty 1859: 75)

De Melho's critique was sent to the missionaries in Tranquebar along with a copy of his own translation. The Tranquebar missionaries agreed that De Melho's translation used excellent and choice language, but they doubted that the 'common people' would understand it.

To settle the question, De Melho's version was 'publicly and solemnly read in the Jaffna Fort Church to a large body of learned Tamils and to other auditors.' According to Simon Casie Chitty, writing in 1859, the assembly had agreed that it was intelligible to the 'common people' and that its language was 'matchless, elegant, pathetic and heart cheering.' That of the Fabricius version, however, 'was a mixture of all words current on the Coast and was extremely uncouth, barbarous and ridiculous, owing to the grammatical errors and the vulgarisms with which it abounded' (Chitty 1859: 75). De Melho's response to the Tranquebar critique of his work, Casie Chitty wrote, was

> that the words remarked on as high by the Tranquebar Missionaries (who certainly were not competent judges) are no other in reality than pure Tamil words, unintelligible to none but to such as understand no other than lame and bastard Tamil. (Chitty 1859: 75-76)

Nevertheless, years later, in 1829, Vedanayagam Sastri wrote that De Melho's 'Columboo Tamil Testament' had 'spoiled our books', by which he meant the translations by Fabricius.

The twofold issue had now been raised: firstly, Who are the 'common people'? and secondly, What is the standard for Tamil prose written across all the dialects that constitute the Tamil language? In religious contexts until now, Tamil poetry had been the 'link language' across diverse social and dialectical communities, and oral and written Tamil prose had been its gloss. The difference between the two was significant, for as Ziegenbalg had observed in 1708 (as translated into eighteenth-century English),

> There is almost so great a Difference betwixt the *vulgar* and *poetical Malabarick,* as there is betwixt *Latin* and *High-Dutch.* For notwithstanding the way of reading be the same, no common *Malabarian* can understand the Composures of the Poets without an Interpreter. And this is the Reason that there are so very few that are able to give a competent Account of the Principles of their Worship; the religious Books being written in so dark and abstruse a Language, as no mean Person is able to dive into. (Ziegenbalg 1718: 2:11)

Ziegenbalg's concern, of course, was typically Protestant, for Protestants insisted that people should be able to 'give a competent account' of the principles underlying their religion, and therefore the Bible should be available to anyone who can read, especially to Christians. But if Scripture is addressed not just to the elite, but to all Tamil-speaking people — to fishermen, merchants, aristocrats, bureaucrats, soldiers, farmers, and laborers, and to high-status and low-status women and men in cities, towns, and villages — what style of Tamil prose should be created? Should it come from the literary dialect of a regional elite like the Velalans of Jaffna or of courtly Tanjore? Or should it come from the dialect of the nonliterate population of coastal mercantile Tranquebar? Or should a new form of Tamil prose be created, one designed in a newly developing cosmopolitan urban center like Madras?

The matter of identity lay hiding inside the question of what kind of language to use for Scripture in the public arena. After all, wherever Tamil-speaking Protestants heard Scripture read, the imagined if not literal gaze of Saivas, Vaishnavas, Muslims, and Catholics from the doors and windows of the church was always in the back of their minds. In a highly sophisticated verbal culture, where language signified a range of identities, how would their sacred Scripture in Tamil represent Protestants to those among whom they lived, and therefore to themselves?

Judging from Sastri's 'Humble Address', his own identity, and that of other Evangelical Velalans in Tanjore, was closely tied to the language of the Fabricius translations. Apart from its strengths or weaknesses, its language signified for him, and others like him, the Pietist culture that Ziegenbalg had begun in Tranquebar over a century earlier, a culture that had been fostered in Tanjore by his guru and 'father' C. F. Schwartz, a German favored by the Tanjore court, esteemed by both the British and their enemy Haider 'Ali, who by the end of his life was widely regarded as 'saintly.' No doubt Vedanayagam's own poems, his status as Sastri or learned scholar, and his acclamation as 'the general and Evangelical Poet to the Congregations' whose poems embodied Ziegenbalg's theology were also implicated.

It is not surprising, then, that such a prominent figure in Evangelical congregations, some of which were over a century old, found it appalling that, after only four years of Tamil study, the 'Junior Missionary' Rhenius had paid 'heathen Moonshees' named Ramachandra Poet and Tandevaraya Pilley ('who blaspheme Christ', he claimed) to guide him in revising the Fabricius translations. Moreover, Rhenius had used a style of Tamil that was — as De Melho might have said — 'detestable and inelegant':

> filled with words not only ungrammatical in meaning, unsystimatical [sic], but also irreligious, perverting the word of God, and blasphemous, and thus made those books to be laughed at by all who hear them, altering them and mixing in them all the Cutcherry Tamil and gentoo words. ('The Humble Address')

'Cutcherry Tamil' and 'gentoo words' referred to Tamil and Telugu slang found in everyday administrative speech and in the language of soldiers and 'pariahs.' Language reveals identity. But Tamils from Madras to Jaffna were divided into many dialects peculiar to both regions and castes, and the nuances of words and linguistic patterns varied according to the dialect, which meant that the specific meaning of particular speech depended on the social context of its utterance.

The problem Tamil-speaking Protestants faced was shared by the 'Moors' or Muslims, which was a claim of religious identity based on a written book. But there was no single social context, or shared Tamil dialect, that would allow them to read that book in a way that would be heard the same by everyone from Jaffna to Madras. The Muslim problem differed, however, because they believed that God's Word is embodied in the Qur'an's Arabic and cannot be translated. Tamil-speaking Muslims might be required to learn the Arabic recitation of Qur'anic passages, but Protestants were not required to learn to read their Scripture in Hebrew and Greek.

In 'The Humble Address', Sastri said that he had written four books criticizing the Rhenius and Haubroe revisions, the first of which was the 'Letter on the Bible Dispute' *(Wedaviautchiapatram* [*Vedaviyattiyāpātram*]).

When Rhenius's translation of the 'Common prayer' (Book of Common Prayer) was published in Madras in 1820, Sastri reviewed it and found 'in one page 10 or 20 and many more mistakes.' He wrote about those mistakes in the 'Letter' he had sent to the missionary Haubroe in Madras, who nevertheless had rejected his suggestions in favor of the advice of the 'heathen' Munshis, Ramachandra Poet and Tandevarayya Pilley.

Three other critiques of their revisions followed in that decade, Sastri reported. To defend his Tamil advisors and himself to the Bible Society that sponsored them, Rhenius had sent to the missionaries and their respective sponsoring societies 'a long treatise in 20 sheets stating that the ancient Missionaries [sic] Translations were contrary to the originals and to the grammatical rules of the Tamil language. . . .' Sastri said that he did not object to the missionaries publishing catechisms or histories in such Tamil, but when literary and common Tamil are mixed and spoiled and then used by congregations and schools for the Scriptures and the prayerbook, that only gives the 'unitarians and Popists' room to laugh, and causes confusion in customary practice.

Moreover, he queried, since none of the congregations at Tanjore, Tranquebar, or Madras had complained about the Fabricius translations, or asked for corrections, why had Rhenius taken it upon himself to 'correct disorderly [sic] all our Religious books which are in use amongst us these 56 years past and make bad what was good?' He noted that Rhenius had defended his actions to the missionary societies in an English treatise, but he then asked how Rhenius's justifications in English can be acceptable when he has not proven himself right in Tamil? 'What distinction is there', he asked rhetorically,

> between the Romish Popes who refuse to distribute the religious books to their people and the Rev. Mr. Rhenius who is dispensing them to people after having perverted the word of God and its nature [?]. Will it not be as the milk mingled with arsenick and given to people who are athirst after Christianity [?].

Those translations created confusion among the people, he said, because most people had been taught to recite texts from memory rather than from books. Consequently, when the missionaries published their experimentations in Tamil, people who had already memorized earlier translations were frustrated and confused:

> These Junior Missionaries . . . composed each at his pleasure the Prayer book, and Catechisims [sic] in different ways; at Madras they print it one

> way and another way at Negarcoil, which after the School boys, Catechumen[s], and Communicants have got by heart according to the strict order given them, the next year they being struck with another though[t] revise them by the said Moonshees and spoil them and put them in print another way; this disorder has increased gradually and the Lord's prayer has been printed in 3 kinds within 5 years.

Once Rhenius had realized that 'all the Congregations rejected [his] unnatural Translations', Sastri then asserted, he tried to cover himself by enlisting Haubroe and other missionaries 'to commit four kinds of Cruelties against the Congregations.'

Four 'Cruelties'

As Sastri stated them, the four 'cruelties' reveal that the 'Junior Missionaries' were voicing new Protestant theological trends in Europe and North America, trends echoing the values that gave rise to the 'Enlightenment' ideologies that had propelled the American and French Revolutions. Those trends favored an egalitarian social vision and ranked the mind as more important than the body. Church services should be 'low' and 'Calvinist' rather than 'high' or 'Anglo-Catholic', and the body should be restrained through a 'Reformed Church' decorum. They judged the century-old Evangelical liturgical and social practices in Tranquebar and Tanjore as 'too Catholic' and 'too heathenish.'

The first 'cruelty' of the 'Junior Missionaries', Sastri said, was to persist with their translations, removing the old versions from the schools and replacing them with their own. They figured, he said, that their new Tamil would replace the old Tamil within 20 years, a generation.

Their second 'cruelty' was to try to unite 'Pallar and Parayar and every description of people into one Caste', and to excommunicate from the Lord's Supper those who maintain their customary differences (a subject we will return to below). Sastri noted that since he had already written a book on those first two 'cruelties' entitled 'New Correction and Amending Caste', he was now speaking more freely on the third and fourth 'cruelties.'

Liturgical Practices

The third 'cruelty' of the 'Junior Missionaries' was to restrict the celebration of festivals, to eliminate at least one, and to prohibit the use of flowers in festivals, weddings, and burials as 'a sin and the lust of the eye' denoting a 'heathen.' Sastri explained that although the 'former Missionaries' had discontinued the observance of saints' days as found among the Catholics, they had kept eight important Christian festivals. 'The Rev. father' Fabricius had listed them in an appendix to 'the Tamil Testament' printed in 1772, which Sastri repeated in 'The Humble Address':

1st The Birthday of Christ or Christmas Day
2nd The Circumcision of Christ or New Year's Day
3rd The Manifestation of Christ or Epiphany
4th Good Friday
5th Easter Day
6th Ascension Day
7th Whit Sunday
8th Trinity Sunday

Of those, Sastri noted, only 'the good Friday' was sorrowful; the other seven were celebrated 'gladly' in both body and soul, and denoted true Christian observance:

> We think that he who would not consider the kindness of God who gave his only begotten son, and be glad in soul and body for the manifold goodness he has done by him, is unworthy even of the name of a Christian.

He illustrated their 'gladness' of body by their celebration of Christmas:

> [we] keep the Church clean and neat, white wash it, adorn it with Christmas flowers, illuminate it with candlesticks, and perform the divine service with becoming modesty, but we by no means celebrate the festivals so pompously as the Roman Catholics do by playing comedy, fireworks, musics such as arabic Taboret, and Cymbal, etc.

The 'Junior Missionaries' tried to change those celebrations. When Haubroe was appointed to Tanjore, he was under the jurisdiction of Rhenius. In turn, Sastri's friend, the 'Malabarian-German' clergyman J. C. Kohlhoff, who had arranged Sastri's second marriage, was under Haubroe's jurisdiction. Haubroe apparently insisted that Kohlhoff support his reforms:

> Notwithstanding no sooner did Mr. Haubroe come to this place, then [sic] he began to raise sedition and hated us without reason and prevented us

> from using even the flowers created by God both in our Marriages and burials, because he was obliged to follow the will of Mr. Rhenius who treats miserably the Congregations of southern India.
>
> The Rev. Mr. Kohlhoff also, without considering the reasons, being on his part, [sic] prevented us from celebrating the festivals of our Lord gladly according to our former customs and locked up the gates of the Church on new years [sic] day of 1827 and directed the people to put up a prayer in the school and ordered to cut off the garlands of flowers which adorned the Church saying that it was an heinous sin.
>
> In this year upon the complaint of the Congregation although the Rev. Mr. Kohlhoff permitted to celebrate the festivals as usual yet Mr. Haubroe did not consent to it and prevented us from celebrating the festivals of the manifestation of Christ which has been celebrated 100 years and which has greatly grieved us and we were obliged to celebrate it in a house.

The new missionaries, Sastri said, considered the festivals days to be ordinary, 'as other days and not as days of importance':

> [they] threaten us like the Romish Priests who say to their people that he who eats animal food on Friday and Saturday is a heretic and guilty of a deadly sin, so they say to us that the use of flowers is a sin and the lust of the eye and he that uses them is a heathen, and thus terrify us by preaching offensive sermons contrary to the word of the Holy Ghost who says by saint Paul: For every creature of God is good and nothing to be refused if it be received with thanksgiving. 1 Timo. 4.4. All these things are the 3rd Cruelty which the Rev. Mr. Rhenius and his companions to do [sic] all the Congregations of this country.

In the eyes of the Tanjore congregation, those eight festivals, which had been celebrated since the early days of the Tranquebar mission, were 'canonical', as their inclusion in Fabricius's translation of the Bible suggested.

The missionaries whom Rhenius led in seeking a new Bible translation were the same ones seeking to diminish the festival calendar and to reduce the sensual aspects of celebration. In Malabarian terms, the 'Junior Missionaries' were not comfortable with a full use of the body's five sense organs *(indriya, poṛi)* in the act of worship, and stressed instead the sixth one, the mind *(manas)*. As Sastri's document reveals, a new Bible translation implied much more than merely new words; it implied a different 'language of the body.' The 'body language' used by those who followed the Fabricius translation was one the 'new missionaries' judged to be suitable for the worship of Siva or

Vishnu in a 'pagan' temple, or for worship in a 'heretical' Catholic church, but not for worship in a Protestant assembly.

Accordingly, the fourth 'cruelty' was to try to remove Tamil music and lyrics from worship and festivities. Sastri began by explaining how their Tamil songs originated:

> The former Missionaries at the first commencement of their receiving gentiles into Christianity, found that the Tamilians were offended at the tunes of the Europeans Hymns, and performed the divine service by singing a few divine songs composed by the Roman Catholics[. A]fter a few years when our Congregation increased day by day, God raised the Poets in our Congregation as . . . the Missionaries themselves gave them prose to versify and used them always in the divine service which rendered it cheerful and edified to [sic] the people. The proof of this may be seen in the old Almanacks, where 10 Stanzas were composed and added at the end, and which were printed at Tranquebar and sent to the Tamilians every year.

Judging from that account, the early Evangelicals had adapted to Protestant use the 'pagan' almanac or *pañcāṅgam* that published the calendar of festivals, feasts, fasts, pilgrimages, vows, auspicious and inauspicious times, etc., along with texts appropriate to the religious tradition concerned. Today, inexpensive *pañcāṅgams* in Tamil may be bought at the beginning of each Tamil year in the month of Cittirai (April-May) and commonly provide all the religious and secular calendars pertinent to the population.

Sastri explained that the songs composed by Tamil poets eventually gave way to hymns translated from the German because the boys educated in the Tranquebar school had been taught the European hymns. When they became adults in the congregations, the hymns they knew took over. But in arenas outside the regular Sunday service, such as festivals, the earlier Tamil songs or 'lyrics' continued:

> When the boys of the charity school grew up in their years, and had improved in the tunes of the Hymns day by day they discontinued the Tamil songs and made use of them particularly at the festivals. In the 40 days of contemplating the sufferings of Christ, or Lent[,] the Catechists, Schoolmasters, etc. according to the orders of the Missionaries accompanied a few boys who had a good voice and sang the mournful songs at every house and raised their minds to the contemplation of the sufferings of Christ; at the passion weeks the said mournful songs were sung after the divine service was over[. T]he Rev. Missionaries themselves have always heard those Tamil songs with joy.

> Besides this, they have ordered to teach the school boys both the Tamil lessons and songs one hour daily after the evening prayer and supper was done, before the children went to repose the day. Schoolmaster from 9 to 10 o'Clock in the night would daily examine the singing boys and gladly correct the errors of them. And in several nights when the Missionaries would come to look after them they would not make any objection to this and would approve of it and say that it was good to improve in their learning at any rate, and go away after hearing their songs gladly for a few Minutes.
>
> When any of the new Missionaries are coming all the teachers with the Catechists accompanied by the school boys, use to go a little way as far as possible to meet and bring them in with joy by singing divine songs[. T]hus the divine songs were sung at our Baptisms, Marriages, and on joyful and mournful occasions. At the particular festivals of Christmas, New Year's Day, etc. as soon as the morning and evening prayers are over the Congregation with the Songsters would go to the Ministers' house, sing one or two Songs and return from thence on receiving their blessings.

Sastri then explained that even though in their liturgies they rejoiced in the body, in contrast to the Roman Catholics their practice was restrained (here he used 'music' to mean musical instruments):

> As Europeans like decent music such as organ, Violin, Flute, etc. harmoniously suiting the tunes of Hymns and use them in divine service, so we like a decent musics [sic] which suits our Tamil songs such as Harp, Pipe, Guitar, Timbrel, Cymbal etc. and use them in such time thinking that it will be acceptable to God and agreeable to the tenor of the 150th Psalm etc. But we have never used those riotous musics which the Roman Catholics use in their festivals such as Arabe, Taboret, Negasarum, Tumtum, Horn, etc. and we wish neither to use them.
>
> Thus, we sing to the Lord in our festivals only by small bell, Cymbal, rejecting even those musical instruments which we might use reasonably for fear of their loudness and this we do after the divine service is over[. A]t the Church we sing only the songs without any music.
>
> Contrary to this our former use which continued since the days of the commencement of Christianity in this country Mr. Haubroe began to treat us in another way, turning Mr. Kohlhoff's mind and endeavouring to gain him to his own side by many reasons in order that we should not use at all Tamil songs since 1827.

According to Sastri, his friend Kohlhoff gave three reasons for the changes he was now demanding. Firstly, Kohlhoff said, the songs are wrongly translated. But, Sastri said, the words of the Tamil songs were correct and Kohlhoff 'raised controversy by affixing his erroneous meanings to them.' Secondly, Tamil Christian poets had followed the customary manner of 'signing' their poems by registering their names in the final stanzas of the lyrics. Kohlhoff judged that to be an act of 'pride and Blasphemy.' And thirdly, he said the use of certain instruments 'is heathenism':

> He not only forbids us obstinately to use any decent instruments even Cymbal with our songs saying that it is heathenism, but also uses what device soever he can in order that we ourselves may put an end to the Tamil singing. Hence he spoiled the pleasures of the Tamilians. I cannot freely say whether [sic: why] Mr. Rhenius and his companions are doing this fourth notable cruelty in preventing to praise the Lord by divine songs even at the festival days which are delightful and impressive to the people.

Sastri concluded 'The Humble Address' with a hope:

> [that] the Congregations may be treated according to their former rule with which the ancient Missionaries have treated us without any objection to the standing rules of the country to the praise of the glorious name of God, and that all the Congregations of this country may be preserved and protected from the Cruelties of the Junior Missionaries, who make us miserable in vain by changing the Religion of liberty into bondage.

As we will now see, 'the standing rules of the country' lay at the heart of Evangelical Velalan concerns. To their minds, following them was 'liberty', while following the new rules of the 'Junior Missionaries' was 'bondage.'

Observance of Caste Distinctions

Let us now return to the second 'cruelty.' In 1824 Vedanayagam Sastri had written the 'Dialogue on the Difference of Caste' *(Sadiausara Sambaveney)* [*Jātiācārasambhāvaṉai*]. The excerpts that follow illustrate his summary of the argument in the preface to that work.

The 'Dialogue', he said, is 'a Discourse between a European Missionary and a Native Doctor of Divinity or Vedasastree of the Vellala Caste.' It contains 'the general arguments . . . impartially given with regard both to Malabar [Velalans] and Velangamatars ['pariahs' of the 'right hand'] . . . which will be agreeable to all. . . .' The reason he wrote it, he explained succinctly though awkwardly, was that the new missionaries had been trying

> to load a heavy yoke upon the Congregations by forcing all the castes or nations of this country to be of one caste to make them eat and drink together and to have those of higher and lower classes connected with each other in marriage, a thing which is quite contrary to the steps followed and orders granted by any of the Rev. Missionaries, such as Mr. Ziegenbalg, Senior Missionary, and others who have been in this Peninsula during these 120 years since Protestantism has been established in this country and which neither Christ has commanded and which is contrary to the custom of the country.

Those who would not agree, he said, had been excluded by the missionaries from Baptism and the Lord's Supper, and from burial in the cemetery,

> thus exciting a cruel enemity [sic], revolutions, and inveterate hatered [sic] and quarrels and preventing the heathens etc. from getting the knowledge of our true religion by putting in their way great and many obstacles and offences and opening wide a door to their mockeries.

Part of the 'new missionaries'' effort was 'to spoil both the scripture and Congregations together entirely. . . .' The congregations themselves were split over the new caste policy — 'some think that this is right and others that this is not and thus are in suspence [sic].'

The 'Dialogue', he continued, consists of three parts. Part 1 presents the ancient history of the Brahmins, 'who are a kind of Jews.' Sastri had probably never met a Jew; his view of them derived from the Protestant reading of the Old Testament through the eyes of the New Testament. Accordingly, the Jews are supposedly much too concerned with ritual purity, with ritual acts of purification from sin, and with keeping themselves apart from 'gentiles', which is the way he viewed Brahmins. 'Caste . . . , its classes, differences and manners', he said, began with the Brahmins and was not indigenous to the Malabarians.

Interestingly, later in the century the Saiva Velalan, Arumuga Navalar, argued a similar idea in a much more sophisticated manner, but against the Protestants. Having assisted a Wesleyan Methodist missionary in Jaffna to revise the Tamil Bible yet again, he knew it in detail; and he perceived parallels between the Israelite temple cultus and the Saiva temple cultus. To his mind, the Jews were a 'kind of Saiva.' Moreover, he claimed that the Protestants had betrayed the religion of their own Bible (Hudson 1994a). Yet both Sastri and Navalar understood 'the Jews' from biblical texts over 2,000 years old. Neither, it appears, knew anything of the way the synagogue cultus, which was the heart of Judaism in their time, interpreted those texts.

Part 2 presents objections to caste division and to the means taught by Brahmins for obtaining the pardon of sin and paradise. It also gives testimonies from 'heathen Philosophers' about image worship, polytheism, and monotheism, or, in his words, about 'the variety of Idols and the Three Morties [*Murti*] and the existence of one Supreme Being.'

Part 3 of the 'Dialogue' consists of answers to nine questions Sastri posed to the missionaries about their new commands: (1) Are they absolutely necessary? (2) Do they fit the rules of Christ? (3) Will they aid the propagation of Christianity? (4) Will they benefit the country? (5) Will they agree with contemporary worldly affairs? (6) Can they be fulfilled? (7) Will there be any benefit in trying to fulfill them? (8) By trying to fulfill them will people not be hurt and suffer loss? (9) Were these rules followed by Christians in Europe or by the missionaries who brought Christianity to Malabar?

The 'Dialogue', he explained, elucidates the differences between castes and describes their manner of living and worship and their customs. He thought it would prove useful to catechists 'in their conversations with heathens' and especially to missionaries from Europe.

Sastri then illustrated the basic argument of the 'Dialogue' with an excerpt from another of his works, 'Twelve Arguments of the Divine Songsters' [*Jñāṉappāṭṭaka Paṉṉirujñāyam*]:

> . . . as one catches an elephant showing another [elephant] and the quail showing another quail, so we who are to convert the heathens to Christianity, why should we be an offence to them before they can be acquainted with our Scriptures? Even the Popish priests are good examples to us in this they dress their clouths [sic], caps, and gowns without causing any offence to the Tamil nations.

He was apparently alluding to Beschi's strategy of dressing as an acharya.

In the opening 'Humble Address', Sastri had already argued that earlier missionaries like Ziegenbalg had been good 'catchers of men' because they had respected the customary divisions of the country. Not only had they followed 'Popish' practice and dressed like a 'Tamilian priest', he said (although Ziegenbalg and other early Germans apparently did not), but like the elephants and quails they had also used Velalans to convert Velalans and 'Gentoos' to convert 'Gentoos', and had

> manifested inexpressible kindness to them and treated them without any difference of their casts [sic], with distinction, and built the Church in the form of the cross and made them to sit in their respective places. . . .

Moreover, they had lived as of a 'high caste among the people of Europe', had used only 'Malabars' (Velalans)[4] as their cooks, and did not eat flesh in public. 'They had acted prudently', he said, 'without causing any offence either to the higher or to the lower according to the saying of the Apostle [Paul], being made all things to all men in order to gain all. I Cori. 9.20.22. 10.33.'

Yet the 'Junior Missionaries', he wrote, persist in uniting 'Pallar and Parayer and every description of people' into one caste, even though they act contrary to the way the 'Honorable Goverment' acts, and contrary to the strict order of the Lord Bishop Reginald Heber in Calcutta, 'according to which the Congregation ought to be treated without intermeddling in the different customs and manners of this country. . . .'

Judging from those statements, the new missionaries were seeking to eliminate all distinctions between high-status and low-status castes among Protestants, and between the 'right hand' and 'left hand' divisions. They wanted to create a single Protestant culture that intermarried and interdined as if it were an egalitarian community. Such social interaction, they apparently believed, would both express and create love and charity.

To bring about such unity, Sastri continued, the new missionaries employ a 'few clever fellows' from the congregations of Tanjore, Tranquebar, Madras, and Palaiyankottai as catechists, assistants, and servants,

> and direct them and the other congregations to unite with Pallar and Parayer, eat and intermarry with them and teach us as this was the only way to go to Paradise and take a few texts on the love and charity and explain them contrarily. This they who should preach on the faith of the Son of God, preach now all the day long more than ten times upon the subject of eating with Pallar and Parayer promiscuously; and reproach the Tamilians very abominably and scandalize them by writing in various Tracts and reports respecting the usages of their Castes, which they send to various places and cause thereby an inexpressible confusion and dissensions and hate those that contradict with an inveterate hatred and call them heathen

4. Sastri used 'Malabar' to denote the 'civilized' people of the *ūr,* and 'Valangamattar' to denote the 'uncivilized' aliens of the *cēri.* He used 'Tamilian' similarly to denote the people of the *ūr.*

> unregenerated, and thrust them from the Lord's supper and a Christian burial, even dismiss them from their situation.

In a selection from another work, 'Your Hour' *(Uṅkalvēlai)*, which dates from 1830 when the congregation had already split, or perhaps even a little later, Sastri explained how that policy affected the Evangelicals in Tanjore. It had to do with seating. First, the new missionaries used a secular context to express their egalitarian values through seating arrangements. Forsaking the practices of the former missionaries, he said, the new ones had scattered the Christians that had already been gathered,

> and ensnared some head men among them to sit at Table with them and eat and drink Tea, and to imagine vainly that they had procured great virtue by it; and though they held distinction by putting chairs for themselves to their wives and children [sic], and by putting Benches for Country borne and Soldiers they began to treat the masters and the slaves of this country equally.

Next, they extended those changes in seating arrangements to the sacred context in Tanjore. For over 50 years, Sastri explained, distinct mats had been used in the liturgical settings at Tanjore for different castes. (That was a variation of Tranquebar's earlier practice, in which some sat on benches, some on mats, and some directly on the floor.) In Tanjore, the Velalans ('Tamilians') sat on 'Sedge' mats, and those who belonged to the Paraiyan 'right hand' division (Valangamattan) sat separately on mats of 'Coldrickoo.' But in the time of the missionary L. P. Haubroe,

> from the year 1830 mats of Rotten [Rattan] were spread all over the Church without seperation [sic], and all were ordered to sit together in the same mat publicly in the Church without any distinction.

Due to Haubroe's reform in seating, the congregation had split into two parts, the Velalans and the Valangamattans. When the congregation asked that a four-foot strip of mat be removed, apparently to separate the two groups, Haubroe had refused. He insisted that if people needed to sit, they must all sit on the same mat, or else all must sit on the ground, and he took away the mat that was spread in the church. Therefore, Sastri lamented,

> We all the Tamilians [Velalans] and their wives sit in the Church on the ground. What greater cruelty is there than this? If the Valangamattar sit on

> the mat we must sit on the mat, if not we must sit on the ground, is it just? But by this will they change the world into heaven? Is it written in the Scripture in vain to render honor to whom honor is due [?]. Rome. 13.7.

The issue posed by rattan mats, it appears, derived from the fact that they were woven from long strands into large sections and placed to form a continuous surface so that all who sat on them would sit on a single interconnected mat. Assuming that 'Sedge' and 'Coldrickoo' mats were of different quality, smaller, and separated, they allowed social distinctions between Velalans and Valangamattans to be articulated, and they allowed for distinctions within the grouping of lower castes itself, for example, between the Paraiyans of the 'right hand' and the Pallans, shoemakers, and smiths of the 'left hand.' The point, Sastri said, was not that the Paraiyans should sit on the ground while the Velalans sat on mats, but that each group should sit on mats or carpets, but separately with their distinctions retained.

Yet it seems clear that the Velalans would have the place of honor. Perhaps in the back of Sastri's mind was the traditional image of the Velalan chieftain, a 'Son of Goddess Earth', who lived, as one Tamil poet put it,

> like a feudal lord with all his vassals round about him. He had therefore slaves and vassals to serve him on all occasions, and these slaves and vassals represented different castes who served him in such capacity whenever occasion demanded. (Pfaffenberger: 38)

In the 'holistic' society of Malabar, Evangelical liturgy had brought the 'chieftains' together with their 'slaves' and 'vassals' before the Table of the Lord, but seated them separately. That arrangement suggested that the 'alien' servants from the *cēri* sat 'round about' their 'Tamilian' masters from the *ūr.* In such a liturgical context, all the castes present, both high and low in status, would expect that honor would go to the 'lordly' and aristocratic Velalans.

Related to seating during worship was the matter of announcing weddings to the congregation. Until now, Sastri wrote, wedding banns or proclamations had been published at the end of the divine service, usually by the ordained priests, who if not Europeans were of course Velalans. When the missionary Haubroe arrived, however, he began to use the principal catechists for the rite, and they might be 'pariahs.' Recently Haubroe had acted with 'much more cruelty': he had intentionally used the 'Valangamattoo Catechist' to publish the banns of 'a few Tamilars' (Velalans), in order, Sastri claimed, to anger them. He noted specifically the marriage of David Pillai's daughter Anna. Her father had begged them not to use a 'pariah' catechist to announce his daughter's banns; and when they did, 'the seperated [sic] part of the Congregation' united among themselves even further.

Judging from Sastri's account, which is obscure regarding some points, the Velalans decided that 'the Priests' would not compromise and would 'endeavour to do greater evils.' Their best recourse was to affirm their Velalan identity after the wedding ceremony, celebrating their caste's customs even more elaborately than usual. As he formulated their decision:

> 'let us do our best as their [they] raise our anger by causing Valangamattar to sit with us in the same mat and by publishing the banns of our Marriage by the Catechist of them, so we shall raise their anger by using pomps', when they come to the Church they come honestly as good people, and after the marriage was performed their use of customs is numberless. What a greater change is this?

In other words, the effort by the new missionaries to eliminate caste observance during liturgies had merely persuaded the Velalans to articulate their own caste identity even more clearly to themselves and the world around them.

Vedanayagam Sastri provided other thoughts on caste observance in another selection, one excerpted from 'Festival Eulogy' *(Pandegey Prasdabam* [*Paṇṭikaippirastāpam*]). That text was his response to the revised order of the Lord's Supper published in 1825 by the Church Missionary Society in Madras. He began by repeating the view Dandapani Swami shared: that the four classes *(varṇa)* were ways to organize many different castes and lineages *(jāti, kulam)* into groups, with the unnamed cluster of 'alien' castes constituting 'the fifth' standing outside. But, Sastri noted, when the Europeans used that model, they used the word 'Paraya' (*Paṛaiyaṉ*, 'Pariah') to designate the entire 'fifth class.' By talking of five *varṇas* or classes, the Europeans implied that there was no distinction between *ūr* and *cēri,* between 'Tamilians' and 'aliens'; and that there is only a single Malabarian society divided hierarchically into five classes. Moreover, by lumping the 'right hand' and 'left hand' groupings of castes together as collective 'untouchables', the Europeans obscured the significant caste distinctions those people made among themselves. Furthermore, the Europeans neglected to include themselves (and the 'Portuguese') in the classification.

That last omission suggested to Sastri that the 'white' Europeans saw themselves as a single civilization over against the 'dark' Malabarians, which constituted another single civilization rather than a society composed of differing peoples from the 'civilized' *ūr* and the 'alien' *cēri.* Not only that, in his eyes European 'white men' were presenting themselves as the group that set the norm for being Christian:

> In Pages 42 [sic] you say that no Brahmins, Chatria, Vasias, Sudras, and Parayers, be partakers of this Table but Christians. In answer to this, I say. . . . Although there are in India more than 100 Castes according to the professions, Politeness, various posture, and habits of the people yet the ancestors have divided them into 4 Classes, as Brahma, Chatria, Vasia, and Sudra, without adding Paraya as a 5th Class. Why did you divide it into 5 Classes pointing out the Paraya Caste? If they must be mentioned should you not also mention Pallas and shoemakers whom Parayers abhor as 6th and 7th Castes? . . . Why did you leave out in this account the European in your Caste? Is this not partiality? . . . You say that Christians only should come to this Table, who are they, are they the white men?

He then asked whether 'the disposition of neglecting the neighbour or making a difference' is not also found among Europeans, or whether good Christians are only in Europe, or only among 'Valangamattar who utterly hate Pallers, Shoemakers and smiths rejecting them as of the left hand.'

Sastri then pointed to two books that set for him the standard of a 'good Christian': 'One Thing Needful' *(Oṉṟukuṟaiyatu)* and 'The Chapter on Wisdom' *(Jñaṉappaṭalam)*. Daniel Pillai in Tranquebar had translated them from German. Daniel Pillai, Sastri said, had been 'Prime Minister to the Court of Justice of the Danish King at Tranquebar.' John Murdoch later identified him as the 'Translator to the Danish Government' who devoted one hour a day for 40 years to translating Christian books. Those published included *The Golden Treasury (Parāparaṉuṭaiyapiḷḷaikaḷiṉ Āparaṇappeṭṭi)* by Carl Heinrich von Bogatzky, published in Vepery in 1800, and consisting of texts, hymns, and prayers for every day in the year (Barnett and Pope: 67); *Meditations on the Christian Character (Can Mārkka Viḷakkam),* published in Tranquebar in 1810; *Meditations on the Passion of Jesus Christ (Ēcunātar Pāṭupaṭṭa Carittirat Tiyāṉam)* by J. F. Starke, published in Madras in 1835; *Hours of Spiritual Refreshment (Jñāṉamucippāṟu Nēram)* by Muller, published in Madras in 1841; and *Spiritual Doctrine (Jñāna Upatēca Viḷakkam)* by C. Schade, published in Madras in 1853 (Murdoch: 11-12). Obviously, Pietism was still alive in Tranquebar and Tanjore.

Sastri insisted that Protestants observed caste among themselves not because of pride or arrogance, but because of custom and necessity. 'We likewise know that every one is the descendant of Adam, and the pride of Caste is nothing. . . .' Yet, he noted, most of the 6,000 villages of the Tanjore kingdom did not contain a single Christian house. 'We know the whole kingdom is filled with heathenism, and civil distinction', he said, yet if those civil distinctions were not observed, as the new missionaries insisted, people would be turned away from coming to Christ.

Those ancient civil distinctions, he continued, correspond to differences in styles of living. Customarily, Velalans do not eat with Paraiyans because Velalans abhor the flesh of kine, which Paraiyans eat, just as Europeans do eat with Paraiyans because they enjoy beef, and eating it is their custom:

> We the natives of this country, though we eat sheep yet we would not eat the flesh of cows. Hence do we love the sheep and hate the cows? Nay, what is it unless we do so by usage: the flesh of kine will not agree with every pious man, this is not by arrogance but because it is not customary from ancient time. We do not like to eat with Parayers indiscriminately, it occasions an aversion. . . . Can you say it is either from piety or affection that you eat with Parayers while you eat the flesh of kine because you like it and it is agreed with the customs of your country [?]. Nay, we would neither do it so for want of piety nor that we hate them, but that we feel loathsome to eat with Parayers in consequence of our abhorring the flesh of kine which is not agreeable to the custom of our country.

Likewise, he continued, Paraiyans (of the 'right hand') and Pallans (of the 'left hand') do not interdine with each other, but not because of 'the uncleanness which exists among them or by the Pride of Caste.' They avoided interdining, Sastri implied, because of the ancient functional division of the single 'social body' that we discussed earlier, a body holding a plow held in its right hand and scales in its left. The two groupings of high-status and low-status castes united in that body straddled the regional boundaries of Malabar. Even though an unresolvable dispute about the status of the two 'hands' in relation to each other persisted, it was not, Sastri argued, a dispute between the 'pure' and 'impure.' All caste divisions, he said, are civil distinctions characteristic of the country. They are not essentially contrary to the Christian message, and if converts are sought, they should not be opposed.

Indeed, 'The Augsburg Confession' of 1530, to which Ziegenbalg and his German Lutheran missionary heirs subscribed, supported Sastri:

> It is taught among us that all government in the world and all established rule and laws were instituted and ordained by God for the sake of good order, and that Christians may without sin occupy civil offices or serve as princes and judges, render decisions and pass sentence according to impe-

> rial and other existing laws, punish evildoers with the sword, engage in just wars, serve as soldiers, buy and sell, take required oaths, possess property, be married, etc. . . . Actually, true perfection consists alone of proper fear of God and real faith in God, for the Gospel does not teach an outward and temporal but an inward and eternal mode of existence and righteousness of the heart. . . . Accordingly Christians are obliged to be subject to civil authority and obey its commands and laws in all that can be done without sin. But when commands of the civil authority cannot be obeyed without sin, we must obey God rather than men (Acts 5:29).

At issue, of course, was the question of which commands of Malabarian civil authority constituted sin for the Christian. Was caste observance enforced by the king of Tanjore not God's will? If not, why not?

Even if the prohibition on killing and eating cattle and the observance of purity and pollution distinctions among castes had been based on Veda, the Malabarian Evangelicals did not understand them as part of the sacred social order of Dharma. They viewed them instead as secular practices in the category of social custom *(vaḻakkam)*. Still, social custom was to some degree sacred to them, because it was the fabric that held Tamil society together, and God, they believed as Lutherans, is the one who ordains the good order of any society.

In his discussion of the rites of the Lord's Supper as newly revised by the missionaries, Sastri attacked their interpretation of the admonition to be 'reconciled to your brother' before eating the bread and drinking the wine. The missionaries said that it meant that Velalans should unite with their servants of the 'right hand' and eat with them 'without arrogance and shame.' Sastri disagreed. How, he asked, can you invite anyone to dinner and then tell him to come without arrogance without insulting him? Will he not inevitably feel abused? How is that sort of invitation consistent with 'the order of the Lord who said unto the Servant, go out unto the highways and hedges and compel them to come in that my house may be filled [?] (Luke 14.23).' Is the uniting of Velalan with Paraiyan and their eating together, he wondered rhetorically, 'the principal doctrine of Christianity?' Is the Kingdom of God food and drink?

'The Foolishness of Amending Caste'

The final selection, the preface to 'The Foolishness of Amending Caste', discusses a specific event that revealed an 1828 dispute among the Velalan Protestants themselves. It was written collectively by Velalans in Tanjore.

They began by outlining their theology by means of three New Testament verses in the Authorized Version, or King James Version, of about 1613. Firstly, 'Destroy not him with thy meat, for whom Christ died' (Romans 14:15). Secondly, 'Give none offence neither to the Jews, nor to the gentiles, nor to the Church of God' (1 Corinthians 10:32). And thirdly, 'Let every man abide in the same calling wherein he was called' (1 Corinthians 7:20). Since we know that the Evangelical Velalans knew the Christian Bible thoroughly, we may pause briefly to consider the verses they had chosen, as they appear in their respective textual contexts, using this time the Revised Standard Version of 1952.

The first verse (Romans 14:15) sets forth the way the Velalans saw the situation in which they found themselves. It comes from the apostle Paul's letter to a Christian community in Rome in the middle of the first century. The community consisted of observant Jews and of non-Jews of various sorts. According to Paul, they were living at an eschatological time when 'the night is far gone, the day is at hand' (13:12).

Unwittingly, Paul had used a metaphor familiar to Indian tradition: they were in the predawn 'hour of Brahma' *(brahmamuhūrta),* the period when devotees arise to prepare themselves for sunrise and the new day through meditation, prayer, and purification. Paul and the Roman Christians, however, believed that the 'sunrise' would be the return of Christ, and that the new 'day' would be the resurrection of the dead, the judgment by God of all, and the establishment of God's Kingdom in a transformed world.

Nevertheless, as the first-century Roman community was awaiting the imminent return of Christ, a dispute had arisen about life in the meantime: Should all believers observe the same practices; for example, should they all eat the same food and observe the same calendar? The question was one that inevitably would arise between Christian Jews and Christian gentiles, just as it later did between Christian Velalans on the one hand and Christian Europeans and Valangamattar on the other.

Those Christians who were Jews and observed the Torah's laws of purity in food and other matters, and kept the commandments regarding Sabbath and festivals, would appear to be socially exclusive of the gentiles. Observant Christian Jews would not, for example, share a meal of meat that had not been slaughtered as Torah prescribed, nor one that mixed milk products with meat products. They would, however, share a completely vegetarian meal inclusive of milk. Christian gentiles, however, may not have considered a vegetarian meal properly festive for a communal banquet. Similarly, the Christian Jews, who observed the Sabbath as 'holy' and set it apart from other days, would likewise separate themselves from Christian gentiles, for whom Sabbath observance seemed unnecessary. For any people who believed that they had not converted to Torah observance but to Christ, Torah observance was not binding.

Though he was a Jew, Paul's faith was so 'strong' that he believed the Torah's laws regarding food were no longer binding for Christian believers, including Jews. Yet he also did not believe that all believers should follow the same practices. Those 'weak in faith' who will not eat meat, he said, are to be welcomed, even if they eat only vegetables; and they in turn are not to pass judgment on the 'strong in faith' who do eat meat. After all, he queried, 'Who are you to pass judgment on the servant of another? It is before his own master that he stands or falls' (14:4).

Paul made the same point about the calendar. Some believers regarded certain days as 'holy' and other days as not, while other believers regarded all days as the same. He who observes 'holy' days or abstains from observing them, he said, does so 'in honor of the Lord and gives thanks to God' (14:6). Since every believer belongs to the Lord and will stand before God's judgment seat, why pass judgment on each other now (14:7-12)?

Paul believed nothing to be unclean; but he also believed that if someone else thought a food unclean, it was unclean for that person. He would not insist that anyone eat what he or she regarded as unclean; moreover, he himself would not eat something anyone regarded as unclean in his or her presence:

> If your brother is being injured by what you eat, you are no longer walking in love. Do not let what you eat cause the ruin of one for whom Christ died. So do not let what is good to you be spoken of as evil. For the kingdom of God does not mean food and drink but righteousness and peace and joy in the Holy Spirit; he who thus serves Christ is acceptable to God and approved by men. (14:15-18)

In other words, the Kingdom of God is not food and drink.

The second verse that the Tanjore Velalans cited in 'The Foolishness of Amending Caste' made the same point again, but with a different emphasis (1 Corinthians 10:32). In a discussion that identified all believing Christians with the Israelites (10:1–11:1), who had been commanded to love God and their neighbour, Paul focussed on what constitutes the good of the neighbour in the matter of eating. It is not what you eat, he said, but how what you eat affects your neighbor's conscience (10:23-30). Therefore, to fulfill the commandments to love God and the neighbor,

> . . . whether you eat or drink, or whatever you do, do all to the glory of God. Give no offense to Jews or to Greeks or to the church of God, just as I try to please all men in everything I do, not seeking my own advantage, but that of many, that they may be saved. Be imitators of me, as I am of Christ. (10:31–11:1).

The third verse they cited (1 Corinthians 7:20) brought in the matter of circumcision and of slaves. In Corinth, the Christians awaiting for 'daybreak' had to figure out in the meantime how to live in the 'dark.' Paul's answer was basically for them to continue in the social role they were playing at the time they had converted: '. . . let every one lead the life which the Lord has assigned to him, and in which God has called him. This is my rule in all the churches' (7:17). Christian male Jews should not try to hide their identity as Jews by disguising their circumcision through an operation practiced within Hellenistic culture. At the same time Christian male gentiles should not seek circumcision. Circumcision was irrelevant among believers because the covenant it signified had been replaced by a new one; and since it was irrelevant, 'Every one should remain in the state in which he was called' (7:20). Among the Malabarians, of course, circumcision was not an issue for any Christian, European or Indian, though it was for Muslims. Yet Paul's teaching made the relevant point vividly: while waiting in the 'dark' for 'sunrise', nothing that identified your 'ethnicity' had to be changed to be a Christian.

More immediately relevant, however, was the matter of slavery. In Corinth, some of the Christians had been slaves when they converted. Should they now be freed? Paul's answer was both no and yes: 'Were you a slave when called? Never mind. But if you can gain your freedom, avail yourself of the opportunity' (7:21). In other words, a Jew or a gentile converting as a Christian did not necessarily submit to a programmatic change in social practice as, for example, a gentile would when converting as a Jew. Changes would inevitably occur over time in the local context, however, as Christians sought to work out what 'slavery' and 'freedom' meant to them where they lived:

> For he who was called in the Lord as a slave is a freedman of the Lord. Likewise he who was free when called is a slave of Christ. You were bought with a price; do not become slaves of men. So, brethren, in whatever state each was called, there let him remain with God. (7:22-24)

We do not know how the Velalans and the Valangamattans in the Tanjore congregation differed in their application of that teaching to their respective positions. In Tranquebar in the early eighteenth century, some Christians had been slaves, but whether any in Tanjore in the early nineteenth century were is not known. Nevertheless, read literally, Paul's view did not require the abolition of caste observances within the congregation during the 'night' before the eschatological 'sunrise.' It would all depend on what 'love of neighbor' meant in that context, on how recognition of difference affected the conscience of one's neighbour.

The Velalan authors of 'Foolishness of Amending Caste' recognized their situation in Paul's letter, and specifically, it would appear, in the Christian Jews contending with the Christian gentiles. The Christian Jews represented the 'Malabarians', and the Christian gentiles represented the 'Junior Missionaries.' United in a single liturgical body, the two constituted a social mixture. People from differing societies in Europe worshiped with people of differing societies in India, and in their own lives they observed differing culinary customs and calendars.

Yet after 1800 years, the religious situation was significantly different from that of Paul's day. The establishment churches from Denmark, Germany, and Britain no longer lived as if the eschatological 'dawn' was imminent; much of their attention turned instead to the issues of institutional continuity and order. They were the leaders of 'Christendom' and assumed, in practice, that whenever the new 'day' would dawn, it would not be soon. The Tanjore Velalans, it appears, had returned in their thinking to the earlier 'predawn' expectation in Rome. They were living in the 'night', they believed, but the 'sun' of God's Word had broken into it dimly; in the Evangelical Church they were experiencing a 'taste' of the dawning Kingdom of God. That 'taste' was the 'taste' of love, which servants of the same master share even though they serve him in different ways as they await his arrival.

Anticipating a later discussion, we may understand the Velalan's 'aristocratic' self-perception by drawing upon Jesus' parable of the Kingdom of God as being like the wise and foolish maidens awaiting the bridegroom during the night (Matthew 25:1-13). If the returning, resurrected Christ is like a Velalan bridegroom 'chieftain' on his way to his wedding feast, the Velalan and Valangamattan Christians are like his servants and slaves waiting in the dark for his arrival, and for the wedding feast that will follow. But some waited in the dark wisely and others waited foolishly.

The 'Foolishness of Amending Caste' had been written in response to an issue raised by John Devasagayam Pillai. He was probably the grandson of the translator Daniel Pillai,[5] and at the time was the Native Superintendant of

5. Murdoch (11) said that Daniel Pillai was the 'grandfather of the late Rev. J. Devasagayam, Tinnevelly.'

Church Missionary Society schools in Tranquebar (Hough: 179). John Devasagayam Pillai had sent a letter in Tamil and English, dated September 18, 1828, to David Pillai, the prominent Tanjore Velalan whose daughter Anna's marriage we noted earlier. John Devasagayam Pillai wanted the letter to be made known to the entire Tanjore congregation because it stated his present views on the matter of caste observance among Protestants, which was 'that the distinctions of Caste originated from Idolatrous customs, and that thereby the Christians run in danger to lose the spiritual life and its growth. . . .'

He urged those Velalans who were holding positions in the Tanjore palace to act with courageous faith by giving up observing caste distinctions. If they did so, he wrote, they 'would neither meet with evil nor lose in their temporal concerns.' Yet, he said, if they did meet with evil or lose their positions, 'God would open another door.' Moreover, he said, abandoning caste distinctions would not hinder 'heathens to embrace Christianity.' He who willingly ate with 'Pallars and Parayers forsaking Caste' would be imitating the patriarch Abraham, who had obediently acted to sacrifice his son Isaac to God and then received him back.

John Devasagayam Pillai, it appears, had come to agree with a missionary in Tranquebar named G. Barenbruck. In the same year Devasagayam Pillai wrote his letter, Barenbruck published a Tamil work in Madras entitled 'Scripture Doctrines Defined and Explained' *(Tēva Vācaṉattiṉ Pōtaṅkaḷ)*, in which he used Scripture to argue against caste observance (Murdoch: 18). Moreover, Barenbruck had recently excommunicated a Velalan catechist on the grounds that he had refused the missionary's request that he dine with a 'pariah' assistant at the latter's house. The Tanjore Velalans recounted the incident this way:

> . . . the Rev. Mr. Barenbrook being displeased at Arulananden Catechist who served faithfully under him for 6 years and 6 years under Mr. Mead therefore 12 years, because then he charged him to go and eat with Devanasen the Valangamattoo assistant, who will prepare a banquet in his house, he shewed his unwillingness to it; he [Barenbruck] thrusted him [Arulanandan Catechist] away from the Lord's Table as one unregenerated and took from him the Mission accounts and treated him differently began [sic] to shew his aversion always to him.

In fear of 'great danger', they said, the Velalan catechist Arulanandan resigned his position and 'with grief and sorrow of mind' left Tranquebar with his wife and five children. Apparently, they went to Tanjore.

The Tanjore writers judged Barenbruck's behaviour in Tranquebar to be 'a cruelty and injustice which never has been witnessed in this country from the commencement of Christianity to this time.' Moreover, they criticized John Devasagayam Pillai because in his letter he not only had comforted himself with the statement from John 16:2, 'that whosoever killeth you will think that he doeth God service', but he also had taken no interest in Arulanandan Catechist's case. He even went so far as to argue that the catechist was the one at fault. According to them, John Devasagayam Pillai's view of the matter was this:

> Arulanandem Pilley resigned his situation and did so very rashly; he was not forced to eat with the low caste; but the Rev. Mr. Barenbrook, as it was his conscientious duty, laid before him several important texts of the scriptures, as he did to me and others, against the distinction of Caste prevailing in this country, and when he made his objections, he was given up and left to his own will.

Nevertheless, the 'Tanjore Evangelical Congregation' had formed their own view of the matter directly from Arulanandan Catechist as well as from the letter. The view they reported appears to have been that of the Velalans, for we have no record of how the Tanjore Valangamattans saw things.

The Velalans gave their view through four points. Firstly, they said, it was cruel to demean a man who had been catechist for 12 years by calling him a 'child' *(piḷḷai)* because he refused to eat in the house of a 'Parrian' *(Paṛaiyaṉ)*. Here *piḷḷai* as 'child' differs from the Velalan caste title 'Pillai.' Yet, as we noted above, Sastri himself had played on its meaning in his poetry. Indeed, Barenbruck himself may have played derisively with that meaning, accusing the Catechist of being 'childishly' true to his caste title, Pillai.

Secondly, they said, it is plain that Arulanandan Catechist was told to dine with a 'low caste man', which means that he was forced to, and 'to force a Vellalen to eat in the house of Parrian, is a great cruelty against religion and the customs of the country.' People of the *ūr* should not be forced to receive food from people of the *cēri.*

Thirdly, they said, Barenbruck's duty lies with instituting religion, not with uniting castes. For them, 'religion' was a matter of faith and inward experience, not of social organization.

Fourthly, 'because the poor Catechist was left and given up to his own will', they said he was in fact forced out.

The congregation, they continued, was grieved to see that John Devasagayam Pillai had 'lost his spiritual eyes' through the 'Junior Missionary.' By arguing that 'the strength of caste is in the meal', he was like Samson, 'who declared to Delilah that his strength was in his hair and lost his two eyes' (Judges 16:16-17). Spiritual blindness, they suggested, lies in identifying the power of God with material forms.

John Devasagayam Pillai was over 40 years old, they said, 'and has observed hitherto the distinction of Caste, without considering in the least that all the learning he acquired, the doctrine he preached, and the examples he shewed hitherto would become sin. . . .' Yet his indifference to 'mingling with the lower castes' (in an unknown event) on the previous nineteenth of August had 'put an hindrance to so many people around him and brought a great shame upon Christianity. . . .' The metaphorical gaze of non-Christians, it seems, was so intense in Tanjore that the Velalan Evangelicals felt shamed when one of their own behaved in public contrary to 'the customs of the country.'

Moreover, they continued, John Devasagayam Pillai had been overcome 'by passages of a book which he never read . . .'; presumably, they meant Barenbruck's 'Scripture Doctrines Defined and Explained.' All of that, the congregation thought, was like 'the guiles of the tempter, by which our first Parents fell into sin.' In other words, the 'Junior Missionary' Barenbruck was the snake in Eden.

The Tanjore congregation's response in Tamil to John Devasagayam Pillai was the 'long memorandum' entitled 'Foolishness of Amending Caste.' They organized it by drawing forth 12 points from his letter and responding to each one. They summarized their responses in the English preface, and that summary will now be the focus of our attention.

The 'foolishness' of the title referred to Jesus' parable in Matthew 25:1-13 about the Kingdom of Heaven, comparing it to ten virgins, or maidens, who took their lamps to greet a bridegroom. Five of them foolishly took no oil with them. That lack of foresight meant that when night came, they had to leave the others in order to buy oil. In the middle of the night, while they were gone, the bridegroom arrived, the feast began, and the door was shut. When they finally returned, they were left outside in the dark. By not thinking ahead, they had excluded themselves from the wedding feast.

John Devasagayam Pillai's ideas about giving up caste observance, the writers implied, were similarly foolish and would lead to similar consequences. He had not calculated carefully the realistic consequences of all Protestants behaving as if they were a single caste *(jāti)*, and a 'defiled' one at that. Inevitably, social cohesion among believers would weaken as internal and external disputes grew stronger, and in the end no one would attend the 'wedding feast.' Among the Protestants, on the one hand, the 'pariahs' would be encouraged to think of their social position differently, as perhaps equal to that of the Velalan 'aristocrats.' They would then demand that their equal status be articulated during the rites of the Lord's Supper. The congregation would then fall apart, and Velalans would feel enormous pressure to forsake the church, leaving it largely confined to 'pariahs.' No one would feast, for love would have given way to jealousy, anger, and hatred.

On the other hand, non-Christians would view the Protestant disruption of caste customs as anarchical. Velalans freely mingling with 'pariah' castes implied elevation of status, which, in turn, implied a threat to the Dharma upon which their well-ordered cosmos and society depended. Non-Christians would then respond with violence; but, of course, their violence would not be directed at the 'aristocratic' Velalans because they had power and access to the royal court. Instead, it would be directed at the 'upstart' Protestant 'pariahs', who were relatively powerless. If an Evangelical Velalan truly loved the Evangelical 'pariah' with whom he worshiped, what was he to do?

The writers believed, it appears, that those who follow the orderly customs of the country will likewise keep the order of the Lord's Supper because, by doing so, they will preserve order in the world at large, and will one day feast in love with the bridegroom. Those who try to contravene custom will not. In their eyes the feast of God's Kingdom in this world does not depend either on caste observance or on its nonobservance, but it may take place in a wide variety of social systems and cultural contexts. Wherever caste observance has long been established as customary law, therefore, it should be maintained. The 'Augsburg Confession' had implied as much. Furthermore, they said that John Devasagayam Pillai was not only foolish but stupid. He was like the disciple of a stupid guru named Paramartha in popular Tamil fables, which the Jesuit Beschi had told in a book entitled 'The Story of the Guru Paramartha' *(Paramārtakuruviṉkatai).* Like Paramartha, Barenbruck was stupidly leading his stupid disciples in circles, going nowhere. The Velalan writers assumed that their English-reading audience would know Beschi's stories because an English translation of them had been published in London in 1822, translated by Benjamin Babington as *The Adventures of the Gooroo Paramartan* (Barnett and Pope: 54). Beschi, the Pietists' enemy a century earlier, was now their rhetorical support.

In their responses to the 12 points they had extracted from John Devasagayam Pillai's letter, the writers used the words 'Malabars', 'Tamil', and 'Tamilian' to means the Velalans and other occupants of the *ūr.* They may be summarized as follows:

> The customs and distinctions of caste are not 'heathenish' and they prevail not only in the higher (Velalan) caste, but also 'and particularly' in the

lower ('pariah') caste, both of which exist because of the will of God (citing Isaiah 54:16: Behold, I have created the smith who blows the fire of coals, and produces a weapon for its purpose. I have also created the ravager to destroy . . .).

The customs of caste are indispensable to the country, 'as otherwise no one would submit to or obey another.'

No one who gives up his caste can live in the world because, 'neither Native Princes nor the English Government and Gentlemen will accept him.'

Anyone who forsakes caste does an injustice to his relations and to himself, brings shame on Christianity, and puts a great obstacle in the way of 'the salvation of the souls of the gentiles.'

The piety of the 'foolish virgin' [as told by Jesus in Matthew 24:1-13], who pretends to renounce the customs of caste for the sake of Christ, is really like the stupidity of a disciple of Guru Paramartha [as told by Beschi] and only brings unnecessary persecution to the 'poor Christians.'

Preaching and insisting on people eating together at the same Table without regard to caste only creates hatred in the hearts of 'Malabars' and pride in the hearts of 'Pariars.'

The yearly innovations of the 'Junior Missionaries' are against religion and a 'heavy yoke' to the congregation.

They are not proper 'fishers of men' (citing Mark 1:17), because they 'entirely eradicate' the work of the 'ancient Missionaries' and quickly scatter the 'few Tamil Christians that were gathered at the peril of death, and will soon remain only with the Pariahs.'

Their doctrine of uniting castes will only create enmity among Christians 'similar to the enmity of the right and left hand caste from ancient time.'

When the 'amity and the familiarity which existed hitherto' is destroyed, the 'time of ruin' will come when they will 'devour each other.'

The missionaries are disobeying the order of Bishop Heber and the Parent Society in Europe 'not to occasion any disorders in this country.'

Their design is to use violence to make 'the Tamilian infamous.'

In conclusion, the writers observed that everything had taken place just as Vedanayagam Sastri had said it would in his 1824 'Dialogue on the Difference of Caste.' The efforts to amend the Fabricius translations by the 'Junior Missionaries' Rhenius and Haubroe had led them to try to change caste, 'with the hope of destroying the name of Tamilians under heaven by uniting the palloo Parrey [Pallan of the 'left hand' and Paraiyan of the 'right hand'] and every description of Caste. . . .' In 1825 the Tanjore congregation had protested the revision of Scripture with the 'Noise of New Correction', and now, they said, it was protesting the revision of society with the 'Foolishness of Amending Caste.'

Interestingly, the question of how to translate the Bible into Tamil had brought the issues of caste custom, seating in church, celebration of festivals, sensuality in worship, and music all together into one document. Because sacred words resonate on many levels of meaning and implication, we may conclude, the translation of sacred words in writing and speech must be done with great care. The cultural context of translation shapes the meanings and nuances of those sacred words, but the understanding of those words on the part of their readers and listeners in that context leads to interpretations. Filtered through the believers' interpretations, those sacred words then return to give that cultural context its shape. Protestants, unlike Muslims, must struggle wherever they find themselves to translate Scripture in relevant ways; and as long as they exist, that struggle will never end.

CHAPTER 10

Final Thoughts

In response to what they believed was an assault led by the 'Junior Missionaries', Vedanayagam Sastri had led other Evangelical Velalans in Tanjore to articulate a theology that was already more than a century old. How far it was shared by Evangelical non-Velalans is not known, although by the end of the century a Protestant Velalan further south did articulate it on behalf of Protestant Velalans and non-Velalans there (Hudson 1982: 244-59).

A Theology of Pluralism

We have seen evidence of that theology among Tamil-speaking Protestants beginning more than 225 years earlier. It was the theology of Protestant Brahmins in Jaffa that Baldaeus reported in 1672, some of whom identified their Brahmin heritage with the patriarch Abraham, just as Vedanayagam Sastri had identified the Brahmins with the Jews. They, too, had kept their caste and marriage customs, and had done so with a firm knowledge of doctrine and Scripture.

About a decade after the Tanjore document we just examined, the Catholic Velalan named Muttusami Pillei (Pillai) expressed a similar theology when he wrote about the life of the Jesuit Beschi in 1840. People may be unified by faith in the story expressed by the Lord's Supper, he said, and yet, at the same time, live separately according to caste divisions (Muttusami Pillei: 271). Fifty-four years later in Palaiyankottai, the Protestant Velalan E. Muttaiya Pillai expressed the same ideas (Muttaiya Piḷḷai; Hudson 1982).

How may we understand that theology? Let me offer an interpretation. The theology assumed a 'holistic' view of the person that did not view caste within the framework of the 'pagan' origin myth of the four ritual classes *(varṇa),* but according to the origin myth of the Bible. According to the 'pagan' myth (*Rig Veda* 10.90), the four classes derived from the four bodily parts of the primordial 'Man' *(puruṣa)* through a fire sacrifice that began directional space and chronological time. Those ritual classes were built into the structure of the universe in the same manner as were the sun, the moon, the seasons, and the varieties of animals. An echo of that myth is heard in Vedanayagam Sastri's metaphor of the elephant and the quail for the use of Velalans to 'catch' Velalans and 'pariahs' to 'catch' 'pariahs.' The metaphor suggests that castes *(jāti),* like biological species, are 'natural' social divisions built into the ever-changing universe.

According to the Bible, however, all people derive from the body of the primordial 'Man' *(Adam),* who was created after space and time as a distinct being within the structure of the universe (Genesis 1–13). Class and caste divisions were not built into the cosmos, but were constructed later by Adam's sons Cain and Seth, by the sons of the patriarch Noah, and by the descendents of those men as they spread over the earth. Yet linguistic and cultural diversity was caused by God and is good, for as the story of the tower of Babel says, God broke the human family into many different languages and spread them over the earth (Genesis 11:1-9). Consequently, as Muttusami Pillei asserted about Europe's class system and India's caste system, one was neither more nor less 'Christian' than the other:

> What prevails as rank among Europeans, may in a manner be compared with the caste of the natives. However, there is a difference between rank and caste; because if any European of high rank associates and eats with a low man of his nation, the former cannot be degraded into or become a man of low rank, as the Europeans have never had any distinction of caste, either before or after they embraced Christianity. The natives are differently situated. If a Brahmin or other high caste native associates and eats with a low caste man of his country, the Brahmin will be considered as having become a low caste man, there being separate sorts of foods for the different castes of this country. There is no such difference in eatable things among people of high and low rank in Europe. (Muttusami Pillei: 270-71)

Significantly, in his view, the European class or rank structure appeared to be more like an immutable fact of nature, as suggested by the *varṇas* of *Rig Veda* 10.90, than like the *jātis* of Malabarian practice, for the latter were variable. According to the European notion, it is precisely because one's class or rank identity is immutable that one may eat freely with anyone. According to the

Malabarian notion, however, the very mutability of caste *(jāti)* prevents one from eating freely with others. How may we understand that difference?

One reason for the difference lay in differing cosmologies. According to the Christian view that had shaped Europe, God created the world and placed humans in it; after the Flood God promised never again to destroy it because of human evil (Genesis 6–8). The survival of the natural world was no longer linked to human morality. In contrast, according to the view articulated by the story of the primordial 'Man' (*Rig Veda* 10.90), it is because the four ritual classes of humans *(varṇa)* are part of the universe's architecture — itself always in flux, but in an orderly manner — that human behavior has a direct impact on the cosmos. Human evil will bring drought, famine, and social chaos; human good will bring regular rains, prosperity, and social harmony.

Another reason for the difference lay in differing concepts of person, and the Malabarian concept appears to have shaped the thinking of the Christians.[1] Briefly stated, to be oneself fully in the Malabarian notion is to be in and of a particular family, which is in and of a particular caste *(jāti, kulam)*, which in turn is in and of a particular place from which one's food comes. One's body — including the mind *(manas)* — is made of the food grown in a particular place; that food nourishes and shapes one's material nature *(taṉmai)*. That nature is shared by one's family and caste, whose members eat the same food. Materially, which is to say mentally and socially, one is what one eats. What one eats and whom one eats it with create one's nature, a nature that is vulnerable because, as a form of matter, it is constantly subject to change. Time *(kāla)* changes every created thing.

One's changeable nature is therefore 'holistic' because one's own physical nature extends into the bodies of those in the family and in the caste with whom one shares food. As is apparently inevitable (at least so far in history), a 'holistic' society articulates the status and nature of individuals, families, and castes hierarchically. Because status and nature are dependent on changeable bodies subject to time, they must be carefully protected. The principal means of protecting them among the Malabarians was by protecting one's own food, and the food of those who extend one's physical self. John Devasagayam Pillai's assertion that 'the strength of caste is in the meal' apparently was correct.

During the formal meal, the defining element for status in the act of eating is *eccil* or saliva, which, as we discussed earlier, defines eaten food as 'leftover' (Pfaffenberger: chap. 5). Anyone who eats another's 'leftovers' has by that act defined him or herself as inferior in status to the other. As the

1. For explorations of Tamil concepts of personhood, see Hudson 1989; Daniel; Trawick; and Dumont 1970.

nineteenth-century British missionary G. U. Pope reported to the Tranquebar missionaries:

> I have heard the Cup of the Lord — the communion of His sacred blood — denounced as Echil by a communicant because one of the lower caste had drunk of it before! Many caste Christians would not hesitate thus to speak. Such persons we should certainly exclude. (Kuriakose: 151-52)[2]

By 'caste Christians' Pope meant mostly Velalans, that is, those who belonged to one of the four *varṇas* of the *ūr.* It was that defining significance of *eccil* which had caused Evangelicals in late eighteenth-century Tranquebar to desire two cups in the Lord's Supper, and to be concerned about who drank from a single cup first. It was *eccil* that made the new missionary demand for intercaste dining threatening in nineteenth-century Tanjore.

A specific incident made the cultural issues clearer. On the rainy morning of January 27, 1835, Daniel Wilson, the fifth Bishop of Calcutta, performed an Anglican service of Confirmation and Holy Communion in Madras Presidency. That evening he recorded the event. Wilson first noted the mixture of Europeans and Tamils at the altar:

> Forty-eight candidates [for Confirmation]. There were 149 communicants [in the Lord's Supper], the chief civil and military personages kneeling at the altar with Soodras and Pariahs without distinction.

By 'Soodras' he no doubt had in mind Velalans and their Telugu equivalents. Then he described a scene reminiscent of Ziegenbalg and Pluetschau's tiny multilingual Sunday services 129 years earlier in Tranquebar:

> The congregation consisted of upwards of 1000 persons, of whom at least 300 were heathen, crowding outside every door and window as far as the eye could see. Seventy were European gentry, the rest were native nominal Christians from twenty villages around.
>
> The service lasted nearly four hours. I pronounced the Confirmation prayer, the Sentences on delivering the elements, and the Benediction, in Tamil.

2. From G. U. Pope, 'A Letter to the Tranquebar Missionaries regarding "Their Position, Their Proceedings, and their Doctrine"', pp. 9-11. I have omitted what appears to be the editor's parenthetical additions to the quote: '. . . denounced as Echil (in Tamil means filthy leavings) . . .', and '. . . (so called) caste Christians. . . .'

The remaining portions of the long service, presumably, were in English. The Bishop noted that he then made a directive that was obvious to him, but to us reveals how culturally restricted the concept of the 'natural' is:

> I told the congregation that I aimed at no distinction of civil ranks; that the Europeans would naturally approach the altar first; that the respectable and educated natives, Soodras and Pariahs, would naturally come next; that servants and persons of the humblest stations would follow; but that there was to be no inseparable barrier, no heathen dread of defilement, only the natural gradations of society which prevailed in Christian churches at home.

That 'natural' ranking in the order in which people would receive the bread and wine was, as he said, the 'natural gradations of society which prevailed in Christian churches at home.' But in a Protestant church in Madras Presidency along the Coromandel Coast, why were the social gradations 'natural' to Europe to be the standard? Why not the 'natural gradations' of the Malabarians? The answer, of course, is that the church belonged to 'The Church of England', whose head was the King of England, a colonizing church whose own conclusions, worked out over centuries, about the practical meaning of 'love your neighbour' and 'the body of Christ' appeared to the British rulers to be as natural as the sun and moon.

Yet, on this liturgical occasion within a sacred arena in 'Malabar', where the ranking was European, the British rulers 'mixed and mingled' things graciously:

> However, the English gentry voluntarily mixed themselves, on purpose to show the natives there were no inseparable divisions in Christianity, but all were one body. Positively, a Pariah kneeled between the Collector and his lady, at the lady's request. Out of five hundred, ten or twelve only left the church, and would not submit to my demands. Such is God's goodness! (Kuriakose: 121)[3]

Let us look at that scene more closely. The Collector was the British agent in charge of collecting taxes for the Government and responsible for civil order in his District. His wife graciously inviting a 'pariah' to kneel between herself and her husband to receive the body and blood of Christ at the holy altar is indeed a striking reversal of the 'natural' order, not only of En-

3. I have omitted what appears to be the editor's parenthetical explanation of the office of the Collector: 'the chief personage of the station.'

gland but also of Malabar. It was a symbolic gesture in a symbolic feast that pointed to a Kingdom not yet come, but briefly anticipated through a symbolic act of 'love.' Yet it is doubtful that any of the people who gathered there, whether British or Malabarian, or Protestant, Catholic, Muslim, Saiva, or Vaishnava, thought that her behaviour in the liturgy would produce any changes whatsoever in the 'natural' social order of the Collector's District, no matter how the concept of 'natural' was understood.

Let us return to Vedanayagam Sastri's discussion of what castes eat. He suggested that in Malabar what one ate and with whom one ate it signified for oneself and for others who, in traditional terms, was truly the 'Son of Goddess Earth.' In 'pagan' practice, the Velalans who ate goats and sheep, or ate no meat at all, did not in any case eat beef. The cow signified their 'mother', the earth that feeds everyone; and the bull signified their 'father', the Dharma that protects her. Those who ate beef were not 'Sons of Goddess Earth' fathered by Dharma, but alien embodiments of sin and disorder who consumed their symbolic parents.

In their thinking, however, there is part of one's identity distinct from ever-changing matter. It is the 'spirit' or 'soul' *(uyir)*, which experiences 'love' *(anpu)*. *Uyir* is the Tamil equivalent to the Sanskrit concept of *prāṇa* or 'breath', which participates in the pure consciousness *(cit)* of the Self *(ātman)* as defined in the *Upaniṣads* of the Veda. Margaret Trawick's discussion of contemporary ideas about *anpu* in a Tamil family, which we will follow below, sheds light on those eighteenth- and nineteenth-century issues of soul and love (Trawick: chap. 3).

Understood traditionally, the *uyir* or soul, like the *ātman*, is nonmaterial consciousness. It emerges within the fetal gross body *(sthūla śarīra)* while it gestates in the womb, taking up residence in the 'heart.' It possesses a subtle material body *(sūkṣma śarīra)*, and throughout one's lifetime it is the center and source of consciousness. A person sleeps, with the gross body *(sthūla śarīra)* at rest, because the *uyir* has withdrawn its consciousness from the sense organs, including the mind *(manas)*. The *uyir* in its subtle body dwells within the gross body and experiences dreams. A person awakens because the *uyir*'s consciousness enters into the sense organs of the gross body to experience the world, most importantly by means of the mind and the eyes.

As Trawick explained, during one's lifetime one's own *uyir* or soul may 'mix' with the *uyir* of others, especially through the eyes. Such mixing is one of the aspects of *anpu* or love. When arranging marriages, therefore, a decision can be made only after the boy has seen the girl and each has been 'seized' by the other through the eyes. The union of two souls embodied as differently as a god and a human may also occur through the exchange of glances or gazes. Trawick discussed the famous story of Kannappan, the 'naishada' or 'pariah' devotee of Siva who saw Siva only after he had literally dug out one of his eyes and put it on Siva's lingam body. She then interpreted the story tellingly: 'In order for you to understand my heart, you must see through my eyes. In order for me to understand your heart, I must see through yours' (Trawick: 116). That describes the relation between a human and a god, but also the relations between a 'pariah' and a Velalan, or between a Malabarian and a European.

Love, as *anpu,* is tender, gentle, and slow; the loving heart is soft, and feelings of others move it. Yet, *anpu* grows in hiding, and sometimes its powers must be contained: in public the husband and wife must conceal their powerful sexual love, so they walk apart and avoid using each other's names; and the mother must protect her beloved child by not gazing on it. Love or attachment between people grows slowly through what Trawick called 'habituation' *(paḻakkam* or *paṛakkam).* Habituation develops from exposure to, and absorption of, certain things so deeply that they become one's own personality. In her informants' view of habituation, Trawick said:

> There was no point in trying to create a better way of life for others because people liked and wanted whatever it was they were used to having. . . . What you looked like and what you did showed to others what your *paṛakkam* was, and hence, what you were. (Trawick: 98)

When shared with another person, habituation makes that person part of oneself, as Trawick observed:

> This was why it was so important to avoid going near bad or untouchable people, it was important not even to talk to them, at least not too much or in too friendly a way — because they might become *paṛakkam.* And then, as the six-year-old Umapathi had told me, "You would become like them." (Trawick: 99)

The powerful bond of *anpu* that habituation builds is gentle and tender, but it is also cruel and forceful. Since habituation is hard to overcome, Trawick noted, 'it was sometimes deemed necessary to violently force people to do what was in their own best interests. When times or situations changed, people had to change also' (Trawick: 100). Ripening as a person can be painful. Yet, even if *anpu* is painful or disputatious, it requires interaction: 'The true sign of love's absence might be the absence of any interaction at all. . . . What *anpu* never meant was extrication of oneself from others or from the processes of life' (Trawick: 101, 105). Moreover, in the presence of love, conventional purity becomes irrelevant, at least in the context of family, where even *eccil* may convey *anpu:*

> ... the defiance of rules of purity conveyed a message of union and equality and was a way of teaching children and onlookers where love was ... *eccil* shared in love would not cause disease but would cure it. People who love each other will eat from each other's plates or leaves without thought of sickness. (Trawick: 105-6)

Love also reverses hierarchy, but without erasing it; it encourages poverty and simplicity, the humility of servitude, and — in the family at least — the mingling and mixing of boundaries into a single whole. People belonging to such a whole, for example, speak in Tamil not of 'my house' but of 'our house', even if the person addressed is not part of the family.

How do Margaret Trawick's observations of a high-status Tamil family in the late twentieth century apply to the Evangelical Malabarians of Tranquebar and Tanjore? Here are some thoughts. Trawick discussed a family, but we have been discussing a congregation. The congregation gathered together as 'God's people' and shared a common sacrament that was ritually a festive banquet, more like a wedding feast than like a supper in the kitchen. Consisting of discrete social groups identified as lineages, the congregation was more a 'village' *(ūr)* gathered for a festival than a family or lineage *(kulam)* gathered for a meal. Within that festively gathered 'village', people retained their finely graded social distinctions through their seating and eating, but shared the effort to create *anpu* among themselves through a common habituation generated by frequent and regular group worship. Yet that did not mean they wanted to create a common habituation that would take the place of their differing ones.

People might pray together but not eat together, and yet love one another. Interestingly, that traditional Malabarian concept resembles a modern Jewish concept: as 'God's people', many Jews differ according to their observance of ritual purity in matters of food. Members of the same synagogue may pray together in the morning, but in the afternoon may eat separately. Loving friendships may exist without differences in ritual observance disappearing. One feature of such a love is the effort to see into the 'hearts' of others and enable them to articulate their respective 'habituations' with dignity.

According to the metaphor of a 'people', one might argue, differing habituations should be sustained in order for 'God's people' to function as such. In a manner resembling *Rig Veda* 10.90, Paul had said that 'God's people' is like Christ's body, composed of many parts with differing functions that must be kept distinct, yet permeated by the same Spirit. And it is capable of love (1 Corinthians 12–13). Though seemingly harsh and cruel, the insistence that differing 'habituations' within a single congregation be maintained even if some may want to change them can be understood as an expression of love, as an affirmation of the dignity of the other's identity along with one's own.

Such thinking was not alien to the eighteenth-century Pietist missionaries, who recognized that the human world is permanently 'fallen', but it appears to have been alien to the 'Junior Missionaries' of the nineteenth century. The latter apparently wanted to shift from the metaphor of 'village' to the metaphor of 'family' to explain a Christian congregation, and a 'Calvinist' one at that. Instead of nurturing *anpu* by sanctifying caste habituation within the gathered congregation, as is done in a Tamil village festival, they sought the mingling and mixing *anpu* of a family meal. The 'father', however, was from Europe and operated within the Calvinist 'lineaments of the modern world', as E. G. Leonard described the 'Calvinist man.' The Calvinist possessed moral rectitude, a sense of vocation, a capacity for social organization, and 'a faith which, nourished on the Old Testament rather than on the New, was more concerned with the grandeur of God than with Christian love' (Prestwich: 9). Also, by means of the church and society, the 'Calvinist man' sought to create, in some sense, the 'Kingdom of God on earth.'

Given their vision of social reform, the 'Junior Missionaries' may not have understood how revolutionary the Evangelicals already were within Malabarian society. After all, if Evangelical Malabarians believed that their personhood was permeable and that social mixing over time could cause them to share the same 'habituation' as others and become like them, they had already broken new religious ground. By coming together repeatedly in the sacred arena, both 'low'- and 'high'-caste people endangered the 'habituation' they had inherited from their ancestors and were duty-bound to maintain, different as they were. Malabarian outsiders, whether Hindu or Muslim, would expect that all the people who gathered repeatedly throughout the week, year in and year out, sharing the same rituals and eating the same bread and wine, would 'naturally' develop the same 'habituation', which to them would be one of sin and disorder. No wonder it was enormously important to the Evangelical Velalans to maintain caste *paḷakkam,* for, in principle, the identity of their own personhood, and that of all those in the past and future who participated in it, was at stake.

Muttusami Pillei's nineteenth-century explanation of why Catholic and Protestant Malabarians did not see any inconsistency between caste observance and their Christian faith confirms Margaret Trawick's discussion. He said that Christians based their observance of caste on the distinction between the 'spiritual' and the 'physical', and on the spiritual interpretation of the command to love one's neighbour as oneself. Like Vedanayagam Sastri, he agreed with Dandapani Swami's statement that all souls *(uyir)* are to be considered as equal to one's own. And for him, equality of souls is the meaning of 'love' for one's neighbour. As he wrote:

> Although the natives do not associate, nor eat with the low caste people of their own country, yet they consider them as themselves with regard to spiritual concerns. The civil distinction of caste cannot therefore be contrary to the second great commandment of God ['You shall love your neighbour as yourself'], as it is not applicable to the associating, eating, etc., but refers to spiritual concerns alone. See chapter 14, verse 17 of St. Paul's Epistle to the Romans, 'For the kingdom of God is not meat and drink.'
>
> In opposition to this Scripture it is asserted that, a Brahmin, Chatriya, Vaisya, or Sudra cannot become a true Christian unless he associates and eats with them the food served on their table, which has been dressed by Pariahs. Surely this is not in conformity with the Scripture of St. Paul. See verse 15, chapter 14 of St. Paul to the Romans, 'But if thy brother be grieved with thy meat, now walkest thou not charitably. Destroy not him with thy meat, for whom Christ died.'

Muttusami Pillei then brought the issue to the heart of Malabarian culture and to the Christian concern for conversion:

> If we relinquish the distinction of caste we shall be unable to marry the daughters of our heathen relatives, and we should be unable to indulge the hope of our heathen relations becoming converts to Christianity. (Muttusami Pillei: 271)

To preserve one's nature outside the caste, one does not eat with those of lower-caste status; to preserve one's nature within the caste, one marries among kin from the region that is the source of one's nature, from one's 'own place' *(contavūr)*. Both family and conversion thus have a stake in whether a meal is shared or not.

In other words, according to Vedanayagam Sastri the Evangelical and Muttusami Pillei the Catholic, there is no such thing as a Christian 'in general.' In this world, being a Christian cannot be abstracted from being part of a specific group, caste, or ethnic, linguistic, or cultural context. When missionaries wrote in their 1825 explanation of the Lord's Supper that 'no Brahmins, Chatrias, Vasia, Sudras, and Parayers, be partakers of this Table but Christians', Sastri read that as arrogant nonsense. There were more than 100 castes in India, he said, including the Europeans. It was impossible to become 'without caste', because even 'pariahs' and Europeans existed in groups formed by birth *(jāti)* — and no single grouping was equivalent to 'Christian.' Christians existed in a variety of groups. What unified Christians was faith, hope, and love, not a single social entity.

Their point, it appears, was that whoever went to the Lord's Table went as a whole person; and one's wholeness extended into one's family, which extended into a caste, of which the Europeans formed one among many others. Each person's body of flesh, we might say, encoded an 'ethnic' social reality that was as much part of a person as internal spiritual elements of faith and attitude. Such a concept, however, the 'Junior Missionaries' found unpalatable.

Other approaches in India to the matter of interdining help us place that Christian Malabarian view in perspective. In the sixteenth-century Panjab, the third Sikh Guru, Amar Das (1552-74), had introduced compulsory inter-dining in a sacred context as a means to express Guru Nanak's teaching that caste status has no bearing on access to the divine Name and to liberation. As W. H. McLeod observed, interdining developed into the convention of the *laṅgār,* in which men and women of all castes 'sit in status-free lines *(paṅgāt)* and eat together when they assemble on the sacred ground of the *dharam-sala* or *gurduara (gurdwāra)*' (McLeod: 12-13). In 1699 the tenth Guru reinforced interdining for the Khalsa community through the rite of drinking *amrit* from a common bowl during initiation. Yet within the Panth or religion, McLeod observed,

> caste is still generally observed in terms of familial relationships and marriage alliances. . . . Whereas the doctrine of the Panth expressly condemns caste, a substantial majority of Sikhs observe certain significant features of caste in practice. (McLeod: 109-10)

Although the parallel to the eighteenth-century Evangelicals is close, they differed from the Sikhs in that they did articulate caste distinctions within the sacred arena of the Lord's Supper through seating and eating.

A closer parallel may be found among the Chaitanya Vaishnavas of sixteenth-century Bengal. According to Joseph T. O'Connell, all castes would share in the ritual eating of consecrated food *(prasādam),* yet did not intermarry or interdine among themselves freely. They quite consciously maintained a 'two-tiered stance toward social relationships', behaving in an egalitarian manner with each other in devotional ceremonial situations and according to Dharma distinctions with each other elsewhere. They did so, he reported, in order to maintain the social order and to avoid misunderstanding and controversy (O'Connell: 22-23). They applied Krishna's advice to Arjuna in the *Bhagavad-gītā* (3.21-26) to imitate God by acting for the welfare of the world, because God is the 'Man' of *Rig Veda* 10.90 who created distinctions through the primordial fire sacrifice. The Chaitanya Vaishnava practice and explanation resembled the Evangelical practice and explanation: caste observance was the custom of the country and countering it is not for the 'welfare of the world' because it brings conflict and hinders the spread of the faith.

Perhaps, after all, the early nineteenth-century theology of caste present among Malabarian Protestants and Catholics for over 225 years should be viewed as their transformation of the view that Saiva and Vaishnava acharyas had taught to rulers at the Tanjore court. In agamic thought, we recall, consecration *(dīkṣā)* purifies the body, qualifies one to follow a new discipline of life *(sādhanā)* for spiritual goals, and raises one's status; yet it does not remove caste identity nor the 'ethnic code' of the body. Initiated devotees gather together to worship in the 'iconic presence' *(sannidhi)* of God, yet they live together separately according to caste.

Since Pietists stressed the development of a sanctified inner life that would express itself ethically, we might also think that the Evangelicals would have agreed with Ramakrishna Paramahamsa, the renowned nineteenth-century Bengali devotee of the Goddess. He said:

> When a wound is perfectly healed, the slough falls off itself; but if the slough be taken off earlier, it bleeds. Similarly, when the perfection of knowledge is reached by a man, the distinctions of caste fall off from him, but it is wrong for the ignorant to break such distinctions. (*Sources:* 70)

But Ramakrishna's man of perfected knowledge was not an ideal for Pietists. They believed in 'justification by faith through grace', not in salvation through knowledge. They believed that they lived in an imperfect and sinful world — and that the caste system, like the class system of Europe, was 'fallen' and imperfect. Yet they hoped that God would nevertheless find them righteous — not, however, because they had attained a perfection of knowledge that enabled them to allow caste distinctions to 'slough off' naturally. Rather, they hoped they would be judged righteous because they trusted in Christ's atoning sacrifice and because, within a 'fallen' society, they as Protestant Malabarians had tried to live a life of love as they understood it.

The Intellectual Impact of Colonizing Europe

The changes wrought by the 'Junior Missionaries' illustrate the fact that once the Protestant cultus had been established in Malabar, its Malabarian members had to deal over the years with the changing intellectual and social climate of Protestant Europe. They were relatively free of one issue, however. Throughout the eighteenth century, the Halle center had refused to allow the Tranquebar mission to be co-opted by European nationalism, for it did not want to repeat the Dutch Reformed Church experience in Ceylon, where the Protestant mission was an arm of the state and suffered accordingly (Lehmann 1956b: 111-12).

Halle's missionaries were German, but with no German colony in India they were supported by the Danish and the English. Their mission began as Lutheran Evangelical and ended as Anglican Protestant. Since the mission was 'international', the narrower intellectual interests of specific Protestant nationalisms had little impact on the Malabarian Protestants, even while the political conflict between the British and the French reinforced the conflict between the Protestants and Catholics, with each regarding the other as heretics.

Nevertheless, that international Protestant mission operated within and through a developing colonial enterprise that had its own intellectual impact. At the beginning of the nineteenth century, Protestant Malabarians had to face Enlightenment thought and values that had developed in the eighteenth century, ideas and values that had developed in the context of the international economy that had created Tranquebar itself. Europe had produced among its intellectual elite the idea of autonomous personhood in which the human body encodes individual 'rights' and 'duties' rather than the collective 'rights' and 'duties' of the holistic family, class, or caste. It was that newly developing notion of personhood that had led the 'Junior Missionaries' in Tranquebar and Tanjore forcibly to change the mats in the church.

In contrast to the Pietist Lutheran belief that forcible means are not necessary because, over time, the preached gospel will change the believer's heart 'so the abuse itself would at last crumble and vanish',[4] in a Protestant theology influenced by Calvinist belief the notion developed that some enforcement was necessary. A person already saved by grace through faith has been saved for character, and the law of God as found in the Bible will be the guide for life, which he or she should strive to fulfill (Walker: 351). The pas-

4. From K. Graul, *Explanation concerning the Principles of the Leipzig Missionary Society, with regard to the Caste Question,* in Kuriakose: 150.

tor's task, accordingly, was to help build character, or, in Tamil terms, a specific mode of 'habituation' *(paḻakkam).*

As the British assumed rule over the Malabarians in Madras Presidency, the alliance of Protestantism with the Company and its militia inevitably produced the view that Protestantism was good for the British empire. James Hough, who was chaplain to the Company in Palaiyankottai from 1816 to 1820, wrote in 1824 that 'the Protestant Missionary is the truest friend to Government' because, while the Soldier, the Magistrate, the Commercial Agent, and the Collector labor for reward, 'the humble Missionary, without any pecuniary remuneration from the Government, devotes himself exclusively to the improvement of the Subjects of the Realm.' By teaching 'all ranks' their 'duty to God and Man', he binds the Natives, or at least those who are converts, not by constraint but 'by an identity of interest, and by the bond of Christian Love' (Hough: 272-73). That was a Company point of view. How far it was the viewpoint of the Protestant Malabarians is not clear, though, as we noted, Vedanayagam Sastri understood the cross and the cup on the bride's marriage pendant *(tāli)* to signify the divine power that enabled the Europeans to conquer India. Still, he may have thought, as did the Velalan E. Muthiah Pillai at the end of the century, that, like all things, British rule too would pass (Hudson 1982).

The efforts by the 'Junior Missionaries' to eradicate caste may be viewed as an attempt to make the Evangelical Malabarians more 'British' and bound more tightly to the Government by an 'identity of interest.' The Evangelicals' resistance to them may then be viewed as the effort to retain their own interest, to remain Malabarian, or even to remain particularly 'Tamilian' in the sense of the residents of the *ūr.* By affirming the older 'international' view of the Halle mission over against the narrower 'nationalism' of the British missions, the Malabarians were attempting to preserve their Evangelical culture from complete identification with the colonial Government.

Nevertheless, Evangelical missions had developed within colonial culture. It is therefore not surprising that at the same time that European merchants were viewing India as a place to gain wealth in moveable property, European missionaries were viewing it as a place to gain wealth in souls. Ziegenbalg, Pluetschau, and other eighteenth-century missionaries had some resemblance to individualist entrepreneurs, whose efforts to accumulate private capital conflicted at times with the interests of the established national Companies. Both capitalists and missionaries viewed India as an impersonal field for investment, yet, interestingly, neither had prepared for it carefully.

Just as Roelant Krappe had stumbled onto the Tanjore coast in 1618 and then turned it to the advantage of the Danish Company, so Ziegenbalg and

Pluetschau rather arbitrarily had gone to Tranquebar and turned it to the advantage of the Evangelical Church. Frederick IV of Denmark had first solicited the University of Halle for missionaries to India, and then changed his mind, and on their way to Copenhagen Ziegenbalg and Pluetschau thought they might be sent to Guyana or Africa. Only when they reached the Danish court did they learn that it would in fact be India. But, of course, they had no way to learn Tamil and could only study Danish on the ship.

As a merchant family might change its mind about a commercial venture, the Danish royal family had changed its mind about missions, switching investments quickly according to fluctuating variables. As far as the Malabarians were concerned, the motivations of the royal family appear to have been entirely impersonal — to its members, it appears, 'East Indians' were interchangeable with 'West Indians' and 'Africans.' If one wanted to 'save souls' in the abstract, it did not matter where the souls were, or whose they were, or what it was they were to be saved from. It took Ziegenbalg a lot of work finally to learn what 'heathen darkness' in 'Malabar' was exactly, and then the depth of its sophistication amazed him.

A similar seemingly commercialized 'universalism' drained of civilizational particularity, it appears, is what enabled Ziegenbalg to adjust to Malabarians rather than to Africans or to West Indians in his life's work. Apparently, he had assumed he could do 'business in souls' wherever he went. Ardently believing that the Wisdom of God acts throughout the world, he thought he could use reason to complete that Wisdom with the Christian story in any 'heathen' culture. His seriousness of purpose, and his enterprise, drove him to study Tamil as no Protestant European before him had, investing in the scholarly study of native beliefs and practices in order to use them rationally to destroy the authority of Dharma for those who were steeped in it. The direct results, among others, of his industriousness were the first translation of Luther's catechism and of the Christian Bible into any South Asian language — making the Bible the largest prose text in Tamil at that time — and the beginning of the Protestant printing press in India (Jeyeraj 1997b: 67; Beyreuther: 97). From those efforts we can trace the mid-nineteenth-century emergence of Arumuga Navalar's vigorous Saiva press, which served his Saiva renaissance, his antimissionary campaigns, and his development of modern Tamil prose.

In early eighteenth-century Malabar, people usually found the Protestant effort to save their souls unappealing. A vignette of C. F. Schwartz talking to a *devadāsi* stated it nicely:

> Schwartz one day met a Hindoo dancing-master, with his female pupil, and told them, that no unholy persons shall enter into the kingdom of heaven.

> 'Alas sir!' said the poor girl, 'in that case hardly any European will ever enter it'; and passed on.[5]

'Hardly any European' implied that some were admirable, and Ziegenbalg and Schwartz represented those Europeans of piety whom Malabarians could admire, something not commonly expected in the colonies. The elements of their Evangelical message — revelation, incarnation, faith, grace, sin, salvation — were not new to Malabarians, of course, although the way Ziegenbalg put them together around the figure of Jesus was. Yet in the early eighteenth century, the context for the Evangelical cultus was the European colony that, for different reasons, Saivas, Vaishnavas, and Muslims found outside the framework of true and admirable civilization.

Partly because of that fact, partly because of declining health, and partly because of continuing disagreements with mission headquarters in Europe, Ziegenbalg wrote in 1718,

> . . . since I know that my work often does not attain the looked-for goal, at times such great sorrow and sadness overtake me that I cannot comfort myself and I experience many sleepless nights. Much patience is required in order to labour tirelessly for souls and not be frightened away when the work seems useless.

As he worked in the shadow of the Danish fort and its state-supported corporate enterprise, his heavy personal investment in the relatively small mission was, he thought, on the verge of tallying more debit than credit. Seven months later, at age 36, Bartholomaeus Ziegenbalg died from an undetermined illness. Evangelical Malabarians, however, were alive and there to stay. Their task was to make their faith sensible to themselves in all their variety, and to do so in the changing contexts of Dharma and Shari'a, of Company culture, and of a cultus directed by missionaries from a Europe in flux.

5. From Hugh Pearson, *Memoirs of the Life and Correspondence of the Rev. Christian Schwartz,* 1:89-94, cited in Kuriakose: 65.

Glossary

***ācārya,* acharya** a teacher-priest whose conduct and knowledge are exemplary for his disciples; a teacher-priest who consecrates men and women into *mantras* to use in āgamic rites, and may perform rites on their behalf.

Āgama written and oral traditions of ritual and thought believed to have been revealed specifically for the present degenerate age (Kali Yuga) by Śiva, Nārāyaṇa, or the Goddess; Āgama complements Veda and extends rites and knowledge from Veda to Śūdras, women, and others by means of consecrations *(dīkṣā)* presided over by an acharya; Āgamic texts teach four disciplines based on *mantras* in an order of progressively demanding commitment: (1) *caryā* or disciplined behaviour, (2) *kriyā* or liturgical ceremony, (3) *yoga* or unified consciousness using visualization *(dhyāna),* and (4) *jñāna* or esoteric knowledge or insight.

ajñāna (akkiyāṇam) literally 'ignorance', especially of esoteric knowledge *(jñāna);* used by Ziegenbalg and others as equivalent to 'heathen' or 'heathenism', meaning people and religions that do not claim Abraham as ancestor, as do Jews, Christians, and Muslims.

Āḻvār 'masters', glossed as 'those drowning [in divine consciousness]'; the name for 12 saint devotees of Nārāyaṇa whose poems comprise the Śrī Vaishnava canon of the 'Tamil Veda.'

amrit (amṛita) 'non-death', a liquid symbolizing longevity and prosperity; used for initiation into the Sikh Khālsa community.

anpu love, affection.

antāti a form of Tamil poetry in which words or sounds at the end *(anta)* of one stanza are the beginning *(āti)* of the next stanza; when the words or sounds of the final stanza begin the first stanza, the poem forms a 'garland' *(mālai)* of sound.

asura a being of darkness, whose realm is in dark waters under earth; an opponent of the *devas.*

Aurangzeb Aurangzeb Alamgir, the 'Great Mughal', who ruled from Delhi in the north from 1658 to 1707; after rigorously subduing his rivals, he ruled over the greatest expanse of Mughal control; he levied tribute on Tanjore and Tiruchirapalli in 1691.

bali a sacrifice of animal life to a deity or demon.

Bali The king of *asuras,* who had taken over Indra's realm in heaven; at his horse sacrifice, Nārāyaṇa appeared as Dwarf (Vāmana), swelled up as Trivikrama, enslaved him, and now protects him in the underworld realm of Sutala.

bhakti devotion through body, mind, and speech focussed on the divine person by which the devotee 'participates' in the presence of the divine; the metaphor of slave to master dominates: the devotee as slave lives 'at the master's feet' (*aṭikaḷ* in Tamil); devotees, and by extension ascetics and saints, are therefore called *aṭikaḷ:* those who live at their master's feet.

braḥman the abstract power of being *(sat),* consciousness *(cit),* and joy *(ānanda)* understood differently by different religions that acknowledge the authority of Veda; its potency or power to emanate all things is called *śakti.*

Brāhmin a member of the ritual class *(varṇa)* of priests and scholars responsible for the knowledge and rites of Veda, commonly called Smārtha Brāhmins; also a priest who serves icons in temples according to Āgama, commonly called a *pūjāri.*

catur the term Vedanayagam Sastri used for his public exposition of Evangelical thought by means of his music and poetry.

Cera one of three ancient Tamil dynasties (Chola, Cera, Pandya), whose realm comprised the west coast.

cēri the settlement or village outside the boundaries of the *ūr* for castes *(jāti)* thought by people of the *ūr* to be alien, uncivilized, and ritually impure.

Chola one of three ancient Tamil dynasties (Chola, Cera, Pandya), whose capital was Uriayur on the Kaveri River and port was Puhar at the Kaveri River delta; the Cholas of the eleventh to fourteenth centuries built their capitals in the delta, notably at Tanjore.

dakṣiṇā a ritual gift to the performer of a ceremony at its completion, which transfers the intended result or 'fruit' *(phala)* of the rite from the performer to the sponsor.

dāna a ritual gift that purifies the giver, for example, the gift of food to a *sādhu,* or money to a temple.

dargah the tomb of a Sufi saint in Islam.

dāsa slave or servant.

dasyu 'aliens' in 'The Laws of Manu' (10.45); people outside the four ritual classes *(varṇa);* uncivilized people constituting 'the fifth' *(pañcamar)* ritual class.

deva a being of light whose realm is heaven above earth; an opponent of the *asuras.*

devadāsi 'the servant of a god'; a woman married to a local form of deity, who served him by dancing and singing during specific liturgies; her sexuality was regarded as highly auspicious and ritually useful; Europeans regarded *devadāsis* as prostitutes.

Devī the Goddess, who in narrative is the wife of Śiva (Umā, Pārvatī, etc.), the virgin sister of Nārāyaṇa (Durgā), or the wife of Nārāyaṇa (Śrī, Lakshmī, Bhūmī, etc.).

Dharma the 'architecture' of space, time, and all things, which governs their orderly change; the role assigned to each part of the moving universe; the teachings about the nature of the universe and human life, for example, morality, ethics, and metaphysics.

dīkṣā consecration into the use of *mantras* for worship; an initiation such as baptism.

Drāviḍa a Sanskrit term denoting the ancient Tamil-speaking dynasties in southern India (the Pandyas, Ceras, and Cholas); Drāviḍa kings were classified by the 'Laws of Manu' as Kshatriyas, who, through neglect of vedic sacrifices, had fallen to the Śūdra ritual class; they were Kshatriya natures in Śūdra bodies.

faqīr the ascetic disciple of a Sufi master in Islam; Europeans commonly used the term to denote ascetics in general, for example, *sādhus* and *sannyāsins.*

guru a general term for a venerated teacher of sacred knowledge, whose students are disciples.

Ḥanafi one of four Muslim schools that follow specific principles to derive law from the Qur'an and the sayings and deeds *(sunnah)* of the Prophet Muhammad.

Hiraṇyagarbha 'womb of gold'; a rite of royal rebirth prescribed by Āgama.

Indra king of the *devas* and other light beings who resides in heaven to the east.

Iṭaṅkaimattār 'those of the left hand'; the Pallans, Kammalans, and other castes *(jāti)* of the *cēri* who aligned with the mercantile Cettis and Cettiyar of the *ūr*, and rivaled the Valaṅkaimattār ('Valangamattar').

Īśvara literally 'the Ruler', a common title for Śiva.

jāti the group of birth; an endogamous caste consisting of various lineages who share a 'nature' *(taṉmai)* that produces a characteristic 'work' *(toḻil)* that is necessary to the good order of society; it may also denote a set of things sharing specific characteristics.

jñāna knowledge or insight, usually understood as esoteric; opposite to it is *a-jñāna,* 'non-knowledge.'

kaṭavūl God or a god, possibly meaning 'transcendent [*kaṭa*] being [*ūḷ*]'; at times synonymous with *deva.*

Khālsa the Sikh community of initiates in the line of the Tenth Guru, Gobind Singh.

Kshatriya the ritual class *(varṇa)* of ruling warriors responsible for political stability and expansion.

Kubera the ruler of *yakṣas* whom the *rākṣasa* Ravana banished from Lanka in the south; he now lives in the mountains of the north as lord of wealth; his vehicle *(vāhana)* is a human *(nara).*

kummi a genre of Tamil poetry based on a joyful hand-clapping folk dance for girls.

kuṛavañci a genre of Tamil dance-drama based on the theme of a man of the bird-catching caste (Kuṛavaṉ), a woman of the same caste who tells fortunes (Kuṛavañci or Kuṛaṭṭi), and a lady lost in love.

liṅgam a circular stone pillar, rounded on top, signifying Śiva as the unmanifest Absolute *(parāparam);* its altar base, the *yoni,* signifies Śiva's power *(śakti)* in the form of matter; the *liṅgam* and *yoni,* when properly consecrated, serve as Śiva and Śakti's bodies for the rites of *pūjā.*

mantra the words of the four vedic collections of poems *(saṁhitā)* used in rites (*Ṛig, Yajur, Sāma,* and *Atharva Vedas*); Sanskrit words believed to embody the sacred power of the deity they denote; *mantras* are received in secret from a guru or acharya, who recites them into the disciple's right ear during rites of consecration *(dīkṣā)*.

Manu 'man'; denotes the progenitor of people who taught the Dharma he had learned from Nārāyaṇa when the world was beginning, compiled in the text *(śāstra)* known as 'Manu's Book on Dharma' *(Mānavadharmaśāstra),* known commonly as 'The Laws of Manu.'

Marāṭhas Marathi-speaking people of west-central India; in the early eighteenth century they created a political empire centered in Poona, invaded the south, and created a Tanjore Marāṭha province ruled by the Bhonsala (Bhonsle) dynasty.

māyā the creativity of *brahman*'s consciousness; positively it denotes the universe as arising from *brahman*'s *śakti,* while negatively it denotes illusion or delusion, perception as false *(mithyā).*

mūrti a material form, especially the form of a being that is worshiped.

Nawāb of Arcot the 'viceroy' *(nawāb)* of the Nizam of Hyderabad, who had been its last Mughal governor; his nawāb was stationed at Arcot on the Palar River northwest of Madras.

Nāyaṉār 'masters', title for more than 63 Śaiva saints whose stories were told by the Velalan poet Cekkilar in the twelfth-century *Periya Purāṇam;* Nāyaṉār poems comprise the 'Tamil Veda' for Śaiva Siddhānta.

Neṭiyōṉ 'The Tall One', denotes Nārāyaṇa who took the form of Dwarf (Vāmana), swelled up, measured out the universe with three strides (Trivikrama), and enslaved the *asura* king Bali as his protected servant.

Otuvār reciters of the *Tevāram* during liturgies in Saiva temples; they were drawn from high-status castes, typically Velalans.

paḷakkam/paṛakkam 'habituation' of a family or individual inculcated through customary behaviour *(vaḷakkam),* which may change others, or itself be changed.

Pallan a low-status caste 'of the left hand' aligned with merchants, as opposed to Paraiyans 'of the right hand' aligned with cultivators.

Pañca-mahā-yajña 'five great sacrifices' prescribed in texts teaching Veda for householders belonging to the 'twice-born' ritual classes (Brāhmin, Vaishya, Kshatriya): to the *devas* through daily offerings, to the ancestors through monthly and yearly offerings, to living beings *(bhūtas)* through food, to humans through the rites of hospitality, and to *brahman* through the study of Veda; the last is theoretically not to be practiced by women, Śūdras, or any 'aliens.'

pañcamar 'people of the fifth', referring to uncivilized 'aliens' not belonging to the four ritual classes *(varṇa)* and living outside the *ūr* in the *cēri* or the wild.

Pandya one of three ancient Tamil dynasties, whose realm comprised the southernmost portion of the Indian subcontinent; its capital was Madurai.

Paraiyan see 'Pariah.'

parāparam the Absolute, the realm *(vastu)* beyond discursive thought glossed in two ways: (1) 'that which is beyond *(parā)* the beyond *(parāt)*', and (2) 'that which is simultaneously beyond *(parā)* and not-beyond *(aparā)*', that is, the most essential mode of being, which is both transcendent and immanent and in that sense a synonym for *brahman.*

parāśakti the transcendent *(parā)* potency or power *(śakti)* of *brahman,* commonly visualized as the Goddess *(Devī).*

pariah from the Tamil *paṟaiyaṉ,* denoting a member of a caste *(jāti)* in the *cēri* whose 'work' is to play the *paṟai* drum at ceremonies for the *ūr* and perform ritually impure tasks; in Tanjore the Paraiyans belonged to the 'right hand' collection of castes aligned with the Velalans; Europeans extended 'pariah' to mean 'untouchables' or 'outsiders' in general.

Pārppār 'those who see', probably meaning *ṛishis;* denotes Brāhmins in general.

pēy [from ***peyya, preta***] a demonic being who resides locally; perhaps the dissatisfied ghost of someone who died wrongly, or at the wrong time, and now preys on humans.

pēykkaṭavūḷ a divine being of demonic nature.

pēytteyvan a divine being of demonic nature.

Pillai a Velalan caste title that also means 'child.'

Poligars ***(Pāḷaiyakkārer)*** local overlords.

rājā-guru the guru of the ruler, usually an acharya, who advises and performs rites for the ruler.

ṛishi a seer; one of the seven first speakers of the *mantras* of the *Ṛig Veda.*

sādhu literally a 'good man', but used, like 'monk', to denote any man of any religion who lives as a renouncer of the householder's life; the *sannyāsin* is a vedic subcategory of *sādhu.*

Śaiva a member of the religion *(samayam)* that believes the Absolute *(parāpa-*

ram or *brahman)* to be the Supreme Person named Rudra Śiva; his supreme power *(parāśakti)* is the Goddess *(Devī)* named Umā, Pārvatī, Durgā, etc.; membership commonly is by means of consecration *(dīkṣā)* into the use of the 'mantra of five syllables' *(Namo Śivāya)*; in temples worship is addressed to Śiva and the Goddess embodied in a *liṅgam* and *yoni.*

Śaiva Siddhānta 'Śaiva Orthodoxy', the school of Śaiva Āgama dominant among Tamil speakers, which uses the pastoral metaphor of 'master' *(pati)*, 'beast' *(paśu)*, and 'rope' *(pāśa)* for its theology of Śiva, soul, and matter respectively.

śakti the power of *brahman* to emanate things from its own being *(sat)* and consciousness *(cit)*.

samayam religion as a system of doctrine and practice.

sannyāsin or ***sannyāsi*** a man who has formally renounced the householder life by means of vedic rites; the term, like *sādhu*, is often used to denote renouncers in general.

Śāstri a scholar learned in scripture *(śāstra)*; a 'doctor of divinity.'

Shāfi'ī one of four Muslim schools following specific principles to derive law from the Qur'an and the sayings and deeds *(sunnah)* of the Prophet Muhammad.

Śibi a legendary king of the Ikshvāku dynasty, the paradigm of the ruler as self-giving protector: a dove fleeing a hawk that wanted to eat him, flew to King Śibi's lap for refuge; the hawk demanded the dove as his rightful food; to feed the hawk and protect the dove, King Śibi weighed pieces of his own flesh to balance the weight of the dove; the dove's weight increased until King Śibi had given himself completely.

Śūdra the ritual class *(varṇa)* of servants and slaves *(dāsa)* responsible for the service of Brāhmins, Kshatriyas, and Vaishyas.

Sufi a mystic within Islam who cultivates the love of God; a Sufi master *(shaikh)* has disciples called *faqīr* and *dervish.*

Sunni the majority of Muslims, who follow the *sunnah* or collection of the Prophet Muhammad's sayings and deeds in *ḥadīth*, which clarify the Qur'an; others, such as the Shī'a ('Partisans'), recognize additional authorities.

Telugu Nāyakaṉs Telugu-speaking peoples of southern India who ruled as subordinate lords *(nāyākaṉs)* under Vijayanagara authority (fourteenth to eighteenth centuries); the Nāyakaṉs of Tanjore were replaced by the Marāṭha Bhonsala dynasty.

Tevāram 'worship', denoting specifically the Tamil poems composed by Nāyaṉārs for Śiva, collected in the Tamil Śaiva canon called *Tevāram,* and sung by Otuvārs during temple worship.

teyvam divinity; a god or *deva.*

toṣam sin or disorder.

twice-born *(dvija)* a male member of the Brāhmin, Kshatriya, or Vaishya ritual classes *(varṇa)* who has undergone the vedic rite of consecration *(dīkṣā)* into the study of the *mantras* of Veda; any member of those three *varṇas;* Brāhmins in general.

upanāyaṇa the consecration *(dīkṣā)* of twice-born males into the study of Veda, including investiture with a thread of three strands worn over the right shoulder and under the left arm.

Upācaṉai (upāsanā) proper service of a deity through liturgy.

upadhyāyaṉ a teacher paid to teach a part of Veda, or knowledge based on Veda, such as grammar.

ūr the ritually bounded settlement or village for castes *(jāti)* that constitute civilization.

uyir the soul or spirit.

Vaishnava member of a religion *(samayam)* that believes the Absolute *(parāparam* or *brahman)* to be the Supreme Person named Nārāyaṇa, who appears also as Vasudeva, Vishnu, Krishna, Rāma, etc.; Nārāyaṇa's transcendent power *(parāśakti)* is the Goddess *(Devī)* Śrī or Lakshmī in her various forms; membership generally is through consecration *(dīkṣā)* into the use of a mantra, commonly the '*mantra* of eight syllables' *(Om Namo Nārāyaṇāya);* among Tamils Śrī Vaishnavism is the predominant Vaishnava religion.

Vaishya the ritual class *(varṇa)* of agriculturists and merchants responsible for generating and distributing food and goods for society.

Valangamattar from Valaṅkaimattār, 'those of the right hand', denoting the 'alien' residents of the *cēri* (such as *Paṛaiyaṉs*), who aligned with the agricultural Velalans of the *ūr* (who had caste titles such as Pillai and Mudaliyar); their rivals were the Iṭaṅkaimattār, 'those of the left hand' (such as Pallans and Kammalans), who aligned with the mercantile Velalans of the *ūr* (who had caste titles such as Cetti and Cettiyar).

Vaṇikar merchants, whose caste name commonly is Cetti or Cettiyar.

varṇa the four ritual classes of society said (in *Ṛig Veda* 10.90) to derive from the head (Brāhmin), shoulders (Kshatriya) abdomen and thighs (Vaishya), and feet (Śūdra) of the primordial 'Man' *(Puruṣa)* at the creation of the universe; *varṇas* as ritual classes differ from *jātis,* which are endogamous castes of birth, although *jātis* are commonly classified according to *varṇa.*

Varuṇa the emperor of *asuras* and other dark beings under the earth who resides to the west.

vastu realm.

Veda the sacred knowledge seen and heard by seers *(ṛishis)* at the creation of the universe, consisting of four collections *(saṁhitā)* of poems or *mantras* used in rites, commentaries on those rites *(brāhmaṇa),* and esoteric explorations of the latter called *āraṇyaka* and *upaniṣad.*

Vedānta the teachings of the *upaniṣads* of Veda, thought to be the esoteric essence of all revealed knowledge.

zamīndāri large tracts of land whose owner *(zamīndār)* payed taxes directly to the ruler, without any intermediary; *zamīndāris* in southern India resembled minor courts, and *zamīndārs* often patronized the arts.

Bibliography

Āgama. 1940. *Paramasaṁhitā [of the Pancharatra]*. Edited and translated by S. Krishnaswami Aiyangar. Gaekwad's Oriental Series no. 86. Baroda: Oriental Institute, 1940.

———. 1965. *Kasyapa's Book of Wisdom* (Kāśyapa-Jñānakāṇḍaḥ): *A Ritual Handbook of the Vaikhānasas.* Translated by T. Goudriaan. Disputationes Rheno-Trajectinae X. The Hague: Mouton and Company, 1965.

———. 1972. *Lakṣmī Tantra: A Pāñcarātra Text.* Translated by Sanjukta Gupta. Leiden: E. J. Brill, 1972.

"The Augsburg Confession" [of 1530]. Reprinted from *The Book of Concord.* Allentown, PA: Muhlenberg Press, 1959. Madras: Gurukul Lutheran Theological College and Research Institute, 1983.

Arasaratnam, S. 'Protestant Christianity and South Indian Hinduism 1630-1730: Some Confrontations in Society and Beliefs.' *Indian Church History Review* 15, no. 1 (June 1981): 7-33.

Ārumuga Nāvalār, Jaffna Nallūr. 1911. *Caivasamayaneṛi. Ciṭamparam Maṛaijñāṉacampantanāyaṉār aruḷcceyttatu. Yālppāṇaṭṭu Nallūr Āṛumukunāvalāravarkaḷ ceyta putturaiyuṭaṉ* [The Path of the Śaiva Religion, by Maraijnanasambandar Nayanar of Cidambaram, with a New Gloss by Arumuga Navalar of Nallur in Jaffna]. 3rd ed. Madras: Vittiyanupalana Yantiracalai, 1911.

———. 1969. *Pālapāṭam: Nāṅkām Puttakam* [Children's Primer: Book Four] [of 1850-51]. Madras: Arumuganavalar Vittiyanupalana Accakam, 1969.

Baldaeus, Phillipus. *A Short Account of Jaffnapatam, in the Island of Ceylon, as It Was Published in Dutch, in the Year 1672.* Translated into English in 1704. Colombo: Wesleyan Mission Press, 1816.

Barnett, L. D., and G. U. Pope. *A Catalogue of the Tamil Books in the Library of the British Museum.* London: The British Museum, 1909.

Bayly, Susan. *Saints, Goddesses and Kings: Muslims and Christians in South Indian Society 1700-1900.* Cambridge: Cambridge University Press, 1989.

Beyreuther, Erich. *Bartholomaeus Ziegenbalg: A Biography of the First Protestant Missionary in India 1682-1719.* Madras: Christian Literature Society, 1955.

Bhāgavata Purāṇa. *Śrīmad Bhāgavata: The Holy Book of God* [with Sanskrit text]. Translated by Swami Tapasyananda. 4 vols. Madras: Sri Ramakrishna Math, 1980-82.

———. *Śrīmad Bhāgavatam.* Translated by N. Raghunathan. 2 vols. Madras and Bangalore: Vighneswara Publishing House, 1976.

Bible. *The Holy Bible: Containing the Old and New Testaments.* Revised Standard Version. New York: Thomas Nelson and Sons, 1952.

Caldwell, Robert. 1881a. *A Political and General History of the District of Tinnevelly in the Presidency of Madras: From the Earliest Period to Its Cession to the English Government in A.D. 1801.* Madras: Printed by E. Keys, at the Government Press, 1881.

———. 1881b. *Records of the Early History of the Tinnevelly Mission of the Society for Promoting Christian Knowledge and the Society for the Propagation of the Gospel in Foreign Parts.* Madras: Higginbotham and Company, 1881.

Chitty, Simon Casie. 1859. *The Tamil Plutarch: Containing a Summary Account of the Lives of the Poets and Poetesses of Southern Indian and Ceylon: From the Earliest to the Present Times, with Select Specimens of Their Compositions.* Jaffna: Ripley and Strong Printers, 1859.

———. 1988. *The Castes, Customs, Manners and Literature of the Tamils.* [Reprint of 1834 and 1934.] New Delhi and Madras: Asian Educational Services, 1988.

Cronin, Vincent. *A Pearl to India: The Life of Roberto de Nobili* [1577-1656]. New York: E. P. Dutton and Company, 1959.

Dandapani Swamikal [of Tiruvamattur]. *Sattiya Sūttiram & Sattiya Vācakam.* [Urai (gloss) by Ti. Ce. Murugadāsa Aiya]. Published during Aruḷmiku. Śāntaliṅga Swamikaḷ Gurupūjai Viḻā. Palani-Kattaiccinampatti: A. Palaniveluttevar, 1971.

Daniel, E. Valentine. *Fluid Signs: Being a Person the Tamil Way.* Berkeley, Los Angeles, and London: University of California Press, 1984.

Davis, Richard H. 1991. *Ritual in an Oscillating Universe: Worshiping Śiva in Medieval India.* Princeton: Princeton University Press, 1991.

———. 1997. *Lives of Indian Images.* Princeton: Princeton University Press, 1997.

De Silva, K. M. *A History of Sri Lanka.* London: C. Hurst and Company; Berkeley and Los Angeles: University of California Press, 1981.

Devanesan, D. V. *Tañjai Vedanāyagam Sāstriyar.* 2nd ed. Madras: Christian Literature Society, 1956.

Devapackiam, Mary. "The History of the Early Christian Settlements in the Tirunelveli District." Master's Thesis submitted to the Department of Tamil, University of Madras, 1963.

Diehl, Carl Gustav. 1956. *Instrument and Purpose: Studies on Rites and Rituals in South India.* Lund: C. W. K. Gleerup, 1956.

Dillenberger, John, and Claude Welch. *Protestant Christianity Interpreted through Its Development.* New York: Charles Scribner's Sons, 1954.

Dubois, J. A. *Letters on the State of Christianity in India; in which the conversion of the Hindoos is considered as impracticable. To which is added, A Vindication of the Hindoos, Male and Female in answer to a severe attack made upon both by The Reverend —— . London: Longman, Hurst, Rees, Orme, Brown, and Green, 1823.*

Dumont, Louis. 1970. *Homo Hierarchicus: The Caste System and Its Implications.* Translated by Mark Sainsbury. Chicago and London: University of Chicago Press, 1970.

———. 1977. *From Mandeville to Marx: The Genesis and Triumph of Economic Ideology.* Chicago and London: University of Chicago Press, 1977.

———. 1986. *Essays on Individualism: Modern Ideology in Anthropological Perspective.* Chicago and London: University of Chicago Press, 1986.

Duncan, James S. *The City as Text: The Politics of Landscape Interpretation in the Kandyan Kingdom.* Cambridge: Cambridge University Press, 1990.

Farnum, Mabel. *The Sacred Scimitar: Life of Blessed John de Brito.* Milwaukee: The Bruce Publishing Company, 1946.

Al Fārūqī, Isma'īl R, and Lois Lamayā'al Fārūqī. *The Cultural Atlas of Islam.* New York: Macmillan Publishing Company, 1986.

Fenger, J. Ferd. *History of the Tranquebar Mission.* Worked out from the Original Papers. Published in Danish and translated into English from the German of Emil Francke (Compared with the Danish original). Tranquebar, 1863.

Ganesh, Kamala. 'Vellalas: A Socio-Historical Perspective.' *South Indian Studies — II,* edited by R. Nagaswamy, 47-58. Madras: Society for Archaeological, Historical and Epigraphical Research, 1979.

Ganguli, Kisari Mohan, translator. *The Mahabharata of Krishna-Dwaipayana Vyasa.* Vol. 10. 5th ed. New Delhi: Munshiram Manoharlal, 1991.

Gaur, Albertine. *Second Supplementary Catalogue of Tamil Books in the British Library.* Department of Oriental Manuscripts and Printed Books. London: The British Library, 1980.

Gensichen, Hans-Werner. '"Abominable Heathenism": A Rediscovered Tract by Bartholomaeus Ziegenbalg.' *Indian Church History Review* 1 (1957): 29-40.

Gnanadickam Sastriar, V. Noah. *Tañcavūr Suvicēṭa Kavirāyarākiya Vetanāyakam Sāstiriyār Carittiram* [Life of Vedanayagam Sastriar, The Evangelical Poet of Tanjore]. Tanjore: V. S. Vedanayagam Sastriar, n.d. [reprint of 1899].

Grafe, H. 'Hindu Apologetics at the Beginning of the Protestant Mission Era in India.' *Indian Church History Review* 6, no. 1 (June 1972): 43-69.

Hooper, J. M. S. *Bible Translation in India, Pakistan and Ceylon.* 2nd ed. Revised by W. J. Culshaw. London: Oxford University Press, 1963.

Hospital, Clifford. *The Righteous Demon: A Study of Bali.* Vancouver: University of British Columbia Press, 1984.

Hough, James. *A Reply to the Letters of the Abbe Dubois on the State of Christianity in India.* London: L. B. Seeley and Son, 1824.

Hudson, D. Dennis. 1972. 'Hindu and Christian Theological Parallels in the Conversion of H. A. Kṛṣṇa Pillai 1857-1859.' *Journal of the American Academy of Religion* 40, no. 2 (June 1972): 195-206.

———. 1981. 'Renaissance in the Life of Sāminātha Aiyar, a Tamil Scholar.' *Comparative Civilizations Review,* no. 7 (Fall 1981): 54-71.

———. 1982. 'Christians and the Question of Caste: The Veḷḷāla Protestants of Pāḻayaṅkōṭṭai.' In *Images of Man: Religion and Historical Process in South Asia,* edited by Fred W. Clothey, 244-59. Madras: New Era Publications, 1982.

———. 1985. 'The Responses of Tamils to Their Study by Westerners 1600-1908.' In *As Others See Us: Mutual Perceptions, East and West,* edited by Bernard Lewis, Edmund Leites, and Margaret Case, 180-200. Comparative Civilizations Review nos. 13-14 (Fall 1985 and Spring 1986). New York: International Society for the Comparative Study of Civilizations, 1985.

———. 1986-92. 'Tamil Hindu Responses to Protestants (Among Nineteenth-Century Literati in Jaffna and Tinnevelly).' *The Journal of Oriental Research, Madras* 56-62 (1986-92): 130-53.

———. 1989. 'Violent and Fanatical Devotion among the Nāyaṉārs: A Study in the *Periya Purāṇam* of Cēkkiḻār.' In *Criminal Gods and Demon Devotees: Essays on the Guardians of Popular Hinduism,* edited by Alf Hiltebeitel, 373-404. Albany, NY: State University of New York Press, 1989.

———. 1992. 'Ārumuga Nāvalār and the Hindu Renaissance among the Tamils.' In *Religious Controversy in British India: Dialogues in South Asian Languages,* edited by Kenneth W. Jones 27-51. Albany, NY: State University of New York Press, 1992.

———. 1993. 'Madurai: The City as Goddess.' In *Urban Form and Meaning in South Asia: The Shaping of Cities from Prehistoric to Precolonial Times,* editors Howard Spodek and Doris Meth Srinivasan, 125-42. Washington, DC: National Gallery of Art, 1993.

———. 1994a. 'A Hindu Response to the Written Torah.' In *Between Jerusalem and Benares: Comparative Studies in Judaism and Hinduism,* edited by Hananya Goodman, 55-84. Albany, NY: State University of New York Press, 1994.

———. 1994b. 'Vraja among the Tamils: A Study of the Bhāgavatas in Early South India.' *Journal of Vaiṣṇava Studies* 3, no. 1 (Winter 1994): 113-40.

———. 1995a. 'The Śrīmad Bhāgavata Purāṇa in Stone: The Text as an Eighth-Century Temple and Its Implications.' *Journal of Vaisnava Studies* 3, no. 3 (Summer 1995): 137-82.

———. 1995b. 'Tamil Hindu Responses to Protestants: Nineteenth-Century

Literati in Jaffna and Tinnevelly.' In *Indigenous Responses to Western Christianity,* 95-123. New York and London: New York University Press, 1995.

———. 1997. 'The Courtesan and Her Bowl: An Esoteric Buddhist Reading of the Maṉimēkalai.' In *A Buddhist Woman's Path to Enlightenment: Proceedings of a Workshop on the Tamil Narrative Maṇimēkalai* (Uppsala University, May 25-29, 1995), edited by Peter Schalk, 151-90. Acta Universitatis Upsaliensis: *Historia Religionum* 13. Uppsala, 1997.

———. 1998. 'Winning Souls for Siva: Ārumuga Nāvalār's Transmission of the Śaiva Religion.' In *A Sacred Thread: Modern Transmission of Hindu Traditions in India and Abroad,* edited by Raymond Brady Williams, 23-51. Chambersburg, PA: Anima Press, 1992. Republished as *Modern Transmission of Hindu Traditions in India and Abroad,* edited by Raymond Brady Williams, 23-51. Princeton: Princeton University Press, 1998.

———. 1999. 'A New Year's Poem for Krishna: The *Tiruppallāṇṭu* by Villiputtūr Vishnucittaṉ ("Periyāḻvār").' *The Journal of Vaiṣṇava Studies* 7, no. 2 (Spring 1999): 93-129.

Ilakkuvanar, S. *Tholkappiyam (in English) with Critical Studies.* Madurai: Kural Neri Publishing House, 1963.

Ilaṅkōvaṭikaḷ 1966. *Cilappatikāra mūlamum N. Mu. Veṅkaṭacāmi Naṭṭār iyaṟṟiya uraiyum.* Ve. Peri. Pala. Mu. Kacivisuvanātaṉ Cettiyār edition. Tirunelveli and Madras: The South India Saiva Siddhanta Works Publishing Society, Limited, 1966 [reprint of 1942].

———. 1978. *The Cilappatikaram.* Translated with introduction and notes by V. R. Ramachandra Dikshitar. Madras: The South India Saiva Siddhanta Works Publishing Society, Tinnevelly, Limited, 1978 [reprint of 1939].

———. 1985. *Cilappatikāra mūlamum Arumpaṭavuraiyum Aṭiyārkkunallāruraiyum.* Notes by U. Ve. Sāminātaiyar. 6th ed. Tanjore: Tamilp Palkalakaik Kalakam, 1985 [reprint of 1955].

———. 1993. *The Cilappatikāram of Ilaṅko Aṭikaḷ: An Epic of South India.* Translated by R. Parthasarathy. New York: Columbia University Press, 1993.

Irakavaiyaṅkār, Mu. *Tolkāppiyap Poruḷatikāra Ārāycci.* Manamaturai: Mu. Ra. Narayanaiyankar, 1960.

Irāmanātaṉ Piḷḷai, P. 1975. *Tāyumāṉavaṭikaḷ Tiruppāṭalkaḷ. Cittāntac Ciṟappurai.* Tirunelveli: The South India Saiva Siddhanta Works Publishing Society, Tinnevelly, Limited, 1975.

Jackson, William J. *Tyagaraja: Life and Lyrics.* Madras: Oxford University Press, 1991.

Jeyeraj, Daniel. 1996. *Inkulturation in Tranquebar: Der beitrag der Frühen danisch-halleschen Mission zum Werden einer indisch-einheimischen Kirche (1706-1730).* Erlangen, Germany: Verlag der Ev.-Luth. Mission, 1996.

———1997a. 'Tranquebar and Tamil Evangelical Inculturation.' Unpublished paper delivered to the Colloquium on Christianity in India, Asha Nivas Conference Center, January 8-11, 1997.

———. 1997b. 'Early Tamil Bible Translation in Tranquebar.' *Dharma Deepika: A South Asian Journal of Missiological Research* (Mylapore, Madras) 1, no. 1 (June 1997): 67-77.

———. 1998. *Ordination of the First Protestant Indian Pastor Aaron.* Edited by Daniel Jeyeraj. Chennai [Madras]: Lutheran Heritage Archives, Gurukul Lutheran Theological College and Research Institute, 1998.

Kane, Panduran Vaman. 1974. *History of Dharmaśāstra (Ancient and Mediaeval Religious and Civil Law).* Vol. 2, part 1. 2nd ed. Poona: Bhandarkar Oriental Research Institute, 1974.

Kulentiraṉ, Capāpati [Kulandran, Sabapathy]. *Kiṛistava Tamiḻ Vetākamattiṉ Varalāṛu [A History of the Tamil Bible].* Bangalore: The Bible Society of India, 1997.

Kuriakose, M. K. *History of Christianity in India: Source Materials.* Madras: Christian Literature Society, 1982.

Lamb, G. H. *C. F. Schwartz.* Madras: Christian Literature Society, 1948.

The Laws of Manu. 1964. Translated by G. Buehler. Sacred Book of the East, vol. 25. Delhi: Motilal Banarsidass, 1964 [reprint of 1886].

The Laws of Manu. 1991. Translated by Wendy Doniger with Brian K. Smith. London: Penguin Books, 1991.

Lebbai, Sayyid Muhammad Ibn Ahmad ('Mapillai 'Alim of Kayalpattanam'). *Fathud-dayyan: Fi Fiqhi Khairil Adyan (A Compendium on Muslim Theology and Jurisprudence).* Translated from the Arabic-Tamil by Saifuddin J. Aniff-Doray. [1873.] Colombo: The Fat-hud-dayyan Publication Committee, 1963.

Lehmann, Arno 1956a. *Es begann in Tranquebar: Die Geschichte der ersten evangelischen Kirche in Indien.* Berlin: Evangelische Verlagsanstalt, 1956.

———. 1956b. *It Began at Tranquebar.* [Translation of edited version of *Es begann in Tranquebar* by M. J. Lutz.] Madras: Christian Literature Society, 1956.

Manasseh [Maṉācē], Dayāmaṇi. *Vedanāyaga Vedasāstri.* Vedanayaga Sastri Bi-Centenary Celebration Publication. Madras: The Christian Arts and Communications Service, 1975.

Mani, Vettam. *The Puranic Encyclopaedia.* Delhi: Motilal Banarsidass, 1984.

Manickam, S. 1993. *Slavery in the Tamil Country: A Historical Overview.* 2nd ed. Madras: Christian Literature Society, 1993.

———. 1988. *Studies in Missionary History: Reflections on a Culture-Contact.* Madras: Christian Literature Society, 1988.

McLeod, W. H. *Who Is a Sikh? The Problem of Sikh Identity.* Oxford: Clarendon Press, 1992.

Mitter, Partha. *Much Maligned Monsters: A History of European Reactions to Indian Art.* Chicago and London: University of Chicago Press, 1992.

Müller-Bahlke, Thomas J. *Die Wunder Kammer: Die Kunst- und Naturalien*

Kammer der Franckeschen Stiftungen zu Halle. Photographien von Klaus E. Goltz. Halle/Salle: Verlag der Franckeschen Stiftungen, 1998.

Murdoch, John. 1870. *Catalogue of the Christian Vernacular Literature of India.* Madras: Caleb Foster, 1870.

———. 1968. *Classified Catalogue of Tamil Printed Books: With Introductory Notices (Reprinted with a Number of Appendices and Supplement).* First edition in 1865, published by The Christian Vernacular Education Society, Madras. Reprinted in 1968, under the editorship of M. Shanmukham. Madras: Tamil Development and Research Council, Government of Tamilnad, 1968.

Muttaiya Piḷḷai, E. (Muthiah Pillai). *Kiṟistavarkaḷiṉ ācāramum, kurumār pōtakamum.* [The Manners and Customs of Native Christians and the Rules and Regulations of European Missionaries]. Palamcottah: Printed by K. S. Sankaranarayana at his Chinthamani Press, 1894. [Reprinted in Madras by Sir David Devadoss, 1950.]

Muttusami Pillei, A. [author and translator]. 'A Brief Sketch of the Life and Writings of Father C. J. Beschi or Viramamuni, translated from the original Tamil.' *Madras Journal of Literature and Science,* April 1840, 250-300.

Neill, Stephen. 1984. *A History of Christianity in India: The Beginnings to* A.D. *1707.* Cambridge: Cambridge University Press, 1984.

———. 1985. *A History of Christianity in India: 1707-1858.* Cambridge: Cambridge University Press, 1985.

Nilakanta Sastri, K. A. *A History of South India: From Prehistoric Times to the Fall of Vijayanagar.* 2nd ed. London: Oxford University Press, 1958.

O'Connell, J. T. *Religious Movements and Social Structures. The Case of Chaitanya's Vaisnavas in Bengal.* Shimla: Indian Institute of Advanced Study, 1989.

OED. The Compact Edition of the *Oxford English Dictionary.* 2 vols. Oxford: Oxford University Press, 1971.

Packiamuthu, David. 'Royal Clarinda.' Unpublished paper presented at the Seminar on Some Indigenous Leaders of the Church in South India, Palayankottai, 29 August 1993.

Paul, Rajaiah D. 1961. *Chosen Vessels: Lives of Ten Indian Christian Pastors of the Eighteenth and Nineteenth Centuries.* The Christian Student's Library no. 25. Madras: Christian Literature Society, 1961.

———. 1967. *Triumphs of His Grace: Lives of Eight Indian Christian Laymen of the Early Days of Protestant Christianity in India, Every One of Whom Was a Triumph of His Grace.* Madras: Christian Literature Society, 1967.

Pelikan, Jaroslav. *The Christian Tradition: A History of the Development of Doctrine.* 5 vols. Chicago: University of Chicago Press, vol. 4, 1983; vol. 5, 1989.

Peterson, Indira Viswanathan. 1993. 'The Play of the Kuṛavañci Fortuneteller: The Popular, the Classical, and the Exotic in an 18th Century Literary Genre.' Unpublished paper presented to the Workshop on Cultural Production and Cultural History in the Middle East and South Asia: 1500-1900. Philadelphia: The University of Pennsylvania, May 1993.

———. 1996. 'European Science and German Missionary Education in the Lives of Two South Indian Intellectuals in the Eighteenth Century: The Cabinet of Curiosities (Kunstkammer) in Halle and Tañjāvūr.' Rev. version. Unpublished paper presented to the Fourteenth European Modern South Asian Studies Conference, Copenhagen, August 1996, Panel on 'Christianity in India.'

———. 1998. 'C. F. Schwartz and the Education of King Serfoji and Vedanayaka Sastri of Tanjore: An Evaluation of the Sources.' Unpublished paper presented to the International Study Seminar on Christian Frederick Schwartz, Thanjavur Tamil University, February 26-28, 1998.

Pfaffenberger, Bryan. *Caste in Tamil Culture: The Religious Foundations of Sudra Domination in Tamil Sri Lanka.* Foreign and Comparative Studies/South Asian Series no. 7. Syracuse, NY: Maxwell School of Citizenship and Public Affairs, 1982.

Prestwich, Menna, editor. *International Calvinism 1541-1715.* Oxford: Clarendon Press, 1986.

Qur'an. *The Holy Qur-an: Text, Translation and Commentary.* By Abdullah Yusuf Ali. 3rd ed. Published by Khalil Al-Rawaf and printed in the United States by McGregor and Werner, Inc., 1946.

Ramanujan, A. K. *Poems of Love and War: From the Eight Anthologies and the Ten Long Poems of Classical Tamil.* New York: Columbia University Press, 1985.

Ramaswamy, Sumathi. *Passions of the Tongue: Language Devotion in Tamil India, 1891-1970.* New Delhi: Munshiram Manoharlal Publishers Pvt. Ltd., 1998.

Rangachari, K. *The Sri Vaishnava Brahmans.* Bulletin of the Madras Government Museum. New Series: General Section, vol. 2, part 2. Madras: Government Press, 1931.

Rangaramanuja Ayyangar, R. *History of South Indian (Carnatic) Music: From Vedic Times to the Present.* 2nd ed. Bombay: Vipanchi Cultural Trust, 1993.

Rao, Velcheru Narayana, David Shulman, and Sanjay Subrahmanyam. *Symbols of Substance: Court and State in Nāyaka Period Tamilnadu.* Delhi: Oxford University Press, 1992.

Richard, Anjala. *Vētanāyaka Sastiriyar Kīrttaṉaik Kaḷañciyam.* Kotagiri: Thanjai Vedanayaga Sastriar Peravai on 10 February 1992 at the Vedanayaga Sastriar Festival, 1992.

Roy, Asim. *The Islamic Syncretistic Tradition in Bengal.* Princeton: Princeton University Press, 1983.

Sabhāpati Nāvalār [of the Tiruvavatuturai Atinam]. 'Varalāṛu' [History]. In *Śivasamayavāṭavuraimaṛuppu,* by Sivajnana Yogi, 1-6. Cidambaram: Siddhanta Vidyanupalana Yantrasala, 1893.

Sathianathaier, R. *Tamilaham in the 17th Century.* Madras: University of Madras, 1956.

Segal, Alan F. *Paul the Convert: The Apostolate and Apostasy of Saul the Pharisee.* New Haven and London: Yale University Press, 1990.

Sjoman, N. E., and H. V. Dattatreya. *An Introduction to South Indian Music.* Amsterdam: Sarasvati Project, 1986.

Sources of Indian Tradition. Volume Two: Modern India and Pakistan. 2nd ed. Edited by Stephen Hay. New York: Columbia University Press, 1988.

Spear, Percival. 1963. *The Nabobs: A Study of the Social Life of the English in 18th Century India.* London: Oxford University Press, 1963.

Spener, Philip Jacob. *Pia Desideria.* Translated and edited by Theodore G. Tappert. Philadelphia: Fortress Press, 1964.

Stein, Burton. *Peasant State and Society in Medieval South India.* Delhi: Oxford University Press, 1980.

Stoeffler, F. Ernest. *The Rise of Evangelical Pietism.* Supplements to *Numen* 9. Leiden: E. J. Brill, 1965.

Sutherland, Gail Hinich. *The Disguises of the Demon: The Development of the Yakṣa in Hinduism and Buddhism.* Albany, NY: State University of New York Press, 1991.

Tamil Lexicon. 6 vols. Madras: University of Madras, 1982.

Tappert, Theodore G. 'Introduction: the Times, the Man, the Book.' In *Pia Desideria,* by Philip Jacob Spener, 1-28. Translated and edited by Theodore G. Tappert. Philadelphia: Fortress Press, 1964.

Terry, Charles Sanford. *Bach: A Biography.* London: Humphrey Milford, 1928.

Thurston, Edgar, and K. Rangachari. *Castes and Tribes of Southern India.* 7 vols. Delhi: Cosmo Publications, 1975 [reprint of 1909].

Tirukkuṛal: Mūlamum Parimēlāḻakaruraiyum. Madras: The South India Saiva Siddhanta Works Publishing Society, Tinnevelly, Ltd., 1964.

Tondiman, T. M. [To. Mu. Pāskarat Toṇṭaimāṉ]. *Vēṅkaṭam Mutal Kumari Varai: Kaviri Karaiyile.* Tirunelveli: S. R. Suppiramaniya Pillai, 1967.

Trawick, Margaret. *Notes on Love in a Tamil Family.* Berkeley, Los Angeles, and London: University of California Press, 1990.

Van Buitenen, J. A. B., translator. *The Mahābhārata,* vol. 2. Chicago: University of Chicago Press, 1975.

Vedanayagam Sastri. 1829. '"Saditeratoo" [*Jātiteruttu*], By Vedenayaga Sastree, the Evangelical Poet Tanjore 1829.' British Museum: Oriental Printed Books and Manuscripts, Cat: OR. 11,742.

———. n.d. [1879?] *Gnanakummy* [*Jñāṉakkummi*] and *Kaliyāṇa Vāḻttutal.* Palayankottai: Church Mission Press, [1879?] [Title page missing].

———. 1850. *Sāstirakkummi: Sastherukkoomme, a Satirical Poem on the Superstitions of the Hindoos.* Madras: American Mission Press, 1850.

———. 1851. T. Devasahayam and Miron Wislow. *Blind Way, Part I-IV. Incantations and True Way* [*Kuruṭṭuvaḻi, I-IV, Mantiram, Meyvaḻi eṉṉum puttakaṅkaḷ atāṅki irukkiṉṟatu*]. Jaffna: American Mission Press, 1852.

———. 1938. *Petlakēnkuṟavañci* [*Bethlehem Kuravanci*] [1800]. With a Preface by E. Vedabothagam. Tanjore, 1938 [reprint of 1820 edition].

———. 1963. *Cepamālai* [Songs for Morning and Evening Worship, collected 1808-55]. Nazareth: Das Press, 1963.

———. 1964. *Petlēnkuṟavañci* [*Bethlehem Kuravanci*] [with] *Jñāṉattacca Nāṭakam, Jñāṉavuḷā, Āraṇatintam, Jñāṉa Antāti.* 2nd ed. Madras: Christian Literature Society, 1964.

———. 1969. *Sastirkkummi* [1814]. Trichendur: Thomas Ratnam, 1969.

Venkatachari, K. K. A. *The Maṇipravāḷa Literature of the Śrīvaiṣṇava Ācāryas, 12th to 15th Century* A.D. Bombay: Ananthacarya Research Institute, 1978.

Walker, Williston. *A History of the Christian Church.* Rev. ed. New York: Charles Scribner's Sons, 1959.

Young, R. F., and S. Jebanesan. *The Bible Trembled: The Hindu-Christian Controversies of Nineteenth-Century Ceylon.* Publications of the De Nobili Research Library, vol. 22. Vienna: Institute of Indology, University of Vienna, 1995.

Yule, Henry, and A. C. Burnell. *Hobson-Jobson: A Glossary of Colloquial Anglo-Indian Words and Phrases, and of Kindred Terms, Etymological, Historical, Geographical and Discursive.* By Henry Yule and A. C. Burnell. New ed. by William Crooke. [Reprint of 1903.] Delhi: Munshiram Manoharlal, 1968.

Ziegenbalg, Bartholomaeus. 1717. *An Account of the Religion and Government, Learning and Oeconomy, etc. of the Malabarians, Sent by the Danish Missionaries to Their Correspondents in Europe.* Translated from the High-Dutch. London, 1717.

———. 1867. *Genealogie der malabarischen Goetter. Aus eingenen Schriften und Briefen der Heiden zusammengetragen und verfasst von Bartholomaeus Ziegenbalg.* [Written in 1713.] Edited by W. Germann. Madras, 1867.

———. 1930. 'Nidi Wunpa oder malabarische Sitten-Lehre bestehende in sechs und neunzig feinen Gleichniszen und Lebens-Reguln, so da vor mehr als sieben hundert Jahren von einem Ostijndischen heyden in Malabarische versen geschrieben aber nunmehro von Wort zu Wort in die hochteutsche Sprache versetzet worden von Bartholomaeo Ziegenbalg.' Tranquebar, 1708. In *B. Ziegenbalg's Kleinere Schriften.* Hsrg. von W. Caland. Amsterdam, 1930.

———. 1718. *Propagation of the Gospel in the East: Being an Account of the Success of Two Danish Missionaries, Lately Sent to the East Indies, for the Conversion of the Heathens in Malabar. In Several Letters to Their Correspondents in Europe. . . . Rendered into English from the High-Dutch and Dedicated to the Most Honourable Corporation for the Propagation of the Gospel in Foreign Parts.* [In 3 parts: 1st ed. of part 1, 1709; of part 2, 1710; and of part 3, 1718.] 3rd ed. London, 1718.

———. 1719. *Thirty Four Conferences between the Danish Missionaries and the Malabarian Bramans (or Heathen Priests) in the East Indies, Concerning the*

Truth of the Christian Religion: Together with Some Letters Written by the Heathens to the Said Missionaries. Translated out of High Dutch by Mr. Philips. London, 1719.

———. 1926. *Ziegenbalg's Malabarisches Heidenthum.* [1711.] Hrsg. von W. Caland. Amsterdam: Koninklijke Akademie van Wetenschappen, 1926.

———. 1957. *Alte Briefe aus Indien. Unveroeffentliche Briefe von Bartholomaeus Ziegenbalg 1706-1719.* Hrsg. von Arno Lehmann. Berlin: Evangelische Verlagsanstalt, 1957.

———. 1984. *Genealogy of the South-Indian Gods: A Manual of the Mythology and Religion of the People of Southern India, Including a Description of Popular Hinduism.* Edited by W. Germann. Translated with new additions and an index by G. J. Metzger. [1st ed., 1869.] New Delhi: Unity Book Service, 1984 reprint.

Zvelebil, Kamil. 1973. *The Smile of Murugan: On Tamil Literature of South India.* Leiden: E. J. Brill, 1973.

Index